CONTROLLED CHAOS

CHIP

KELLY'S
FOOTBALL
REVOLUTION

MARK SALTVEIT

DIVERSIONBOOKS

Also by Mark Saltveit

The Tao of Chip Kelly

Diversion Books
A Division of Diversion Publishing Corp.
443 Park Avenue South, Suite 1008
New York, New York 10016
www.DiversionBooks.com

For more information, email info@diversionbooks.com

First Diversion Books edition July 2015.
Print ISBN: 978-1-62681-823-1
eBook ISBN: 978-1-62681-822-4

For Noreen Kelly S. M., whose avid football fandom is only the latest in a lifetime of inspiring surprises.

CONTENTS

"No battle plan survives contact with the enemy... Everything is uncertain except such will and energy as the commander carries in himself."

—Prussian General Helmuth von Moltke the Elder

"Everybody has a plan. Until they get hit."

—Mike Tyson

"We went into [Pamplona] like coaches. We got there on Friday. We walked the course, we plotted it all out exactly where we would be on each turn. We wanted to make sure we knew exactly what we were doing and make sure we could get into the stadium.

...

"[When] all the bulls were on the course, it was just total anarchy. Every plan we had that we were going to execute was out the window and we were just running for our lives. Much the same thing that happens when the ball is kicked off. You better have a contingency plan, because if your [initial] plan doesn't work, you're going to get hit with a horn."

—Chip Kelly

INTRODUCTION

Chip Kelly is the most intriguing coach in football today. Discarding tradition and conventional wisdom for a series of decisive, unpredictable, and possibly reckless changes, he is determined to seek every possible advantage for his team.

Kelly and his staff are famously tight-lipped about their sports science innovations, as well as offensive and defensive schemes, but there is a meticulously organized plan behind it all. He's not going to tell you what that plan is, but if you watch his methods closely and listen carefully to what he says, you can work out the rough shape and some fascinating details.

My first book, *The Tao of Chip Kelly* (Diversion Books: 2013), used a number of Kelly's famous "Chipisms" to explain the football philosophy he developed over decades of college coaching, and show how it manifested itself in his four years with the Oregon Ducks and first preseason in Philadelphia.

Since then, I've been following Kelly's Eagles closely (and writing about them weekly). This book looks at the collision of his remarkable vision with the reality of NFL competition. Success against college kids does not guarantee anything when a coach moves to the pros, facing elite talent and brilliant coaching minds on even the worst teams. (Just ask Steve Spurrier.) Even the last two Super Bowl-winning coaches (Pete Carroll and Bill Belichick) struggled in their first NFL head-coaching jobs.

This book focuses on Kelly's second year in Philadelphia, the 2014 season and the crucial off-seasons before and after it, which is when the real work of coaches gets done. It was not an easy year for the Eagles. The excitement of Kelly's first season and the division title they won faded amid roster controversies, injuries, and uneven play by the team's stars. At the same time, unexpected successes and strengths buoyed the team and brought dramatic wins, such as the 27-0 shutout of the New York Giants.

Football is a game of people, not theories, and 2014 was the year that Chip Kelly's brilliant innovations smacked into the hard realities of ego, money, and human frailty—including his own. We won't know for years if this was just a speed bump on his road to glory, or the moment when dull, difficult reality caught up with a flashy and arrogant coach.

Either way, this year told us a lot about the character, strengths and weaknesses of a fascinating figure—a lot more than we would have learned from simple, easy success.

Chip Kelly is not backing down or giving up on his vision. He's doubling down, taking over as the Eagles' GM, with a complete control over the team shared by only two other NFL coaches: Carroll and Belichick. Eagles owner Jeffrey Lurie has gone all in on Chip, and the coach only has three more years under his contract to show results. Win or lose, the twists and turns are going to be dramatic.

There are good reasons for the kinds of checks and balances that slow down most coaches and limit their ability to rapidly change their team. Most of the time it's a bad idea to remove those safeguards, for the same reason it's usually stupid to cut off the lock on ovens that prevents you from opening them during the 800-900° Fahrenheit self-cleaning cycle.

And yet, there was a pizza enthusiast in Atlanta who did exactly that[1] so that he could bake a proper crust, which is impossible at the usual 550° maximum. Jeff Varasano may have melted down a couple of ovens figuring out how to do that, but today his restaurant (Varasano's) is rated as one of America's "elite 8" pizzerias by Rachael Ray.[2]

---

1   "Jeff Varasano's Famous New York Pizza Recipe" by Jeff Varasano, October 18, 2006. Section 4: The Oven. Retrieved from www.varasanos.com/PizzaRecipe.htm

2   "The Search for America's Best Pizzaria" by Ed Levine and Adam Kuban. *Everyday with Rachel Ray*, March 2010.

Jeff Varasano hit the sweet spot, where he destroyed a couple of ovens but didn't burn his house down, and this allowed him to develop an elite pizzeria. It will be to fascinating to see if Chip Kelly can do something similar with the Eagles, building an elite team without burning down the NovaCare Center.

WHAT IS CHIP KELLY DOING?

When the Philadelphia Eagles hired Charles "Chip" Kelly as their head coach in January, 2013, he had never worked for an NFL team before. He'd only been a head coach at any level for four years, at the University of Oregon.

It was one of the most successful major college coaching debuts ever. The Ducks had previously been a second-tier PAC-12 team; Kelly led them to a 47-6 record and a top-5 ranking every year. They only narrowly lost the college National Championship Game (NCG) to Cam Newton's Auburn Tigers in Kelly's second year, and destroyed Kansas State in the Fiesta Bowl less than two weeks before the Eagles hired him.

It has always been hard to get an accurate picture of Kelly, in large part because he is very tight with information. The coach has a ton of personality but he's rarely willing to share it with anyone outside of his team and staff. Sportswriters, used to boilerplate answers and endless clichés, often rely on inaccurate stereotypes when trying to describe his teams.

The most common image of the coach is as an offensive genius: an X's and O's wizard like Steve Spurrier, the successful college coach who famously flopped in the NFL. College football is wildly experimental compared to the conservative NFL, and Kelly has been at the vanguard of implementing "spread" offenses— positioning his players all over the field to force defenders into making difficult one-on-one tackles.

Statistically, this description is accurate, but it misses a big part of the story. Kelly's teams have racked up plenty of yards and points, both in college and the NFL, but he has an equally particular—and equally successful—approach to defense that is usually overlooked. His deceptive alignments and "two-gapping" 3-4 defense have been as important to his success as his offenses have.

And in fact, the coach's play-calling is based on simplicity rather than intricate design. His teams run seven or eight basic plays with multiple options, over and over, hidden behind flexible formations and the relentless tempo at which Kelly's teams play. Contrary to popular opinion, his teams emphasize the run over the pass, and don't require a mobile quarterback.

In addition, Kelly looks for any successful methods from outside of football that he can bring to his coaching. He told a round table of reporters that

> I make it a habit of trying to study high-performance organizations, and it doesn't have to be football. It can be the military. It could be a business. It could be sports teams from other sports.

Coach Kelly uses business innovation strategies from the likes of Jim Collins (*Good to Great*), Stanford academic Carol Dweck (*Mindset*), business ethicist Dov Seidman (*How*), former University of Oregon athlete Greg Bell (*Water the Bamboo*) and author Simon Sinek (*Leaders Eat Last: Why Some Teams Pull Together and Others Don't*). The *Wall Street Journal* reported that he calls on a group of college professors for insights from their particular fields.[1]

Other sports are a natural source of inspiration. The Eagles use a signaling system involving a sort of fan of multicolored plastic blades. It was sent to them out of the blue by the volunteer women's softball coach who created it. Kelly saw its potential and started using it immediately.

Kelly has also borrowed ideas on spreading out players from NBA coach Erik Spoelstra, an Oregon native who won two NBA Championships with the Miami Heat. And he consulted in August of 2014 with Graham Henry, the legendary coach of the New Zealand All Blacks, the dominant international rugby union team.

1   "The Philadelphia Eagles' Secret Coaches: Professors" by Kevin Clark, *Wall Street Journal*, September 16, 2014.

One major inspiration is the U.S. military, especially the Navy SEALs. In 2013, he hired Shaun Huls—a Navy SEALs strength coach and trainer who focused on reducing non-combat injuries—as the NFL's first "sports science coordinator." It makes a lot of sense. Soldiers in the Special Forces often have NFL-size bodies and undergo similar, if not more intense, training. (The SEALs impose sleep deprivation; Kelly asks players to get 8-10 hours a night.) In the NFL, the stakes are winning, fame and money, but Seals and Rangers will literally die if their training is not as effective as possible. That's bound to focus the mind and generate the best techniques.

The coach even takes concepts from popular movies, generally silly comedies such as *Night Shift* ("Feed the tuna mayonnaise!"),[1] *Pirates of the Caribbean* ("there are rules for pirates and there are guidelines for pirates"),[2] and *Beverly Hills Cop* ("I know this team is not going to fall for the banana-in-the-tailpipe trick").[3]

Most importantly, Kelly has formed a complete vision of his ideal football program, which he has built from the ground up. A set of rock-solid principles he has honed over a lifetime of playing and coaching football nonstop since he was a boy. Evidence based. Experienced based. But never based on conventional wisdom.

As he told a round table of Philly reporters in 2014[4]:

> I was probably a pain in the ass as a little kid, I would imagine. I questioned everything. I've always been a why guy, trying to figure out why things happen and what they are and just curious about it from that standpoint...
>
> When I became a head coach, I had never been a head coach before and I had no experience being it, so I'm going to ask a million questions about how do you do this, and how does the training room, and how

1   "A Man on the Move" by George Schroeder, *Eugene Register Guard*, October 18, 2009.

2   "Chip Kelly-speak highlights at Ducks camp" by Stephen Alexander, *Portland Tribune*, August 7, 2012.

3   "Chip Kelly's top 15 quotes in his first year as Eagles head coach" by Jimmy Kempski, Philly.com, January 16, 2014.

4   "Three Chip Kelly Leftovers" by Sheil Kapadia, *Birds 24/7*, July 25, 2014.

do you operate, because that wasn't really under my domain when I was an offensive coordinator. In most situations, it's, 'OK, that makes sense.' But I just wanted it to be explained why, like what's your protocol and how do you do it? Anything that's going to touch the football team, from there, I think you develop what you want, and your philosophies and how you want things to work.

In other words, he is reinventing football, building it up from first principles and practical experience with a samurai-like dedication to his craft. He trusts only what he sees with his own eyes and experiences in games. A few fundamentals stay the same, and the rest is open to change—players, formations, weather, even the rules of the game. "Just tell me the rules and I'll play by them," Kelly is fond of saying.

What stays the same, then? Football is a series of several dozen 4-6 second bursts of intense activity by a team of young men working together. There's no place for ego, selfishness, or focus on personal statistics. Faster and smarter are always better. "Bigger people beat up little people," but matchups are more important. If you plan yours well, a quick little guy (such as 5'6" Darren Sproles) can run past or even out-muscle a big lumbering player. Everything else is negotiable.

The result is a football program whose innovations are immediately apparent from the moment you walk through the doors of the NovaCare Center. The fast food that previous coach Andy Reid had served in the team's cafeteria has been replaced by healthy meals and charts about nutritious food groups. (Reporters love to mock the customized protein shakes as "special smoothies.") The Eagles break with NFL tradition by having vigorous workouts the day before a game, and taking off the day after (Monday, instead of the usual Tuesday).

Practices are extremely fast, filled with blaring music, and separated into twenty-six short periods announced by a robotic voice. Each is dedicated to specific tasks: stretching, special teams

(ST), seven-on-seven scrimmages, passing drills, or (very rarely) instruction. The team uses a variety of gadgets to teach key skills, from remote-controlled cars to three garbage cans stacked on top of each other at an angle to the bizarre-looking "bug men".

Linebacker Emmanuel Acho told Phil Sheridan of ESPN that

> It's controlled chaos. We have the music blaring. Sometimes, you can hardly hear your teammates. But that means everything on Sunday is a lot slower. When you come out here and you can hardly hear the call, then on Sunday, when you're playing at home and it's quiet when you're out there, then it's very simple. I think we do a good job of stressing ourselves in practice so the game is easier.

Kelly has no ego about being a creator. When told he is innovative, he is quick to tell you that he didn't invent any of the stuff his teams are doing, and he's right. Soon after being hired in Philadelphia, he repeated something he has said in many forms over the years:

> If you weren't in the room with Amos Alonzo Stagg and Knute Rockne, then you stole it from somebody. We didn't invent this.[1]

(Those two coaches invented maneuvers such as the forward pass, the center snap, and the reverse about a hundred years ago.)

So what exactly does Chip Kelly do, then? He focuses on the process, all the things that happen before a game begins—from the selection of players to how they eat, drink and sleep. Practice methods. Weight training. Injury prevention and recovery. The intangibles of team psychology and bonding.

He questions and tests everything that goes into a football program, under the motto "science before tradition." And then he implements the best ideas he can find, more thoroughly and ruthlessly and with better understanding than anyone else.

---

1 "Kelly: We're Not Revolutionizing Anything" by Sheil Kapadia, *Birds 24/7*, July 12, 2013.

What makes Chip Kelly's program unique is not his new ideas, but the clarity of his vision and his effectiveness in putting it into practice. Or as he put it in a 2013 round table discussion with reporters:

> We're not revolutionizing anything. All we're trying to do is make sure we're kind of crystal clear on our plan of what we're doing, and we understand what we're doing.[1]

It's a concept so simple, so obvious even, that you wonder why everyone doesn't do the same. Well, simple doesn't mean easy. Kelly's approach takes a lot of hard work, and it looks weird from the outside. Football is a socially conservative world, rooted in the small towns of the South and Midwest. It's full of blue-collar guys and country boys. Radical change is a hard sell.

Kelly has no easily understood overall philosophy to sell, either. Chip's "philosophy" is a collection of small, hard-won insights he has accumulated from decades of real life experience playing and coaching football. He offers to explain any and everything he asks players to do, and they confirm that he lives up to this promise. He also does well at boiling the principles down into the sorts of catchy phrases that business gurus get rich off of, slogans such as "win the day," "the faceless opponent" and "habits reflect the mission."[2] But it can still be hard for players to understand why he needs everyone on his team to wear the same color socks, or avoid taking shortcuts across the lawn.

Chip Kelly's program asks a lot of his players, and not everyone is willing to go along. He demands that his players devote their lives to football the way he does, that they subordinate their ego to the team and allow their sleep and piss and brainwaves to be monitored. In a group of athletes where pretty much everyone has had extraordinary talent, drive and success since they started high

---

1   "Kelly: We're Not Revolutionizing Anything" by Sheil Kapadia, *Birds 24/7*, July 12, 2013.
2   These football mantras are collected and explored in *The Tao of Chip Kelly* by this author (Diversion Books: 2013).

school, that's a lot to ask.

It's all based on the idea that a lot of small advantages will add up to one big advantage, and ultimately a Super Bowl or two. That all this weirdness and sacrifice and hard work will not only help the team win, but also be fun for the players and exciting for fans. It worked at Oregon, and there have been glimpses in Philadelphia.

Nonetheless, the NFL is full of incredibly smart and talented people dedicated to making sure that they win and Chip Kelly loses. New methods open up new possibilities, but also new vulnerabilities. Coach Kelly signed a five-year contract with the Eagles, and the first two years went by without a playoff win.

Philadelphia's owner Jeffrey Lurie has committed to Chip Kelly whole-heartedly, giving him a large contract, the NFL's biggest coaching staff, millions of dollars in new equipment, and power over his team matched only by Pete Carroll and Bill Belichick.

The coach has free reign to implement his vision, and he's racing ahead as fast as possible to do so. Kelly's full program will either succeed dramatically or fail spectacularly, and we will know soon enough. There are no excuses left. It's all on Chip, and he wouldn't have it any other way.

YEAR I

2013

When the Eagles hired Kelly in January of 2013, there were a lot of skeptics. Dozens of football pundits wrote him off as another Steve Spurrier or Bobby Petrino, an offense-minded college trickster who neglected defense and was too cute and clever for NFL opponents.

Kelly needed a special kind of mobile quarterback (QB) to run his beloved read option play, they argued, and pro linebackers were so big and fast that they would cripple his QB very soon. RGIII was their exhibit A—knocked out of the playoffs before the end of his first year as a running quarterback for Washington. Like Spurrier, they said, Kelly would last a year or two and crawl back to college with his tail between his legs. If he was lucky, he might get the job at USC or Texas.

Heath Evans of NFL.com was perhaps the most outspoken[1]:

> I am going on the record calling Chip Kelly one of the worst hires in pro football history.

When did Evans come to this stark opinion? After weeks or months of careful analysis? No. *Two hours* after Kelly's hiring was announced.

His ridiculous rationale started with the "fact" that:

> Kelly had the biggest recruiting advantage ever known to a college coach.

---

1   "Philadelphia Eagles' hire of Chip Kelly could be NFL's worst ever" by Heath Evans, NFL.com, January 16, 2013.

No wonder he had such an edge on Alabama and USC and Stanford, when he out-recruited those schools year after year, right? (I'm being sarcastic; hopefully it is self-evident that no one has had a recruiting advantage on Alabama, or the SEC in general, in this century. Only USC, Ohio State, and Florida State might even be considered close.)

There was no need to wait for the Eagles' 2013 division championship to refute this "hot take"; it was ripped apart before 2:00 pm the same day by SB Nation's Jason Kirk.[1]

Even Cleveland writer Terry Pluto—who put together the hilarious book *Loose Balls*, an oral history of the American Basketball Association's wildest days—got caught up in the negativity. Before signing with the Eagles, Chip negotiated hard with the Cleveland Browns but walked away from their head coaching job without any deal. That decision looks especially brilliant today, given the team's turmoil in 2013 and 2014. Pluto wrote "Cleveland Browns better off without Chip Kelly."[2] Instead, they hired Robert Chudzinski, a longtime NFL assistant coach. The Browns went 4-12 and he was fired after a year. In 2014, under new coach Mike Pettine, the team's record improved to 7-9, but they lost their last five games in a row.

After just one year, Kelly had proven these critics wrong, if not idiotic. They had focused on the most obvious aspect of Kelly's teams—their explosive offense—while missing the rest of his programs' distinctive features: a gambling, bend-but-don't-break defense (in the style of the great Eagles DC Jim Johnson), relentless focus on special teams, and unique approaches to practice, nutrition, and what the team calls "sports science."

Kelly was implementing a lot of other changes as well, notably a switch from the Eagles' "wide-9, 4-3" defense to the coach's preferred "two-gap 3-4" front. In that system, there are only three down linemen on the front line, and they aren't expected to sack the

---

1 "Chip Kelly, 'worst ever' hire: NFL people, please study up before you dismiss" by Jason Kirk, *SB Nation*, January 13, 2013.
2 "Cleveland Browns better off without Chip Kelly" by Terry Pluto, *Cleveland Plain Dealer*, January 6, 2013.

quarterback much. Their job is to occupy blockers and stymie the run, while the four linebackers behind them defend short passes and harass the passer. The system demands great skill from the three up front linemen while denying them much of the glory that comes from quarterback sacks. But if it works right, you have essentially added an extra player to your defense.

Expectations for this defense in year 1 were not high, since the team was only able to replace three of the seven starting linemen with players more suited to the new scheme. Optimists hoped that Kelly's offensive prowess would simply allow the team to outscore opponents in a series of shootouts, until future seasons when the transition was completed.

The new coach's first training camp was consumed with a quarterback competition between veteran Michael Vick, the fastest-running quarterback in NFL history, and Nick Foles, an unknown third-round pick out of Arizona, who had struggled through several games in 2012 after Vick was knocked out with an injury.

Though Chip Kelly had praised Foles when Oregon played against his Wildcats, Vick was the clear winner. He was the dual threat quarterback everyone thought that Kelly's offense required, with extraordinary speed and a great arm, but the team struggled to a 1-3 record before Vick got injured. Foles was NFC Player of the Week in a win against Tampa Bay, then played poorly for three quarters against Dallas before suffering a concussion. The *Associated Press* summed up his game this way:

> ... there won't be a quarterback controversy in Philadelphia after this one. Nick Foles was awful and left with a head injury.[1]

After Matt Barkley had a couple of bad games and Vick was reinjured, the Eagles stood at 3-5 and Kelly's team seemed to be floundering.

Then Foles returned against Oakland and tied the record for

---

1 "Cowboys knock out Nick Foles, stymie Eagles to claim 1st place" *Associated Press*, October 20, 2013.

most TDs (seven) in one game, a performance that put him the NFL Hall of Fame by the end of the week. It was just his ninth start as a professional, right after missing two games with a concussion. He never looked back, seizing the starting job and uncorking one of the most efficient performances in NFL history, with twenty-seven touchdown passes to only two interceptions.

He was the Pro Bowl MVP in his second year of pro ball and led the NFL in passer rating at 119.2—the third highest in NFL history, and better than Tom Brady has ever done. Players on rookie contracts can't be extended until they finish their third year, but Foles was headed for a big payday at the end of the 2014 season if he could produce anywhere near that level.

Foles was not the only player to have a good year. The team's stars (wide receiver DeSean Jackson and running back LeSean "Shady" McCoy) had career-best years in Kelly's hyper-speed, run-based spread offense, and the first-time coach had gone a long way toward instilling a positive culture of teamwork, subdued egos and healthy living.

The defense did surprisingly well too, giving up fewer than 33 points in eleven of their last twelve games. Slot cornerback Brandon Boykin had six interceptions, tied for second place behind only Richard Sherman of the Super Bowl-champion Seahawks.

Everything fell into place in the second half of the season, aside from a puzzling loss to the Minnesota Vikings, as the regular season hurtled forward at the pace of Coach Kelly's no-huddle, tempo offense. The team finished the year on a 7-1 run, with a mixture of luck—Aaron Rodgers getting injured before the Green Bay game—and grit, as in the three-point victory over a tough Arizona team. The Birds demolished Chicago 54-11 and won the magical "Snow Bowl" against Detroit, after a blizzard dumped several inches of the white stuff on Lincoln Financial Field right before game time.

The grand finale was a clutch victory over über-rival Dallas to make the playoffs (and just as importantly, keep the Cowboys out). The momentum of this team and its visionary coach felt unstoppable as they entered the playoffs, so the sudden end to the season was startling—the top step of the stairs that you expect, but isn't there.

The Birds fell to the wily veterans of the New Orleans Saints on a last second field goal, 24-26, and suddenly everyone was going home. But the year had been filled with unexpected successes and there was a general sense of optimism in Philadelphia. The team's innovative rookie coach had led the Eagles to a division title and a 10-6 record, after a dismal 4-12 season in 2012 that got longtime coach Andy Reid fired.

This positive mood was a rare luxury in the City of Brotherly Love, despite Reid's tremendous record of success in the first ten of his twelve seasons as the Eagles' coach. Even in 2010, the last good year, a *New York Times* reporter described Philly as a place "where anxiety has a permanent place in fans' hearts."[1] Brandon Lee Gowton, the editor of the popular Eagles blog *Bleeding Green Nation*, puts it this way:

> Some people are not happy unless they're not happy.[2]

Of all the writers who made early predictions about Chip Kelly as a coach, Greg Rosenthal of NFL.com was the shrewdest:

> I'm not sure what the Kelly era will be like in Philadelphia, but Eagles fans can get ready for a wild ride.[3]

Whatever you think of Chip Kelly as a coach, it's clear that Rosenthal nailed it. Year two in Philadelphia was about to prove how prescient he was.

---

1 "Eagles' DeSean Jackson Balances Soft Hands With Sharp Talk" by Joe Drape, *New York Times*, January 8, 2010.

2 Brandon Lee Gowton [@BrandonGowton]. August 7, 2015. Retrieved from https://twitter.com/BrandonGowton/status/497554357173637120

3 "Around the NFL: Chip Kelly hired as Philadelphia Eagles' next coach" by Greg Rosenthal, NFL.com, January 16, 2013.

WARNING SIGN

JANUARY 6, 2014

The Philadelphia Eagles' 2014 off-season began with an ominous development. Very few people even knew about it at the time, just a handful of Eagles coaches and front office staff. And they weren't talking.

It was such a little thing, just one guy missing a meeting, but looking back it foreshadowed all the chaos that exploded two-and-a-half months later.

For the fans of Eagles Nation, that day was actually a happy moment, full of optimism despite Philadelphia's tough playoff loss two days earlier. Overall, the Eagles had had a very good year in 2013. Not perfect. They had a lot of work to do in the off-season, but as Chip and his assistant coaches began evaluating players, every indication was that things were on the right track and moving forward.

Except for DeSean Jackson. Fans and sportswriters didn't find this out for months, but after cleaning out his locker, Jackson walked out of the NovaCare Center, blowing off his mandatory exit interview.

This was a slap in the face to his coaches. And while team officials did a remarkable job of keeping the incident quiet—even reporters with excellent confidential sources didn't know about it until months later—the team clearly took it as a warning shot by DeSean and his aggressive new agent, Joel Segal.

What the public did know was that earlier that day, in the locker room during cleanout, Jackson had told every reporter who would listen that he wanted and deserved more money and more security (meaning guaranteed money). He wanted more even though he had signed a $48.5 million, five-year contract just two seasons earlier under the previous coach, Andy Reid.

DeSean had received (and spent) nearly all of his guaranteed money in the first two years of his team-friendly contract. Bob Grotz of the Norristown *Times Herald* wrote that "There was speculation he caved and signed the last deal because he was strapped for cash."[1] Now that the guarantees were gone, the team could cut him at any time without paying him another dollar.

Under his new coach Chip Kelly, Jackson had just finished his best year ever, with eighty-two catches for 1,332 yards and nine TDs. Football careers are short, he had delivered, and Eagles Nation loved him, so why shouldn't he get paid accordingly? Or at least get more of his contract money guaranteed?

Eight months earlier, Jackson had fired Drew Rosenhaus, the agent who negotiated that 2012 deal for him, and signed with rival agent Joel Segal. Agents only get a percentage of the deals that they negotiated. As long as DeSean's old contract remained in effect, Segal got nothing and Rosenhaus got 3% of DeSean's earnings, despite the fact that he had been fired.

To fans and reporters, none of whom knew about the exit interview, Jackson's comments about deserving more money just sounded like DeSean being DeSean.

Beat reporter Les Bowen of the *Philadelphia Daily News* says that Jackson wasn't demanding anything. Instead, a number of reporters asked him "very aggressively" about the contract and Jackson replied that a raise seemed fair. Bowen told me:

> The main thing I remember from that day was, everybody knew Vick was gone, and that this was the last day with Michael Vick. And [DeSean] kept hanging around Vick's stall, and talking to Vick, and putting his

---

1   "Philadelphia Eagles DeSean Jackson wants new contract" by Bob Grotz, *Norristown Times Herald*, January 6, 2014.

hand on Vick's shoulder. This was like, a huge thing for him, that Vick was leaving.

Philadelphia Inquirer beat reporter Zach Berman told me that Jackson spoke about his contract only in response to Berman's direct question; the receiver did not volunteer his complaints.

> I asked DeSean the question about the contract because I believe he had no guaranteed money remaining on his deal, or a very small amount. So essentially he was in a situation where he had no leverage. I mean, the team could have released him– as they did–or traded him. And to add to that, he had just changed his agent, and usually when you change your agent, there's an impetus towards it as well. And I thought his answer was reasonable. He didn't come in there kind of mouthing off about the contract. I asked him the question.

Jackson made the same point in an Instagram post the next day, after controversy erupted. At the same time, Berman noted,

> DeSean had no problem answering this question. I mean, there's some times when you sense as a reporter that a player doesn't want to talk about this, and DeSean had no problem answering this question.

The Eagles let reporters roam around the locker room after games and at cleanout, and once word spread that the WR was asking for more money, reporter after reporter came up to ask him about it. The *Inquirer's* other primary beat reporter, Jeff McLane, later reported that:

> Jackson gave essentially the same answer to several waves of reporters that approached him as he cleaned out his locker stall.[1]

But there were some small—and maybe important—differences between what he told the different scribes. Tim McManus and Sheil

---

1   "Source: New contract for DeSean Jackson unlikely" by Jeff McLane, *Philadelphia Inquirer*, January 9, 2014.

Kapadia of *Birds 24/7*, the highly respected football blog hosted by *Philadelphia Magazine*, quoted Jackson as saying:

> I think my agent Joel Segal has a great plan going into this off-season. I still feel like I'm a top receiver in this league… I definitely feel something's deserving, so we'll see how that plays out and hopefully we can work things out smoothly and not have to worry about anything out of the ordinary.[1]

At his own press conference later that day, his last of the season, Coach Kelly dismissed the dispute with a joke.

> I don't talk about contracts, I'm never going to have a discussion over it. I do think everybody in this room should be paid more, though.[2]

Looking back now, and knowing that Jackson was just about to slap his coaches in the face, the wide receiver's comments about his agent's "great plan," and avoiding "anything out of the ordinary" sound a lot more like a threat.

Twice in the previous ten years, the team's front office had learned the hard way that a demanding wide receiver (WR) with a new agent is a very dangerous situation.

They had been burned both times, once with Terrell Owens in 2005, and again with DeSean himself in 2011. Both times, the team's star wide receiver switched to agent Drew Rosenhaus, demanded more money, and threatened a holdout. Both times, the Eagles held firm. Both times, the player started acting out and the team suffered.

Owens, a great wide receiver who had led the Eagles to their last Super Bowl appearance, publicly criticized his quarterback Donovan McNabb, wore a Cowboys jersey after the Eagles lost to Dallas, and got into a locker room fistfight with former teammate Hugh "Turbobird" Douglas, who was delivering a message to Owens as the front office's "goodwill ambassador". (A team source told Chris

---

1   "Jackson Wants A New Deal" by Tim McManus and Sheil Kapadia, *Birds 24/7*, January 6, 2014.
2   "Eagles' Jackson wants to renegotiate contract" by Nick Fierro, *Allentown Morning Call*, January 6, 2014.

Mortensen that Douglas, a 6'2", 281-lb. defensive end (DE), was more of a "Badass-ador."[1]) Despite T.O.'s half-hearted apology, the team suspended and later released him, getting nothing in return.

DeSean Jackson's first contract dispute played out a little differently. With one year left on his modest rookie contract after the 2010 season, Jackson (and Rosenhaus) had demanded a new deal.

DeSean staged a training camp holdout that collapsed right before big penalties on the wide receiver would have kicked in. Still, he pouted his way through the 2011 season, scoring only two touchdowns. After several years of playoff success, the Eagles started the 2011 season 4-8 before winning their last four to salvage a .500 record.

In the opinion of reporter Les Bowen, the holdout led to the demise of team president Joe Banner. Bowen told me that

> [Coach] Andy Reid wanted this resolved, and wanted DeSean full-hearted and single minded. This kept dragging on and on and on and on and the season went bad, and I think Andy was very exasperated that Joe couldn't get this thing done.
>
> … Andy made it clear that this was a huge problem for him, and when they got rid of Joe, one of the first things Howie did was give guys new contracts who were dissatisfied. That was going to be their new model, was not be the team that pissed people off…

Instead of standing firm at the risk of losing DeSean the way they lost T.O., the Eagles rewarded his behavior with a five-year, nearly $50 million contract. Howie Roseman, who had a reputation as a fierce political infighter, gained power, and Joe Banner—a childhood friend of owner Jeffrey Lurie—was fired. Despite the damage to the team, Jackson (and his agent) got paid.

Andy Reid had a kind of surrogate father/son relationship with DeSean. Jackson's dad died of cancer in 2009, a time when Reid's

---

1   "Owens-Douglas fistfight contributed to suspension" by ESPN News Services, ESPN.com, November 7, 2005.

son Garrett was struggling with the drug addiction[1] that would kill him three years later.[2]

Now in 2014, Reid was gone and those disastrous money disputes were fresh in the front office's memory. A new contract would not come as easily this time.

Chip Kelly, who has no children, was less indulgent than his predecessor. If Reid had been a father figure, Chip was a strict stepdad who couldn't understand why this spoiled kid got away with so much crap.

If DeSean thought he was too big for the new coach to challenge, then he hadn't followed Chip Kelly's career at Oregon. In his first head coaching job ever, Kelly had suspended or dismissed his biggest star four different times; RB LeGarrette Blount (suspended for most of the year right after Kelly's very first game), starting quarterback Jeremiah Masoli and All-American CB/returner Cliff Harris (kicked off the team), and RB LaMichael James (suspended). LB Kiko Alonso didn't even have time to become a star before Kelly suspended him for a year.

The big question was, could Coach Kelly take the same approach in the NFL? He had less control given league rules, a union, legal contracts with players, as well as an owner (Jeffrey Lurie) and General Manager (Howie Roseman) who had final say on personnel issues.

DeSean Jackson challenged Kelly as soon as the new coach began practices in 2013, refusing to learn all three wide receiver positions as Chip wanted. The coach moved quickly to establish his authority. He immediately demoted DeSean to the second and third teams in practice. Jackson demanded a face-to-face meeting to ask why. Afterwards, he described their talk:

> When I went in there, he said he expects everybody to buy into the system and do everything the right way.

---

1 "Andy Reid's ordeals and triumphs" by Ashley Fox, *Philadelphia Inquirer*, July 18, 2010.

2 "Garrett Reid, son of Andy, found dead" by ESPN Wire Services, ESPN.com, August 6, 2012.

> And if there is any little thing a player doesn't want to do, that's his way of reacting to it. The best thing I did was go talk to him instead of just sitting back and being mad.[1]

The message seemed to have been delivered. Jackson learned a lot of new routes and moves, not just going deep but using the threat of that to open up shorter passes. And Jackson had a career year, going to the Pro Bowl for the third time.

His disruptive attitude had continued, though. Most famously, he yelled at his position coach (WR coach Bob Bicknell) on national TV during the 2013 Vikings game, and shoved a member of the Eagles' staff[2]—it looks like former Seahawks Pro Bowl WR Koren Robinson—who tried to restrain him. Jackson made it clear that he did not fully buy in to Kelly's demanding program.

But by the end of the season in January, 2014, fans and reporters had forgotten about the receiver's rebellions as they speculated about what the new coach would do in the off-season.

1   "After Early Demotion, DeSean Jackson Says He's 'All-In'" by Tim McManus, *Birds 24/7*, June 4, 2013.
2   "DeSean Jackson blows up on Eagles' sideline" by Chris Chase, *USA Today For The Win*, December 15, 2013.

RADIO SILENCE

JANUARY 7, 2014

One reason no one knew about Jackson's no-show was that Chip Kelly and his staff stopped talking to the press. In the 2013 off-season, right after he was hired, Kelly had made the rounds, giving some speeches and talking to reporters both off and on the record. Had they asked their colleagues in Oregon, though, sportswriters would have realized how unusual this was.

While he can be expansive, funny and discursive at press conferences, Chip has rarely spoken publicly anywhere else during his head coaching career. He does a few television appearances and radio spots, controlled environments that he can easily manage, but otherwise Kelly only speaks publicly when he absolutely has to. In January, 2014, Chip Kelly had been a head coach for six years, and had only given two reporters the time and access to write a feature about him.

Both appeared shortly after he took his first head coaching job, at the University of Oregon. One was in the *New York Times*, and the other in the local Eugene, Oregon newspaper (the *Register Guard*). They remain essential reading for anyone interested in Kelly.[1]

---

1   "Man on the Move" by George Schroeder, *Eugene Register Guard*, October 18, 2009; and "Speed-Freak Football" by Michael Sokolove, *New York Times*, December 2, 2010. The author of this book published a longform profile of Kelly at Philly.com in 2014, called "What Makes Chip… Chip" without direct access to the coach. Later in the summer of 2014, Kelly gave a third interview to *Sports Illustrated*/MMQB heavyweight Peter King. King started his account of the discussion with an all-time great humblebrag: "I've had only two extended conversations with Kelly since he was named coach of the Eagles 19 months

Now in his second off-season, Kelly returned to his usual pattern, unavailable to the press and public. He focused his time on scouting college players who might be available in the upcoming draft. Through all of the controversial events of the next two months, he did not issue a single comment, which basically drove the press corps crazy. They were used to frequent—if often boilerplate—comments from Andy Reid, who lasted a remarkable twelve years in Philadelphia, and the best-connected writers had well-developed confidential sources with the team as well.

Now that was all gone, and reporters were not happy.

Kelly runs a tight ship with very few leaks. Purported "inside information" is very rare and rarely reliable. Chip watchers learn to observe the small details on the team's website and focus on what *isn't* talked about as much as what it. Greg Bedard is one of *Sports Illustrated's* top reporters; he has managed to get on-the-record quotes from figures as tight-lipped as Bill Belichick and Tom Brady. But after he wrote a five-page profile of Chip Kelly, he told a Philadelphia sports radio station that doing a piece on the coach "was one of the toughest assignments I've had, his inner circle doesn't give anything up."[1]

This silence baffles traditional reporters, because Chip is actually very good at press conferences. He's direct, confident, disarming and often funny, with the verbal chops of a TV color commentator and the stoic, "actions over words" values of a lifelong "football guy." Reporters think he always helps himself with public appearances, so why not have more of them?

Kelly, the son of an Irish-American attorney, also has a great knack for parrying questions, though his style is all football coach and no lawyer. He frequently teases reporters and calls out insinuations or pompous wording the way your buddies might, if you were enjoying a few beers while watching a game. He ridiculed

ago. To say I know him well would be folly. But I'm starting to get a feel for him." "Scenes from an Ongoing Tour of Training Camps" by Peter King, *Sports Illustrated The MMQB*, July 28, 2014

1   97.5 The Fanatic Morning Show [@975Mornings]. May 26, 2014. Retrieved from www.twitter.com/975Mornings/status/603186096592289792

one scribe for asking about a player's "organic" development, and jumped on another who used the phrase "harken back." He would probably mock the word "scribe" in the last sentence.

When he doesn't want to answer a question, Coach Kelly will look for a flaw in the wording or find some other way to turn it back on his interrogator. Or he'll reject the premise of the question, saying "We don't look at it that way," and reframe the whole discussion.

Reading articles about the Eagles, it often sounds like the reporter is quoting a one-on-one conversation he had with Chip.[1] He isn't. All of the quotes you see in articles come from the same public press conferences, or from a single, embargoed round table discussion Chip holds with the 15-20 beat reporters every spring. Aside from that round table, fans can watch almost every one of these press conferences on the Eagles' website at any time. The only advantage that reporters have is the opportunity to ask a question.

After January 6th, Kelly didn't make a single public remark until March 15th, when he received the Maxwell Football Club's Earle "Greasy" Neale Award as professional coach of the year. Eleven days later, on March 26th, he took questions from reporters at the NFL Owners' Meeting, as required by league rules. And then he was quiet again until April 28th, when the Eagles came out to Philadelphia's Prince Hall School for their annual playground build.

In between those three press conferences, there were a lot of dramatic changes to the Eagles' roster. DeSean Jackson was only one of many personnel problems faced by Chip Kelly and his coaching staff, and Kelly preferred to focus on scouting and free agency instead of worrying about what fans and sportswriters thought.

Actual games are only a small part of the NFL experience. Teams play fewer than twenty hours of actual game time in a year, and much of that is standing around between snaps. But fans immerse themselves year round with fantasy football, the combine and draft speculation, and most importantly arguing with other fans

---

1   All of the Eagles beat writers in Philadelphia are men, though Jenny Vrentas of the national website MMQB has written some of the best-sourced (scoopingest) articles on Chip Kelly.

about what their team should do.

With the Eagles silent, all news about the Eagles had to come from reporters. It's unnerving to write about Kelly's teams. Given his secrecy, we are all just making educated guesses at best.

This stark news vacuum caught the media in a particular historical moment of intense and rapid change. Print newspapers had long dominated the media in the town where Benjamin Franklin fashioned the first modern American newspaper (the *Pennsylvania Gazette*) in 1729.

During Andy Reid's twelve years as the Eagles' coach, the *Philadelphia Inquirer*—its main paper, founded in 1829—had lost more than half of its circulation. The "Inq" and its tabloid rival, the *Philadelphia Daily News*, are now run by the same owners and share a website (Philly.com). In those same twelve years, the combined papers were sold to new owners six times and saw their advertising revenues drop more than 75%. They still do much of the best reporting, but continued layoffs and budget cuts are constant and inevitable.

Sports radio and TV are clinging to their market share nervously, while blogs and podcasts expand rapidly despite uncertain finances and wildly uneven journalistic standards.

Radio and TV are much more expensive to produce than words, but they boast the biggest journalistic prize in town—access to Chip Kelly. Perhaps because the appearances are short and the situations are easier to control, Kelly makes himself available only three places outside of press conferences, all on the air—and then only during football season.

Every Monday morning for five minutes, he calls in to Angelo Cataldi's highly rated sports talk show on WIP radio. Cataldi, a former *Inquirer* sportswriter, has the second-highest-rated morning drive time program in Philadelphia among men 25-54, a prized demographic.

Once a week, Kelly has a one-on-one video interview on the Eagles website with in-house broadcaster Dave Spadaro, who has been working for the Eagles since the 1990s. Spadaro is a smart analyst in a tough spot. As the official mouthpiece of the team, he naturally has to adopt a positive tone, and the habitual naysayers in Philadelphia heap abuse on him in online discussions. It's a dream job in many ways but not an easy one, and Coach Kelly is not inclined to make it easier.

His demeanor in the interviews makes it clear he would rather be down the hall in the video room looking at game film, or really anywhere else on earth. The appearances range from interesting to painful, with gruff one-word answers when the coach is not in the mood to chat.

Also on the website is the "Kellystrator" segment, a fascinating feature that the coach clearly enjoys much more. He reviews game film with a former player (Brian Baldinger or Ike Reese), using a high-tech monitor to diagram plays and step through the video in slow motion. It's a revelation—Chip becomes expansive and enthusiastic, explaining nuances that even hardcore fans might have trouble noticing on their own.

During the off-season though, even these short features go dark and journalists are left on their own to find things to write about. Coach Kelly's Eagles aren't hostile to reporters so much as they simply aren't interested in playing by the usual rules. In a town full of smart, aggressive reporters and colorful personalities who enjoy talking, the absence of leaks from the team is nothing short of astonishing.

Sportswriter Matt Mullin of PhillyVoice.com links the team's approach to a classic battle strategy dating back at least to *The Art of War*, Sun Tzu's ancient book of Chinese military philosophy. The concept is to hide your plans, then act suddenly and decisively.

> Be extremely subtle even to the point of formlessness. Be extremely mysterious even to the point of soundlessness. Thereby you can be the director of the opponent's fate.

It's hard to know if the silence confounded opponents, but it definitely threw the print reporters off. The new media writers, used to being on the outside all along, seemed to adapt a bit better.

REBUILDING THE ROSTER

JANUARY 15, 2014

Rather than chatting with the press, Kelly and his staff were focused on evaluating the results of the 2013 season, and looking at players they might acquire through trades, free agency, or the draft.

January and February are the slow season for NFL teams that aren't in the Super Bowl, and many coaches and players were escaping the snowy 2014 winter on tropical islands. But Chip Kelly watchers were not surprised to learn that he was already diligently working to beef up his squad in free agency and the draft. Kelly told a reporter that he and his staff had sketched out in advance what they planned to do for the entire off-season from January 7th until the moment that training camp opened on July 25th, 2014.

There was a consensus among pundits and reporters, as well as fans, about the Eagles' biggest holes in talent—the gaps that desperately need to be filled:

1. A dominant pass rusher, specifically an outside right linebacker for the 3-4 scheme.
2. One or two safeties.
3. A kicker to replace the fading Alex Henery and his weak leg.
4. One or two cornerbacks (CBs).
5. A tall, fast wide receiver (or perhaps a very elusive slot receiver).

There was not even much controversy in the approach to the

draft; take the best player available (in character as well as talent), rather than stretching to fill the very well noted gaps. The Eagles had been burned in the recent past by drafting for need over talent.

The 2011 collective bargaining agreement between the league and the NFLPA players' union created a radically different market for players. Rookies now sign 4-year contracts at very low salaries. If they play well and stay healthy, free agency promises a giant payday of tens of millions of dollars (depending on position). But the strict salary cap limits teams to only a couple of these stars. With a salary cap of $133 million for all fifty-three players, how many $12 million/year superstars can a team afford?

There were unintended consequences as well. Trading top players became almost impossible, because their large contracts come along with them.

And running backs (RBs) lost value, because statistically most start to decline rapidly from age twenty-six—right about the time their inexpensive rookie contracts expire. Why invest $40 million in a fading asset?

Draft picks became more valuable, as one good pick could give you four years of a great talent for under a million dollars a year, depending on the round. Seattle built their Super Bowl franchise on a number of shrewd lower round picks such as star CB Richard Sherman (a fifth round selection).

The problem is that it's very difficult to predict which college stars will succeed in the NFL. Pro players are so much bigger and faster. Imagine the best one or two players on a top twenty college team; those guys are just average in the NFL. Most players can't adjust.

Many of the players Chip inherited from Andy Reid did not fit his radically different offensive and defensive schemes. Reid ran a West Coast, passing-based offense and had recently switched (disastrously) to an unusual Wide-9 defense. But it's difficult to replace more than a handful of the players on a team's fifty-three-man roster with high-quality talent, which is why many had expected another losing season in 2013.

The team did amazingly well in Kelly's first year with ten of his eleven offensive starters inherited from Andy Reid's team, but this was more of a bullet dodged than a successful strategy, especially on defense. Kelly's OL was completely healthy all year and his unique offensive style managed to surprise opponents in his debut season, masking the fact that the defensive secondary was the second worst in the league.

But NFL teams adapt very quickly, even during a game. Take Chip Kelly's pro debut, against Washington on Monday Night Football. Even though his fast-paced, run-based spread was well known from his years at the University of Oregon, he stunned the Skins with fifty-three first-half plays—more than some teams run in an entire game. The Eagles led 26-7 at the break, and even those 7 points came from a fluke play (a deflected pass was ruled a fumbled lateral and run back for a TD). Washington adjusted at halftime though, and the Eagles barely hung on for a 33-26 win.

Kelly is known for fast and decisive actions, but he also has a very precise notion of the players he wants—their height, weight, speed, agility, hand size, character, intelligence and attitude—which can make it harder to fill positions.

He likes his wide receivers and defensive backs unusually tall (over 6'1" and 5'11" respectively) and physical, seeing an NFL trend toward dominating, oversized wideouts such as Calvin Johnson, Jr. (aka "Megatron") and 2014 rookie Kelvin Benjamin, both 6'5". Only big defensive backs such as Seattle's Richard Sherman (6'3") can hope to keep these speedy giants in check. In Kelly's system, receivers are expected to block defenders when not targeted for a pass; otherwise you have two, three or even four of your eleven players contributing nothing at all on a play. According to WR Josh Huff, this was drilled into Oregon's players as well.

> Chip always said, 'If you don't block, you don't get the rock.'[1]

---

1   "Kelly's former players feel at home with the Eagles" by Les Bowen, *Philadelphia Daily News*, August 28, 2014.

Tailbacks should be compact and muscular one-cut runners who catch short passes and screens and move "north-south" (straight-ahead into gaps in the line) rather than "east-west" (side to side, dodging tackles).

Offensive linemen (OL) must be athletic and skilled at zone-blocking instead of the typical assignment to block a single player. In his 3-4 defensive fronts, the linemen must be good at "two-gapping"—stopping runners on either side of the blocker facing them—while linebackers should be equally adept at rushing the passer or dropping back into pass coverage. This allows the defensive coordinator to disguise who the pass rushers will be, but it also rules out a lot of defenders who are great at pass rushing or coverage, but not both.

LESSONS FROM
A PLAYOFF LOSS

Despite the Eagles' regular season success, they had met their match against New Orleans. The Saints' Sean Payton is one of the few coaches in football who is clearly Chip Kelly's equal as an innovative play caller, and the well-organized veteran team was able to expose many of Philadelphia's weaknesses.

Kelly's philosophy of a spread offense hopes to use every inch of the field, aiming to force solo tackles in the open field and create one-on-one mismatches. But the team's losses, especially against New Orleans in the playoffs, revealed several positions where even one-on-one matchups weren't favorable.

The Eagles had well-known deficiencies in their pass defense, and coached around them vigorously, so Payton surprised everyone by emphasizing his team's less accomplished run game. Mark Ingram, Khiry Robinson and Darren Sproles combined for 171 yards on thirty carries and ground out the final drive for the winning field goal against the Eagles' smaller nickel defense.

While the Saints' runners were able to excel in the grittier playoff atmosphere, averaging 5.7 yards per carry, Philadelphia's shifty LeSean McCoy—who led the NFL in rushing that year—managed only 77 yards (3.7 YPC).

Payton also exposed the inexact fit of many players in Kelly's system. Nick Foles was accurate and decisive all season, but he is no one's concept of a mobile quarterback. Four of the Eagles' five starting offensive linemen had faster 40-yard dash times than Foles' 5.14. Chip answered this criticism by noting that "Foles is not fleet of foot, but he's fleet of mind." In the heightened pressure of the playoffs though, it would have been much better to be fleet of both. Foles added only 3 yards against the Saints in an offense designed to give the quarterback running opportunities.

Kelly's concerns about needing big receivers were borne out, too. DeSean Jackson is one of the fastest receivers in football and a potent deep threat, but he's 5'10" at best and maybe 180 pounds with a heavy backpack on. New Orleans 6'1", 208-pound cornerback Keenan Lewis jammed Jackson at the line of scrimmage and completely shut him down. DeSean also makes no effort to block when he's not targeted for a pass, a pet peeve of Kelly's and a weakness that other coaches have openly mocked him for.[1]

Though Foles targeted Jackson on the very first play from scrimmage, the receiver didn't catch a single pass until late in the third quarter—after Lewis left the game with a concussion. On the very next play, DeSean caught a 40-yard bomb, followed by a short pass on the following snap. The Eagles scored twice to take a late one-point lead, helped by another 10-yard pass to Jackson and a 40-yard pass interference penalty on the man defending him.

But Jackson's late success only highlighted how effectively Lewis had shut him down. In one of the most important one-on-one matchups of the season, the Eagles were hopelessly outmatched. Without the fluke concussion, and the NFL's newly strict concussion protocol designed to protect players against brain damage, Philadelphia's comeback would have been impossible.

Other players struggled, too. Rookie nose tackle Bennie Logan, a surprise success all year, was pushed back repeatedly on runs. #2 receiver Riley Cooper—also having a career year under Kelly—scored the Eagles' first TD, but he dropped a wide-open pass that should have been a huge gain.

And kicker Alex Henery continued his steady deterioration, missing a field goal and booting short kickoffs after the Eagles' two fourth quarter touchdowns, leading to big returns by Sproles.

---

1 "Washington Coach Jay Gruden Slams DeSean Amid Laughter" by Mark Saltveit, *Bleeding Green Nation*, September 19, 2014.

All of these deficiencies combined into one disastrous sequence midway through the first half. The Eagles had driven down to the New Orleans 29 yard line with 2:19 left in the first quarter. On 2nd and seven, LeSean McCoy took a handoff from Foles and cut back to the right, where DeSean had gone out for a short sideline pass and McCoy had a massive opening.

The entire right side of the field was wide open for 15 yards— Shady had only the safety to beat, in the open field, for a touchdown. He's one of the best skill players in football at juking a single tackler in space.

But instead of blocking the cornerback covering him, Jackson simply stood and watched as LeSean McCoy ran in his direction. CB Keenan Lewis left Jackson, ran over and tackled LeSean after a 6-yard gain. After a couple of short runs, the Eagles' drive was stalled by two consecutive losses as a screen pass to Celek was stuffed, and Foles got sacked for an 11-yard loss. On fourth down and twenty-five, Henery missed a 48-yard field goal—and the Eagles lost the game by 2 points.

Chip Kelly does not like losing. He hasn't done much of it, with a 67-19 record in six years as a head coach of the Oregon Ducks and Philadelphia Eagles, and you could argue that he overreacted to his team's failures. Whether that's fair or not, many of his personnel moves can be seen as direct reactions to his team's few losses.

In his first NFL draft, Kelly traded up to grab USC's quarterback Matt Barkley, whose Trojans had scored 51 points against Kelly's Ducks six months earlier. USC still lost that game because Oregon scored 62, but you couldn't blame that on Barkley. The young QB has done little of note in the NFL, though, turning the ball over repeatedly in rare appearances as the Eagles third string QB.

Similarly, the playoff loss to New Orleans—a down note in a good year—became the blueprint for many of Chip Kelly's 2014 roster moves.

And that's just what owner Jeffrey Lurie wanted. The Eagles had a remarkable string of playoff appearances under Lurie and previous coach Andy Reid, but they only reached the Super Bowl once, and lost. The team has never won a Super Bowl, though they garnered three NFL championships before the merger with the AFL. The last was in 1960.

EXPIRING CONTRACTS

FEBRUARY 27, 2014

The first order of business for Howie Roseman and the Eagles' front office was deciding what to do about players whose contracts had run out, or would soon. Unless they agreed to new deals, Jeremy Maclin and Riley Cooper would be free to sign with any team they liked on March 11th. And two key offensive linemen would be entering the final year of their deals, likely to leave in the spring of 2015.

The Eagles' 2013 front five was an accomplished, close-knit group that performed well, taught each other, and moved its blocking downfield at an astonishing rate. They had a rare chemistry, and the Eagles recognized that by signing gifted young center Jason Kelce to a seven-year extension, and locking up thirty-three-year-old future Hall of Fame left tackle Jason Peters for the rest of his career. The rest of the front line—Evan Mathis, Lane Johnson and Todd Herremans—were already signed through 2016 at least.

That was a smart move. Chip had built a rock-solid core for the team, with strong offensive and defensive lines. These were hard-working guys with good attitudes, who loved what Chip was doing for the team. They weren't just great players; they had great chemistry, and several worked out together voluntarily during the off-season.

At the time Kelce signed his extension, GM Howie Roseman marveled at his work ethic, even in the off-season[1]:

---

1   "Jason Kelce, Sweatpants And $37.5 Million," by Sheil Kapadia, *Birds 24/7*, February 28, 2014.

I come down to breakfast every day and he's here, he's working. And it's February. And it's because he loves to be here. He loves the game of football. He has an incredible passion for this city, for this football team.

For his part, Kelce has a clear chemistry with Coach Kelly, and he has been his most vocal supporter on the team. He told reporters:

Chip, as soon as he got here, the culture that he brings, this ever-changing, ever-trying to improve yourself not just as a player but as a teammate, as a leader, as a person, I think that whole thing that's pounded into your head over and over again, that's really what I try to be like as a player and as a person.[1]

The next step was wide receivers. 2014 was an interesting draft year, with one of the deepest classes of big, fast WRs to come out of college, ever.

Meanwhile, 2013 breakout star Riley Cooper and No. 2 WR Jeremy Maclin—who missed Chip Kelly's first season with an ACL tear—were already free agents.

Maclin was small and speedy, with production similar to—but slightly less than—DeSean's. He was a little bigger and a little more versatile than Jackson, but not as fast. One knock on him was a perceived lack of toughness after the catch; reporter Jimmy Kempski gave him the nickname "self-tacklin' Maclin" back in 2012.

WR Riley Cooper wasn't much to look at on paper. He had the size Coach Kelly prefers, at 6'4", 230 lbs, but wasn't especially fast or great at separation. But he and QB Nick Foles had a special chemistry in 2013 for some unexplainable reason, and it's hard to throw that away when it falls into your lap. After Nick Foles took over at quarterback mid-year, Riley Cooper gained more yards than DeSean in six out of nine games—and the Eagles went 7-2.[2]

---

1   "Kelly's Influence Felt Behind the Scenes," by Sheil Kapadia, *Birds 24/7*, March 3, 2014.

2   Brandon Lee Gowton [@BrandonGowton]. March 22, 2014. Interesting chart from the BGN fanposts. Look at the split between Foles and Vick when it comes to Jackson/Cooper. http://cdn2.sbnation.com/imported_

Unlike Jackson, Cooper was effective in the red zone (inside the 20 yard line). In the condensed space approaching the goal line, Jackson's deep speed was no use, while Cooper's height helped win the contested catches and "jump balls" more common there. Cooper had eight touchdowns on forty-seven receptions, only one fewer than DeSean scored on eighty-two catches. Surprisingly, Cooper caught deep passes at the same rate as Jackson, too, boasting more yards per catch (17.6 vs. DeSean's 16.2).

Cooper's connection with Foles was clearest in the Detroit "Snow Bowl" game in 2013. Nothing went right on offense for the Eagles through most of three quarters, until Foles decided to trust Riley. He basically just launched a 44-yard bomb into a raging blizzard, and somehow Cooper found it, dropping out of the snowflakes like a plane landing in the fog. That play turned around the entire game; the Eagles were down 14-0 with five minutes left in the third quarter, then scored 34 points in the last twenty minutes to win.

Cooper was an accomplished baseball outfielder in college, and one theory was that this gave him the advantage in finding balls in the air. At the same time, he hadn't shown much ability in the first three years of his career. He totaled 835 yards in 2013, but only 679 in 2010, 2011 and 2012—combined.

The team accomplished its goals in re-signing Maclin and Cooper, but in retrospect did a poor job of negotiating the contracts. It's likely that in their eagerness to gain bargaining power with their #1 receiver, they gave it away with #2 and #3.

GM Howie Roseman gave Cooper a massive $22.5 million, five-year deal with $8 million guaranteed. According to the website OverTheCap.com, this was the twenty-ninth largest of 290 wide receiver contracts, as of 2015, but no one thinks Riley Cooper is in the top 10% of receivers.

Most dangerously, the contract made it almost impossible to cut Cooper for two years. His big guarantee and cap hit was in the

---

assets/2117793/13323851234_4175f601ec_o.jpg [Tweet]. Retrieved from www.twitter.com/BrandonGowton/status/447427363786477568

2015 season, so that the team actually would have to pay more if they cut him than if they kept him on the roster that year.

With Maclin, it was the opposite problem. The team offered him a multi-year contract, but he insisted on a one-year "prove it" deal. This could cost him a lot of money if he wasn't able to come back completely from his ACL tear, but if he performed well he was poised to get a huge free agent deal.

It seemed like a good bet to him. Maclin played in a spread offense similar to Kelly's in college, at Missouri, and he had just seen DeSean have a career year in the new system, 30% better than anything he'd done before, despite having a worse attitude than Maclin's.

HURRICANE DESEAN

On March 1, a little known and fast-rising reporter named Jimmy Kempski published a story[1] that blew the fragile quiet into shards. In a nutshell, he said that, having signed Maclin and Cooper to new contracts, the Eagles looked like they might be ready to trade DeSean Jackson.

You might think that's a standard, even boring, football story. A team might trade a player. *Might.* Even granted that he's a star, what's the big deal?

DeSean was not just a star, however.

He had earned incredible love from fans with flashy plays and hilarious showboating. The movie *Silver Linings Playbook* is a testament to his iconic status. To signify their love of the Eagles, the movie's characters invoke his name over and over as if they were praying rosaries to the Saint of Sudden Touchdowns.

Above all, Jackson owed his fame to a single play in a game on December 19, 2010. It is now known as "The Miracle at the New Meadowlands" because of the Eagles' improbable comeback. With 8:17 left in the fourth quarter, they were down 31-10 to the New York Giants, and the game seemed clearly lost.

Then Brent Celek caught a touchdown, Riley Cooper grabbed the onside kick, and quarterback Michael Vick had two crucial runs—35 yards, then 4 yards for another TD. The Eagles forced New York to punt, threw another TD to Jeremy Maclin, and forced one more punt with fourteen seconds left and the game tied at 31. You'll never guess what happened next.

---

1 "Eagles' signings of Jeremy Maclin and Riley Cooper could signal a DeSean Jackson trade" by Jimmy Kempski, Philly.com, March 1, 2014 .

The kick went to DeSean, who actually dropped the ball. Then he picked up his fumble and ran 65 yards through traffic for a touchdown, to complete what NFL.com calls "one of the greatest comebacks in NFL history."

Jackson not only scored, he had the presence of mind to run sideways before entering the end zone to run out the last seconds of the clock and prevent the Giants from responding with their own miracle.

It's impossible to overstate how dramatic and emotional that return is. On April 9, 2013, football fans nationwide voted it the greatest NFL play of all time.[1]

Jackson has always been a controversial figure, even in college playing for California in the PAC-10 (later PAC-12). Plenty of fans wished he would work harder, focus on football, and exhibit less diva-like behavior. His soft-holdout during 2011 was a particular focus of scorn, because it clearly hurt the team's performance.

Even so, no reporter, talk radio jockey or blogger had considered the possibility that the Eagles might get rid of Jackson—not even when he said he wanted a new contract and hinted that something "out of the ordinary" might happen if he didn't get it.

So in March of 2014 you had a news vacuum, and a lot of mystery about what Chip Kelly might do. Out of the blue, some guy writes that the coach might trade away the city's most beloved player? The always-intense Philadelphia sports media went on full mobilization. The two major sports radio stations—WIP, and WPEN, better known as 97.5 The Fan—were overwhelmed by the response.

James Seltzer, a producer at WPEN, told me that in his two years at the station, the DeSean situation has been the single biggest story in any sport.

> From a sports radio story perspective, there's been nothing like it, and it went literally for a month of solid DeSean talk.

---

1   "Miracle at the New Meadowlands voted the greatest NFL play of all time" by Justin Klugh, Philly.com, May 9, 2013.

BREAKING NEWS AND CONFIDENTIAL SOURCES

Chip Kelly's staff is very tight-lipped, and it's difficult for anyone to get inside information. A few newspaper reporters broke most of the scoops during the Andy Reid years—Jeff McLane and Zach Berman at the *Inquirer*, Les Bowen of the *Daily News*, and Geoff Mosher at Comcast SportsNet (CSN Philly). With Chip Kelly as coach, new writers joined them, mostly guys who wrote for the blogs of print publications: Tim McManus at *Birds 24/7* (a blog of *Philadelphia Magazine*), Jimmy Kempski of Philly.com (the website for the two big papers), and Eliot Shorr-Parks of NJ.com (a website for several Jersey newspapers). The newer reporters seem more adept at finding non-traditional sources, and they're definitely better at gleaning bits of information from social media sources, such as DeSean Jackson's frequent Instagram postings.

Players such as Evan Mathis and Matt Barkley show up from time to time on Reddit's /r/Eagles forum (or "subreddit"), as does Kempski. It's a place for interaction—Barkley got mad and challenged Kempski to a football-throwing duel after one bit of pointed criticism—but it's also a place where people can send anonymous tips without going through email. Twitter serves a similar function.

Kempski's initial story about DeSean was careful and understated. He did not trumpet confidential sources, or present the piece as breaking news. Under the title "Eagles' signings of Jeremy Maclin and Riley Cooper could signal a DeSean Jackson trade," he wrote a long, analytical essay that described the four possible results of those free agent signings—labeled (a), (b), (c) and (d) —and then suggested a fifth.

> As we learned over the last few days, the answer ended up being "D." Or did it? Is there perhaps a bombshell on the horizon, in the form of "option E?"
>
> E) Both Maclin and Cooper stay, DeSean Jackson goes.
>
> The Eagles are not going to shop Jackson. The instant they do, they'll forfeit any negotiating advantage they may have in trying to recoup acceptable value in return. This is especially true with a personality like Jackson, who comes with a history of character concerns. However, if another team came calling, the Eagles certainly wouldn't laugh and hang up.

This was presented as his opinion and analysis, not a scoop that Jackson was on his way out. But Kempski then proceeded to reveal that he did in fact have a confidential source connected with the Eagles who was suggesting something more dramatic. The very next line reads:

> There's an opinion among some in the Eagles organization that Jackson's personality is not a great fit with the locker room culture that Chip Kelly is trying to cultivate, and the Eagles could be open to trading him.

In the coded language of journalism, Kempski was sending several signals. By presenting this mostly as his analysis, he indicated that he did not have enough information—two independent, credible sources, named or anonymous, is the standard—to report that the Eagles were going to get rid of Jackson.

But he clearly had more than nothing. The certainty of his opinions, and his reporting of "an opinion among some in the Eagles organization," implied that he was carrying a message from the Eagles' front office, aimed at general managers of other squads.

> If another team came calling, the Eagles certainly wouldn't laugh and hang up.

It almost sounds like junior high school shenanigans, where Hannah runs up to ask you if you like Maddie and let you know that if you asked Maddie out, she'd probably say yes.

The Eagles were in a difficult spot. Any team that traded for DeSean would inherit his contract, which was too expensive by league standards. Jackson was basically a top ten wide receiver getting top five money. To trade, a team would have to give up a draft pick or player for the right to pay DeSean more than he was worth.

As Kempski noted, shopping DeSean around would have looked desperate. Potential trading partners would probably refuse to deal, knowing that if they just waited, the Birds would have to cut him. Then they could negotiate a new, cheaper contract and keep their draft picks.

Whatever subtle messages Kempski or the front office may have intended to send, Eagles Nation erupted with an outburst of emotion and bewilderment. WIP and 97.5 The Fan talked of little else for a month or two. Howard Eskin, a famous and mercurial radio host, replied to a tweet by Kempski about his story with the following message (edited for grammar) that implied his own front office sources:

> Possibly trading DeSean Jackson is not connected to the signings of Riley Cooper and Jeremy Maclin. I hear the team may be at the point [of wanting to trade him] because of his drama.
> @howardeskin. 12:56 P.M. March 1, 2014.

Others were in denial, dismissive or angry. On Twitter, "BGN Radio" podcaster John Barchard made a bold bet with the universe.

> If DeSean gets traded this year, I will wear a diaper, paint my chest with the saying "I'm a moron" and walk down Broad St. -Market to South
> @JohnBarchard. 3:34 P.M. March 2, 2014.

On March 4th, slot receiver Jason Avant was cut after a long career as one of the Eagles' most reliable and hard-working players, a true locker room leader. His production on the field had declined steadily, though.

The CSN TV show *Philly Sports Talk* noted the impact on DeSean's future. Host Michael Barkann asked reporter Derrick Gunn if Avant had served as a peacemaker between Jackson and WR coach Bob Bicknell. Gunn replied:

> On more than one occasion, yes. Yes. And the problem with that is… DeSean Jackson doesn't really listen to anybody. Jason Avant was probably the only guy who could get his attention. Over the last several years, the Eagles have had a number of ex-players try to talk to DeSean.
>
> DeSean Jackson does what DeSean Jackson does and I think that's eventually going to be his downfall. Not just with the Philadelphia Eagles, but in the NFL because the word is out on him. The word is out across the league on DeSean Jackson: "We don't know if he's the kind of guy we want in our locker room. We don't care how talented he is."

Four days after Kempski's bombshell, and one day after Avant's release, reporter Geoff Mosher of CSN Philly moved the story forward with a report that DeSean was "one false step away" from being cut outright. Despite that bold headline, though, the actual text of the story was much less confident:

> … it all seems to add up to this conclusion: DeSean Jackson, you're on the clock… all of [GM Howie] Roseman's recent moves and hints suggest that the super speedy wide receiver isn't part of the team's long-term vision. For a variety of reasons, mostly financial, Jackson's days with the Eagles are likely numbered.

No source was cited, and none of the sources I spoke to thought the report was based on solid information. (Mosher declined an interview request.) The article contradicted even itself, with a headline implying that Jackson's behavior was the problem, while the body of the article described the reasons as "mostly financial."

The biggest problem with Mosher's story was simply this;

according to my sources, the Eagles had already decided to get rid of Jackson in February, because Jackson wasn't physical enough, earned too much money, and didn't buy in to Coach Kelly's system.

No additional "false steps" were needed at all. The only thing standing between him and being cut at that point was the team's hope of a trade.

It's likely that Mosher had the same source as Kempski, or that his informant and Jimmy's were both passing on information from a common original source. But Mosher's story was blunt—a competing reporter who asked that his name not be used called it "half-baked reporting"—and it didn't capture the essence of the situation.

Mosher's story viewed the DeSean situation as a replay of the Terrell Owens mess. But Owens played hard and well up to the day he was suspended, and he delivered in the playoffs. He was not overpriced for his production. T.O. *was* in fact one step away from dismissal, for purely disciplinary reasons, and then he stepped over that line.

On March 5th, Eagles GM Howie Roseman ridiculed Mosher's report on Angelo Cataldi's radio *Morning Show*:

> Well it's funny because what I did last night when I got home is, I played the "one false step away" game with my wife. So I said, "what am I one false step away from?" and she said, "Certainly kicked to the curb."
>
> I'm one false step away from getting hit by a bus. I don't know where that report came from. Obviously everything that we're doing we're going to do in the best interest of the Eagles. Don't want to get into every rumor and kind of go through each player one by one, but certainly there was nothing there from anyone in this building that that report came from.[1]

The stories by Kempski and Mosher triggered an extraordinary response from Jeff McLane of the *Inquirer*, who is basically

---

1   "Howie Roseman Played The 'One False Step' DeSean Jackson Game At Home" by Angelo Cataldi and the Morning Team, *CBS Philly*, March 6, 2014.

Philadelphia's best known and best connected reporter. In a March 5th story in the *Inquirer* and a subsequent early-morning tweet, though, the main reporter for Philadelphia's newspaper of record was anything but cautious or carefully sourced.

It's more accurate to say that he thundered like an Old Testament prophet.

> DeSean Jackson rumors have little weight. Not usually into refuting rumors but the madness had to be stopped: http://po.st/dX3ohR #Eagles
> @Jeff_McLane. 5:21 A.M. March 6, 2014.

There were no grays in McLane's story, no caveats. He was 100% confident. And 100% wrong.

> The Eagles are not actively shopping DeSean Jackson, nor do they have any intention of parting with their Pro Bowl wide receiver this off-season... Jackson is not close to being cut, and even if he was one misstep away from forcing the Eagles to move him, they most certainly would not release him without getting something in return.

He was also apparently unaware that DeSean had skipped his exit interview. (That fact was not reported anywhere until three weeks later.)

> There has been no indication from Jackson or his agent, Joel Segal, that he plans to hold out.

What made this blast even more astonishing was that McLane admitted right in the story that he had no sources with the team.

> The Eagles do not respond to rumors. It wouldn't be in their best interest to feed a reporter this sort of information without attribution—as a "team source"—because refuting speculation would be acknowledging it.

So what did he base his conclusion on, then?

> ... after talking with almost a dozen sources from

around the league, it's clear the Eagles aren't interested in dealing the 27-year-old Jackson—not by a long shot.

It appears that McLane spoke with agents and GMs around the league, people who might be involved in a potential trade as well as former members of the Eagles organization such as Joe Banner (a childhood friend of Eagles owner Jeffrey Lurie) and perhaps Andy Reid staffers who had moved on to Kansas City with "Big Red." McLane's story was entirely wrong but it was exactly what many fans wanted to hear.

McLane's fatal mistake was thinking that if Mosher's and Kempski's reports were accurate, the Eagles would have already contacted other teams about potential trades. But the Eagles were keeping their powder dry. As Kempski's story said directly, they knew that actively shopping the wide receiver would ruin his value. They were waiting for the phone to ring.

Jeff McLane has a uniquely contentious relationship with Coach Kelly. Not that any reporters are buddy-buddy with Chip; he has been wary at best toward the press since his first day at Oregon. Andy Reid was a really warm, nice guy from the media's point of view, and well-connected reporters such as McLane had excellent access to information when he was coach.

Chip is at best a sparring partner for reporters. Though he has one of the league's highest ratios of great quotes per press conference, his teams have very few leaks. Access to inside sources dried up, and the change had to be very frustrating for a well-connected reporter.

That's just Chip, but for McLane it seemed a bit more personal, perhaps because he was the top reporter in town with the best access until the day Chip showed up. For his Twitter avatar—the little picture that appears next to your username—McLane often uses a cartoon of the coach looking worried and wearing a bicorn hat, the style associated with Napoleon (and, especially in cartoons, insane people with delusions of grandeur who think they are Napoleon). There was an incident later in the season, during a part of the story we haven't gotten to yet, where Kelly asserted his power over the team. In response, McLane tweeted that cartoon with this caption:

> Think it's time to break this baby out again. It's Chip's Ship, for good or bad.
>
> @Jeff_McLane. 3:50 P.M. January 2, 2015.

The dislike appears to be mutual.

Kelly can be playful, often teasing reporters the way you'd give crap to your buddies. But teasing is tricky. The coach spoke to reporters later in the year, at a particularly rough part of the 2014 season when he wasn't too happy about the way thing were going. Kyle Scott of the website *Crossing Broad* called it "the Saddest Chip Kelly Press Conference Ever."[1]

McLane was pressing Kelly on how whether he might change his lineup for the next game, and tried to poke Coach Kelly a little bit in that same teasing way. Chip was not having it; he turned to ice. When Coach Kelly turns his glare on a reporter, even the toughest tend to falter a bit or try to explain themselves.

Martin Frank of the *Wilmington News Journal* described what happened next in an article titled "Chip Gets Testy, Says No to Young Players:"[2]

> Then the reporter responded that the question was in the vein of Kelly only looking to the next game. To which Kelly responded: "Was that a wise-ass comment?"
>
> Then he stared at the reporter for a few seconds before adding: "I just told you before, we haven't done anything game plan-wise."

Under the scientific laws of Chip Kelly Special Relativity, a five-second wordless stare from the coach into your eyes at a press conference lasts seven or eight hours in normal space-time. A writer who was in the room described the scene this way:

---

1 "This Was the Saddest Chip Kelly Press Conference Ever" by Kyle Scott, CrossingBroad.com, December 22, 2014.

2 "Chip gets testy, says no plans to play young players" by Martin Frank, *Delaware News Journal*, December 22, 2014.

Chip doesn't necessarily like reporters, but he has a special lack of fondness for McLane. There was like 5 seconds of silence with them just staring at each other. And literally every person in the room is just sitting there like, "Oh boy." ... I don't think Chip loves any of the reporters, but I think he loves Jeff the least.

FREE AGENCY

MARCH 11, 2014

Roster moves don't really get started until the middle of March when teams are able to sign unrestricted free agents. Chip Kelly and GM Howie Roseman continued to implement their distinctive strategy:

1. Don't swing for the bleachers by competing for the highest priced stars,
2. Stick to young players,
3. Aim for versatility,
4. Get good citizens and leaders.

Philadelphia Eagles fans were not thrilled with this approach.[1] They wanted the excitement of big, splashy, name-brand signings, and in 2014 there were plenty[2]—by other teams. Denver tried to beef up its defense—so badly embarrassed in the 2014 Super Bowl against Seattle—by signing Dallas defensive end DeMarcus Ware ($30 million), Patriots cornerback Aqib Talib ($57 million) and Browns safety TJ Ward (a paltry $23 million). To replaced Talib, the Pats signed Darrelle Revis away from Tampa Bay on a one-year, $12-million deal.

Some Eagles fans had wanted the team to sign Revis, who was unquestionably an outstanding cornerback, a position the Birds were hurting at. But Revis cost New England $12 million for one year, and if he played as well as hoped, that could be expected to go

---

1   "Open letter to Jeffrey Laurie and Howie Rosen: Stop messing up free agency" by Jimmy Kempski, Philly.com, March 13, 2014.
2   "Free-Agent Frenzy" by Bill Barnwell, Grantland.com, March 12, 2014.

up the next year.[1]

The salary cap for all 53 players was $133 million in 2014. Revis' $12 million would be almost 10% of the entire team's payroll—for 1 out of 53 players. He would have made more than anyone else on the Eagles, a fact likely to cause resentment against the new guy.

Instead of Revis, Jairus Byrd (*plantar fasciitis*) or TJ Ward (who was purely an in-the-box safety, not what Philadelphia wanted), the Eagles signed safety Malcolm Jenkins, who New Orleans had let walk in order to make room for Byrd. Jenkins' contract was only $16 million over three years. He was not considered elite, but his 2013 playmaking was actually better than Revis'—2.5 sacks, 2 FF, forty-eight tackles and two INTs that he returned for 35 yards.

He was also barely twenty-six, versatile, fast and healthy and a natural leader who was a captain for the New Orleans backfield—not to mention, a snappy dresser who sells his own custom line of designer bowties.

That last key point is crucial (the leadership, not his snappy dressing). The Eagles already had two second-year safeties and were looking to draft one or more rookies. A youngish veteran leader who could quarterback the DBs was just what the team needed to work with Wolff and potentially two or three rookies.

There was more—the Eagles released safety Patrick Chung, to widespread delight, re-signed monster punter Donnie Jones and picked up two ace Special Teamers who might also provide depth on defense—Seattle safety Chris Maragos and Houston outside linebacker (OLB) Bryan Braman.

Maragos was a special teams leader for the champion Seattle Seahawks, while Braman was a 6'5", 251-pound toothless wild man (and former Abercrombie and Fitch model), who grew up being homeless for large parts of his childhood, and was kicked out of college after being convicted of "manufacture" of magic mushrooms. (He signed a lease for the house used in the operation,

---

1   As it turns out he did, and it did. In 2015, Revis signed a five-year, $70 million deal with the NY Jets that had $39 million guaranteed. For 2015 alone, he will make $16 million.

and says people he trusted took advantage of him.)

On YouTube, he is famous as the guy who tackled a punt returner without a helmet[1]—*leading with his head*. Asked by Philly reporters about his special teams philosophy, he said "Kill, Maim, Destroy."[2] As a kid, he tried to tackle a fire hydrant. This guy was frightening, in a good way.

Chip and Howie Roseman stuck to their guns, picking reasonably priced younger leaders despite the howls of impatient fans. They had learned the lessons of Seattle, who won a Super Bowl by emphasizing shrewd draft picks and internal development over big free agent signings.

It's not just the expense that makes free agency so dangerous, though that's a big part of it. Players are best when they come into their strength on your team—more humble and hungry, appreciative of the fans, better team players. So the Eagles were looking for players with upside, athletes with good character who may have changed positions or languished behind a star.

The big name free agents come in as stars already, having paid their dues and wanting that bloated paycheck. They know nothing of what their new team has been through, and—often earning more than some of the team's existing stars—are natural targets of resentment.

A little later in free agency, the Eagles signed Miami CB Nolan Carroll ($5M, 2 years) and traded a fifth-round pick for New Orleans' Darren Sproles.[3] Carroll (twenty-seven years old and good sized at six-foot-zero) was a decent press corner who made plays, but also had some flaws.[4] He wasn't expected to replace Bradley Fletcher or Cary Williams as a starting corner, despite their weaknesses, but he

1   "bryan braman no helmet no problem" by theoutcast32. October 12, 2012. Retreived from www. youtube.com/watch?v=C6p-FyBDwWE
2   "Bryan Braman on Special Teams Mentality: 'Kill, Maim, and Destroy'" by Brandon Lee Gowton, *Bleeding Green Nation*, March 13, 2014.
3   "Initial thoughts on the Eagles' acquisitions of Darren Sproles and Nolan Carroll" by Jimmy Kempski, Philly.com, March 13, 2014.
4   "What Nolan Carroll brings to the Eagles" by James Walker, ESPN.com, March 13, 2014.

was unquestionably a big upgrade over the Eagles' previous depth corners—Roc Carmichael and Curtis Marsh. Dime packages with a sixth defensive back had just not been a choice for the Eagles in 2013, and Carroll made them possible. He also played on special teams for Miami as a gunner and returner.

The big excitement though was over Sproles, the NFL player closest to Chip Kelly's college star De'Anthony Thomas and a perfect fit in Chip Kelly's offense.[1] Never mind that Thomas himself was available in the upcoming draft.

Both men were short, fast RBs great at kick returns and catching short passes. But DAT was much less muscular, unproven in the pros and didn't have that great a season in his last year at Oregon. Besides, who knew who might draft him ahead of Philadelphia, in what round?

New Orleans coach Sean Payton called Sproles "the smartest football player I've ever met," and from 2011 to 2013, he had led the NFL in total yards after catch. (LeSean McCoy was fifth, with two-thirds of his YAC production in those three seasons coming in 2013 under Chip).

On the other hand, Sproles was thirty and his yardage had declined the two previous years, which is probably why the Saints let him go. This trade also gave up a mid-round pick in a very deep draft. The Eagles had only six left in the draft, though Sproles' signing signaled that Bryce Brown—or even DeSean Jackson—might be on the trading block for more choices. On the third hand (you mutant freak), Sproles only cost the team $3.4 million a year.

The Saints were preparing to simply release him. Roseman and Kelly saw value that no one else did, and got a star for a late round pick.

Cheaper free agents have the same advantages as rookies—they grow into their power on your squad, if you're careful to find players who fit your scheme and have untapped potential. None of them are sure things, which is why they come cheap. Chung, Isaac Sopoaga

---

1   "Inside Slant: Darren Sproles in open field" by Kevin Seifert, ESPN.com, March 13, 2014.

and Kenny Phillips were (inexpensive) busts in 2013, but the team scored with Connor Barwin, James Casey, and ace punter Donnie Jones. Cary Williams and Bradley Fletcher had been serviceable and certainly better than their predecessors.

While GM Howie Roseman pursued free agents, Chip Kelly was deep into preparations for the draft. For Kelly, that's a hands-on process wherever possible. He doesn't like to rely on written scouting reports or statistics. He's out at the NFL Combine, the Senior Bowl, and every college pro day he can get to. As late as August 30th, roster cut down day, he took the train to Annapolis with Player Personnel Director Tom Gamble to watch Navy play his buddy Urban Meyer's Ohio State team.

The coach, with no family to take care of, racked up more than 11,000 travel miles attending at least a dozen college pro days around the country during March and April.[1] This was unusual for a head coach. Most teams send just a scout or perhaps a key prospect's position coach.

Kelly's travel schedule impressed no less than Gil Brandt, NFL. com's senior analyst, who tweeted:

> Don't think I've ever seen a head coach attend more pro days than #Eagles' Chip Kelly has this year. At #LSU's today.
>
> @Gil_Brandt. 1:12 P.M. April 9, 2014.

Coming from Brandt, that's a hell of a statement. He's not some young, slick-haired TV blowhard. Brandt, who turned eighty about the time Chip Kelly was hired by the Eagles, was the Dallas Cowboys' chief talent scout and personnel executive for twenty-eight years, from the time the team was founded in 1960 until Jerry Jones took over. And he scouted for the Rams before that, back when Dwight Eisenhower was president. So when Gil Brandt says Chip outhustled every other coach he's ever seen, that's a powerful endorsement.

Asked about pro days in late April, Kelly first downplayed

1   "Eagles' Chip Kelly has traveled to at least 12 pro days" by Bryan Fischer, NFL.com, April 9, 2014.

his frenetic attendance, but eventually expanded on why he found them valuable.

> ... it's tough for me to be in a room and argue for or against a player when I've never seen them in person. I've watched the tape but there's so much more than just watching tape. Find out the people that coached him, find out what the janitor in the complex says about him, find out what the people in the cafeteria say about him, find out what he's like from a learning standpoint, find out as much information as you possibly can, and if you don't then shame on you.

CHIP SPEAKS

MARCH 15, 2014

Free agency provided only a temporary break from the DeSean Jackson madness. The Maxwell Football Club, one of the oldest and most prestigious organizations in the sport, gave Chip Kelly its Coach of the Year award on March 15, 2014. He spoke to the press afterwards for the first time since locker cleanout in January. It did not escape the press that he "sidestepped" questions about DeSean, to use Zach Berman's term.[1] Reuben Frank of CSN-Philly described the scene this way:

> At the Maxwell Club presser Friday in Atlantic City, N.J., Chip Kelly was given every opportunity to affirm DeSean Jackson as a big part of the Eagles' plans moving forward, but he ducked the question about Jackson's future with a joke (see video). That's a common Kelly device—ducking questions he doesn't want to answer with jokes. Not sure it means the Eagles are disenchanted enough with Jackson to move him, but he could have said, "Come on, DeSean's our guy, he's not going anywhere," and ended the speculation. And he opted not to.[2]

This was Chip's pointed "joke" about DeSean:

He's a priority at receiver, before Maclin, behind

---

1 "Eagles' Chip Kelly: Jenkins, Sproles good fits" by Zach Berman, *Philadelphia Inquirer*, March 16, 2014.
2 "10 observations from the Eagles' offseason" by Reuben Frank, *CSN Philly*, March 15, 2014.

Cooper, or is it Cooper before Maclin, or Maclin before Cooper? So I'll check what you write, and I'll tell you how we feel about it.

The "you" in that answer did not refer to the press in general. It was pointed directly at the reporter who asked that question: Jeff McLane. Jimmy Kempski added a very interesting behind-the-scenes note to his story about the awards ceremony:

> The reporter who asked the DeSean Jackson question was the *Inquirer's* Jeff McLane, who had previously reported that Jeremy Maclin was a priority over Riley Cooper when the two players were still unsigned by the team. The Eagles ended up signing Cooper first, but that doesn't mean that McLane was wrong. The Eagles could have certainly valued Maclin more, but were just able to get a deal done more quickly with Cooper. Kelly took the opportunity to needle Jeff a little, and in the process, say absolutely nothing about Jackson. It was really a brilliant answer.
>
> The Eagles have had plenty of opportunities to simply say, "DeSean Jackson is an Eagle and will remain an Eagle, end of story."
>
> But they haven't.

On March 18, CSN Philly's Derrick Gunn reported—based on "a league source"—that the Eagles had "notified the Pro Bowl wide out early last week that it's not shopping him but is listening to potential suitors."[1]

This was the same thing Kempski had said seventeen days earlier, but Gunn added a crucial detail—that the Eagles had also tried to trade DeSean in 2013.

> The Eagles last year took inquiries about Jackson and were initially asking for a second-round pick, the source said, but dropped their demand to a middle-round pick but were still unable to trade him. Jackson's diva

---

1   "DeSean Jackson Trade Rumor: Eagles Are Listening to Offers" by Dave Mangels, *Bleeding Green Nation*, March 18, 2014.

reputation and his salary make him difficult to deal.

Meanwhile, Kempski was taking an unbelievable amount of abuse for merely reporting what his sources told him. He received several death threats at Philly.com. Gianfranco Schirripa's tweet was relatively mild:

> This DeSean Jackson trade stuff needs to stop. It only started because this idiot @JimmyKempski wrote an article stating it "could" happen.
> @Francoo91. 9:39 A.M. March 18, 2014.

Just when it seemed as if a consensus was forming (among reporters anyway) that Jackson would be traded, the story took a strange turn with a report from inside the DeSean camp. Ike Reese, a former player now working as a broadcaster, reported on his radio show that it was all a big misunderstanding.[1]

> He's [DeSean Jackson] talked to Chip [Kelly] this off-season," Reese said, citing a source close to the situation. "He's talked to Chip and Chip told him you don't have to worry about all the rumors that are out there. You're here. He's been assured, at least he's been assured at that time [when they talked], that he wasn't going anywhere.

Les Bowen of the *Daily News* confirmed that report on Twitter[2] based on his own source—which was probably the same source—and then very quickly refuted himself.[3]

> I've now heard from a more "official" DeSean Jackson source. Source says contrary to what I was told earlier, and what Ike Reese reported on 94WIP, DeSean HAS

1 "Chip Kelly Assured DeSean Jackson He Won't Be Traded, According to Report" by Brandon Lee Gowton, *Bleeding Green Nation*, March 19, 2014.
2 Les Bowen [@LesBowen]. March 19, 2014. I am told @Ike58Reese is right, Chip Kelly has indeed called DeSean Jackson and told him not to worry about trade reports. [Tweet]. Retrieved from www.twitter.com/LesBowen/status/446321695746719744
3 "Apparently, Chip Kelly has not talked to DeSean Jackson, after all" by Les Bowen, *Philadelphia Daily News*, March 19, 2014.

NOT talked to Chip Kelly about trade speculation. Says DeSean has tried to, but Chip has been too busy with free agency, etc.

Yes, this is confusing. It was even more confusing while it was happening.

On March 23rd, Jeff McLane abruptly changed directions.

The Eagles have intensified their efforts to trade Pro Bowl wide receiver DeSean Jackson in the last week, according to three independent NFL sources.

Intensified? What about McLane's emphatic insistence that Jackson wasn't going anywhere? After that piece, he had taken a week off from writing new articles to figure out what was going on. Now he reported that the Eagles were shopping DeSean, without acknowledging that he had ever said anything different.[1] "Not one of Jeff's shining moments," a team source told me.

Buried deep in his story, though, were several interesting nuggets that showed how hard McLane had been working to get back on top of this story.

Jackson has his allies on the team, but he lost some when he suggested that he deserved a new contract two days after the season ended, one teammate said.

The Eagles decision-makers were also irked by his contract demands and increasingly by his lifestyle, displayed ever-so prominently on social media. Eagles general manager Howie Roseman even went to a few players close to Jackson to see if they could get him to cool it on his Instagram account, for instance.

…

Eagles owner Jeffrey Lurie has been described as one of Jackson's biggest supporters and played a significant part in extending his contract in 2012. He had a three-minute one-on-one conversation with the receiver after the Vikings game in December when

---

1 "Eagles actively shopping DeSean Jackson" by Jeff McLane, *Philadelphia Inquirer*, March 23, 2014.

Jackson had a sideline altercation with receivers coach Bob Bicknell.

McLane ended on a pugnacious note:

> ... at the Maxwell Awards in Atlantic City, he [Chip Kelly] sidestepped the question with a joke about an earlier *Inquirer* report...
>
> Kelly won't be able to avoid reporters next week at the NFL owners meetings in Orlando. He is mandated to answer an hour's worth of questions during a round table interview on Wednesday.

Two days later, on March 25, the narrative took a 180-degree turn when DeSean suddenly reported (on his Instagram account) that he had talked with the coach and everybody was happy again.

> Good to Talk to Big Chip today!! Say or hear what ya want!! The Picture speaks for itself !! Winner BirdGaNg!!

McLane, Bowen and Gunn all reported that DeSean was telling teammates that he was staying in Philadelphia. McLane wrote that:

> The wide receiver called a few teammates on Tuesday morning to tell them he was staying with the Eagles a day after he spoke with coach Chip Kelly.[1]

Clearly, Jackson misunderstood what Kelly was saying. The coach always chooses his words very carefully. According to Bowen,

> [A] source in DeSean's camp says Chip told him to not worry about anything, keep working, and be ready for camp.[2]

Nothing in those words said that Jackson would stay with the Eagles. That was just advice on how to stay professional, whether he was traded or not, but it reassured Jackson, who seemed to want to return (after earlier posting photos on his Instagram account

---

1   "Source: Jackson telling Eagles teammates he's staying" by Jeff McLane, *Philadelphia Inquirer*, March 25, 2014.

2   Les Bowen [@LesBowen]. March 25, 2014. [Tweet]. Retrieved from www.twitter.com/LesBowen/status/448476709298642944

suggesting other teams he might play for).

Jackson's evident excitement suggested that he was being played by his new agent, Joel Segal, who apparently convinced him that all these maneuvers would get him re-signed in Philly for more money. It had worked in 2011, after all.

In 2014, though, there was no way that the Eagles could pay Jackson more. His contract was already way over market, which was why no one wanted to trade. And it's a safe bet that Jackson didn't sign with a new agent in order to take a pay cut, whether he got more guaranteed money or not. Joel Segal's only hope for getting paid was to force the Eagles to release him.

On March 26, 2014, Kelly had his mandatory hour-long session with reporters at the NFL annual meeting. Not surprisingly, he was swarmed by scribes who asked about Jackson directly. His response seemed a little unenthusiastic:

> I like DeSean. DeSean did a really nice job for us. But we're always going to do what's best for the organization... It's never been about just one guy.

Asked about the receiver's work ethic, he added,

> He played 16 games for us, he practiced every day. I had no issues with him.

Not the most intense compliment you could ask for.

JACCPOCALYPSE

MARCH 28, 2014

The final twists in this strange tale took place on March 28th. Eliot Shorr-Parks and A.J. Perez wrote a controversial article for NJ.com titled "DeSean Jackson's gang connections troubling to Eagles."[1] The article reported that Jackson had flashed gang signs in games and on Instagram, that he had been interviewed by detectives in California about two different gang-related murders, and that he had been convicted of marijuana possession in 2009.

Less than an hour later the team released this statement:

> After careful consideration this off-season, Eagles decide to part ways with DeSean Jackson. The team informed him of his release today.

Many concluded that the gang ties were the reason for Jackson's release—or, worse, that the team had slandered Jackson on his way out the door, to justify the cut. Yet, while the NJ.com certainly got attention (and readers) with the gang angle, and they trumpeted it in the headline, the actual story emphasized poor attitude in practices and the locker room, not gangs.

> ... sources close to Jackson and within the Eagles' organization say, it's Jackson's off-field behavior that concerns the front office.
>
> A bad attitude, an inconsistent work ethic, missed meetings and a lack of chemistry with head coach Chip

---

1   "DeSean Jackson's gang connections troubling to Eagles" by Eliot Shorr-Parks & A.J. Perez, NJ.com, March 28, 2014.

Kelly are the reasons, sources told NJ.com. And when the Eagles looked more deeply into why Jackson was missing meetings, they found that his friends were becoming a more powerful—and negative—influence in his life.

The NJ.com story was—and continues to be—very controversial. "Gang ties" was an explosive charge in March, 2014. Beyond the racial subtext of linking Jackson to the Crips gang, the charge came as New England Patriots TE Aaron Hernandez sat in jail, awaiting trial for first degree murder in the death of Odin Lloyd. (He was convicted in April of 2015.) After Hernandez's arrest, *Sports Illustrated's* Greg Bedard had reported that

> Personnel sources from multiple NFL teams tell SI that they had off-field concerns about Hernandez. In particular, the questions pertained to alleged gang activity of some of Hernandez's associates in his native Bristol, Conn.[1]

Every single item in the NJ.com story—except the team's alleged concern over gang connections trumpeted in the headline—was solidly documented. In fact, the newspaper somehow found a Los Angeles detective, Eric Crosson, who was willing to go on the record and discuss Jackson's (very tenuous) ties to two killings.

But the facts in the story were thin, while Crosson's language echoed *Sports Illustrated's* story on Hernandez, implying much more than it stated. The detective sounded a bit like a 1950s newsreel about the terrible menace of biker gangs:

> You don't want to see anybody throwing up gang signs like he did in the Redskins game last year. Those were neighborhood Crip gang signs and he flashed them during a game. He may not be affiliated with the gang, but they don't [ordinarily] take kindly to those not in the gang throwing up those gang signs.

There has never been any evidence or even rumors of Jackson's

---

1   "Hernandez's background scrutinized by NFL teams before draft," *Sports Illustrated,* June 19, 2013.

involvement in violence. If anything, he may have exaggerated his involvement to help promote his struggling gangsta rap music label, Jaccpot Records. But with Hernandez in jail, even a discussion of whether DeSean had links to a gang was highly toxic.

If the gang allegations *were* leaked to discredit DeSean, the gambit didn't work. Radio producer James Seltzer from 97.5 The Fan, one of Philadelphia's two big sports talk stations, said that among the station's callers,

> No one believed the gang story... Not that there weren't some gang ties, but no one believed that was the reason Chip let him go.

The main result of the gang angle was widespread criticism of the Eagles for their presumed role in leaking it, whether that was true or not. Shorr-Parks told me directly that the team was not his source:

> The Eagles did not give me any information whatsoever about it [the gang allegations]. I did not get that from them. I almost don't like to talk about the leaking thing, just cause it's so absurd... If they were going to leak something, why would they give it to me?

Shorr-Parks, a young ex-blogger writing for the website of some New Jersey papers, had a point. Among full time Eagles beat reporters, he was the youngest and least well known. If the team was going to leak a story, he was about #9 on the list of likely targets.

There was another story on CSN Philly the day Jackson was released.[1] It got much less attention (and criticism) than the NJ.com report, but in some ways its charges were more damaging.

Derrick Gunn elaborated on his earlier report about DeSean's missed exit interview, and added a new charge:

> There have been a number of nightclubs in the area that have basically told DeSean or told DeSean through second parties, "We don't want you back in our nightclubs because he is a disruptive factor."

---

1 "Some Philly clubs cut DeSean before Eagles did" by Derrick Gunn, *CSN Philly*, March 28, 2015.

AFTERMATH

APRIL 2, 2014

Five days after he became a free agent, DeSean signed with Washington for $6 million per year, a 40% pay cut, which explained why no one wanted to trade—because they would have been stuck with his full $10-million-a-year original contract.

Jackson's release did not slow down the controversy. There were raging debates over how much the loss would hurt the Eagles offense, whether the team could have gotten something for him in a trade, and the validity and source of the gang allegations. These arguments continued on and off all year; a running gag all season long in the Eagles-centric Twitterverse was to repeat OhWowHmm's tweet of April 25th, 2014 whenever the discussion erupted again:

> *pops out of a birthday cake* hey lets talk about desean jackson
> @OhWowHmm. 6:10 A.M. April 25, 2014.

Sports talk radio producer James Seltzer of 97.5 The Fan said that he believes the DeSean story carried so much weight because, before it,

> What a lot of people thought was, "he's going to bring this crazy offense, and he's an offensive genius." I don't think people understood that, for Chip, the team culture is far more important than anything offensive, and DeSean's release was the first experience that we all had with that belief.

After Jackson signed with division rival Washington, several Eagles players shared some very nasty (anonymous) opinions about him with CBSPhilly.[1] One said:

> You see little kids and how they cry and whine when they don't get their way, that was D-Jax.[2]

Jackson was described as disrespectful to Kelly in front of the team, a guy who was happy if the team lost but he caught three touchdowns, "a 'me-guy' with an attitude problem."

To counter that narrative, Jackson's team arranged a sympathetic interview by controversial TV personality Stephen A. Smith, a former *Philadelphia Inquirer* sportswriter, on ESPN.[3]

The interview didn't go so well, despite careful choreography that included Jackson maintaining Zen-Buddhist-like calm and dressing up in a sweater vest and Urkel-like glasses. He looked like an eager-to-please junior accountant working at his first job, an image that must have confused the crap out of his biggest fans.

Smith focused almost exclusively on the gang red herring and even those questions didn't go so well. Does he associate with gang members, Smith asked Jackson?

> Not if they are doing negative things... I'm definitely aware and know certain gang members, but as far as me being affiliated and me being a gang member, never not have once been.

What about the alleged gang signs he flashed?

> ... if you see signs or if you see me in pictures with affiliated gang members or whatever the case may be, that sign I am throwing up is to connect me with me and my boys.

---

1 "New report details Chip Kelly's problems with DeSean," *CSN Philly*, April 4, 2014.

2 "Sources: DeSean Jackson Was A Problem For Kelly, Eagles In Locker Room" by Joseph Santoloquito, CBSPhilly.com, April 4, 2014.

3 The interview does not appear to be on ESPN's website as a video any longer; there is a story based on it. "DeSean: Not In A Gang," ESPN News Services, April 4, 2014. There are also copies of the interview currently on YouTube.

That's not a very good denial.

In fact, Jackson's answers in this carefully controlled setting did more to raise issues of gang ties than to dismiss them. This suggests that such was the plan of Jackson's team all along—either to build the credibility of his rap label, or to change the subject from criticisms of the wide receiver as selfish and unwilling to work hard for his team.

Smith did ask whether DeSean had been late for meetings, as teammates had alleged.

> For sure I have been late. I'm not going to lie about that.

Chip Kelly's meetings are famously short and prompt, so this would have been a real problem for the coach. When Kelly was still at Oregon, reporter Rob Moseley wrote that:

> The UO staff holds meetings each afternoon at 4:30. Kelly might be there at 4:28, in which case anybody who arrives at the scheduled start time risks entering an empty room.
>
> "We've gotten into staff meetings and spent less than a minute," running backs coach Gary Campbell said. "A 15-minute meeting? That would be a marathon."
>
> "If we ever met for 15 minutes," Aliotti said, "I think we'd all faint."[1]

This approach continues. In the summer of 2014, the *Inquirer's* Jeff McLane wrote that while the Eagles "practices may be as physically grueling as any in the NFL," the players' "work days are shorter than most because the meetings are quick and efficient."[2]

When the actual firing went down, Jackson told Smith, Kelly called him up and said the team was going to move forward without him, that they thought it was best for everyone concerned. "I was sitting there waiting for a reason why," Jackson said plaintively.

---

1   "The focus of the flurry: Everything moves quickly for Chip Kelly" by Rob Moseley, *Eugene Register Guard*, December 26, 2010, page C1.
2   "Walk Chip's Way: Eagles' Kelly a stickler for discipline" by Jeff McLane, *Philadelphia Inquirer*, July 20, 2014.

Watching him, it was hard not to think "How cute! He's never been fired before."

Jackson had run into the sharp edge of Kelly's inside vs. outside communication policy. People inside the NovaCare Center, coaches and players, get a full explanation of everything Chip does and the privilege of asking why. DeSean himself took advantage of this in Chip's summer 2013 practices, after Kelly demoted him to the second and third team for not learning all three receiving positions.

But once DeSean crossed the line and was off the team, he was on the outside and got no explanation at all. He might as well have been a reporter. Kelly maintained his off-season silence for a full month after Jackson was released, despite the storm raging around him. Without any games or practices there were no press conferences scheduled, and Kelly simply doesn't speak to writers at any other time.

The silence wasn't broken until April 28th, when the Eagles had their annual playground build, where players and staff construct a park for a Philadelphia neighborhood. Kelly took questions afterwards, and he said Jackson was let go for "football reasons." With the NJ.com gang story fresh in fans' minds, that answer received a lot of skepticism, but there are reasons to think that it was at least partially true. Jackson doesn't fit Kelly's size specifications at wide receiver, and the coach had moved on from, or refused to fully use other talented players who didn't have the right size either—notably cornerback Brandon Boykin, whose behavior had been impeccable.

Most of DeSean's production in 2013 came in the first part of the season when Michael Vick was still the starting QB. Jackson disappeared in the crucial last three games of the season, against Chicago, Dallas and (in the playoffs) New Orleans, with barely 100 yards in all three games combined.

He was, by all accounts, shut down by New Orleans CB Keenan Lewis "on an island"[1]—that is, one on one, without any safety help. This was a possible indication that Jackon's tremendous speed may

---

1   "Keenan Lewis shuts down DeSean Jackson, but departed with injury" by Joe
     Soriano, NFLSpinZone.com, January 5, 2014.

have been tapering off a bit. If nothing else, Lewis' physical defense on DeSean was a template that other DBs could be expected to use going forward.

And it seems unlikely that the Eagles would want to smear Jackson, if you look at how Chip Kelly handled troubled players at Oregon.[1] It was never his style (or the University of Oregon's) to speak or leak damaging information about a player, even the ones who were dismissed from the team. Especially them, in fact.

On the contrary, the Ducks organization has been famously discreet. During his sophomore year at Oregon, tight end Colt Lyerla was absent at the start of fall training camp. All that Coach Kelly would say in public was

> Colt, who had a great summer for us, he's got a couple things to take care of... He's excused and should be here shortly.[2]

Lyerla ended up missing 20 days of fall camp for what was later rumored to be drug rehab. Once he returned, he went on to have the best season of his college career. Even the following year, after Lyerla quit the team and was arrested for possession of cocaine, the Ducks said nothing negative.

Publicly at least, Kelly has maintained this tradition in Philadelphia. A year after these events, he still had yet to say a negative word about any of the players who had left the Eagles. He seems to follow the stoic silence of the old time warrior—pour one out for the fallen and keep your conflicts private. Anything else is, well, worthless *gossip*. Kelly wouldn't even concede that DeSean was smaller than his ideal size for wide receivers, when asked directly by a reporter.

> It is a size league and you've got to look at those things in certain situations. But again, to get into specifics

---

1   "How Chip Kelly Handles Troubled Players" by Mark Saltveit, *Bleeding Green Nation*, March 31, 2014.

2   "Colt Lyerla absent from Oregon's first day of camp" by Adam Jude, *The Oregonian*, August 6, 2012; "The Mysterious Colt Lyerla" by Stephen Alexander, *Portland Tribune*, September 7, 2012.

isn't fair to DeSean and it isn't fair to anybody in this situation so I'm never gonna do that. When we release a player, and when anybody else is released, we don't talk about why we released them or why we didn't release, or why we kept them, so… That's just not how it's gonna operate with us and I'm never gonna be that way.

In the hothouse atmosphere of the Philadelphia press, though, Kelly's silence was criticized as "arrogance" or even evidence of conflict.

Q: If it's purely a football decision, why did you wait a month to address it, to explain it to the fans?
A: Because I've never, did I have a press conference when we released Jason Avant or Patrick Chung? No. That's just not the way I am. I'm not gonna have a press conference when we release players from our organization. It's just not, I've never felt that way, and I'm never gonna do it…

With the advantage of hindsight and new information that has come to light since Jackson's release, we can put together a pretty clear picture of what happened. The Eagles tried to trade Jackson in 2013, but had no luck. After he had a career year (which made him more tradeable) and then implicitly threatened a holdout, the team decided he had to go.

But under methodical planner Kelly, the Eagles were likely waiting until they had a replacement plan in place before making a final push to trade Jackson. Remember that Jimmy Kempski's initial story was published on March 1st, immediately after the Eagles signed Jeremy Maclin and Riley Cooper to contracts. Darren Sproles was acquired on March 13th. Jackson wasn't released until March 28th.

The effort to trade him was probably doomed all along. Despite his improved production, Jackson's contract was still too high by at least $4 million a year (the discount Washington signed him for.) Jackson's public demand for more money in January must have given teams pause as well, and once they knew the Eagles were shopping him, his value collapsed as Kempski had predicted. If the reporter's initial story came from an attempt by the Eagles' front office to hint at a trade possibility, that maneuver was a disastrous, ham-fisted failure.

Las Vegas bookmakers did not think the Eagles would have much trouble filling Jackson's shoes; the Vegas over/under for 2014 (according to Bovada) was 1,000.5 yards and seven touchdowns for DeSean, vs. 900 yards/6 TDs for Maclin alone.[1] Washington's odds of making the Super Bowl actually went *down* after they acquired Jackson, from 40-1 to 50-1.

But this was still a high stakes gamble. DeSean would have two chances a year to get revenge on his old team, and the very narcissism that made him a locker room problem guaranteed that he would never try harder than during his revenge games against the Eagles.

---

1   "NFL Betting: DeSean Jackson Does Not Boost Redskins' Super Bowl Odds" by *Bovada Sports*, April 15, 2014; "Place Your Bets: Eagles 2014 Player Props" by Andrew Kulp, *The 700 Level*/CSNPhilly, August 27, 2014.

DRAFT SPECULATION

APRIL, 2014

For hardcore fans, the months between the end of one season and the start of the draft feel like an eternity of baseless speculation, what-ifs and angst over every conceivable draft pick.

Of course, if you like endless discussions with your buddies about obscure players, undeterred by actual on-the-field results that can prove you wrong, it's the best time of the year.

There had been so many mock drafts that a bunch of writers in Philadelphia started an #MDMD competition, where they draft mock drafts into teams of mock drafts, which will compete against each other in, I don't know, some kind of recursive fantasy football league.

2013 had been the first NFL draft class of Chip Kelly's NFL career, though of course, the players were selected by GM Howie Roseman (with the coach's input).

Because Kelly had roster control, his input counted more than usual. Roseman could draft a player the coach didn't like, but he couldn't be sure that guy would even make the final fifty-three-man roster, much less play a lot of snaps. Any player drafted before the fifth round who didn't make the roster would instantly be considered a major bust, and an embarrassment to Roseman.

Of course, the reputation of a draft class usually changes over time. Immediately after the Eagles' 2013 draft, it had been considered very successful, and that verdict was reinforced when third-round pick Bennie Logan took over as the starting nose tackle halfway through his rookie season. But as time passes, the results have looked less and less impressive.

The top three picks—RT Lane Johnson, TE Zach Ertz, and Logan—remain very successful, and fifth-round safety Earl Wolff showed flashes of talent in 2013 before injuries hobbled him. But the other four picks—QB Matt Barkley, and seventh rounders Jordan Poyer, David King and Joe Kruger—have added nothing. Barkley was the only one still on the roster after one year.

He actually moved the team down the field well enough, in two partial games in 2013, but he turned the ball over constantly, including each of his first four drives. Barkley played just a half against the Giants and only nine minutes against Dallas, but managed to fumble three times (losing one) and throw five interceptions (one called back by penalty) during that short stretch. He has barely seen the field since, even in blowouts.

Now, in 2014, the Eagles had the twenty-second pick in the draft. Depending on who you read, the Eagles were sure to trade up for flashy QB Johnny Manziel (even though they had Nick Foles, a young and inexpensive quarterback who led the NFL in passer rating) or Anthony Barr (the UCLA RB who converted to OLB) or Odell Beckham (a speedy WR with the same physical limits as DeSean Jackson) or safety Ha Ha Clinton-Dix (great player, silly name).

Or they were guaranteed to trade down into the second round to get an extra pick or two, and take big wide receiver Cody Latimer from Indiana or Jeremiah Attaochu, a raw pass-rushing OLB, or Kelvin Benjamin, a huge WR. No, that's not it, they were obviously going to stay put with the twenty-second pick in the draft and pick either of two WRs—Marqise Lee of USC or Brandin Cooks of Oregon State. Or Beckham or Barr if they fell. Or cornerback/safety Kyle Fuller of Virginia Tech.

Even Chip's general principles were disputed. He was sure to pick a bunch of Oregon players: Terrance Mitchell, De'Anthony Thomas, and Colt Lyerla. No, he actually preferred Pac-12 players who did well against the Ducks, such as Cooks and Lee and Bishop

Sankey. No, he just wanted bigger guys who beat up little guys.

Some of this was media invention, such as the Manziel speculation, which was constructed by reporters twisting Chip's words at his late April press conference.[1]

A reporter had asked him about Manziel, and Kelly replied sarcastically that they were interested in any possible player. The reporters present actually laughed. Then the interviewer persisted, and Kelly softened, saying that yes, he had recruited Manziel to Oregon, and it "broke my heart" when he chose Texas A&M instead.

Writers took this exchange as an excuse to say that Kelly really wanted Manziel, which was clearly false, but they sold some ads and delivered some cheap page views.

But much of the misdirection was, in fact, artful dodging by the Eagles' front office, undoubtedly leaking contradictory information to different reporters to muddy the waters. Because none of those predictions came true. But the team didn't want to give away any unnecessary information.

The reality is that it's almost impossible to predict who a team with a later pick will choose until the teams ahead of them make their selections. There are just too many possibilities.

---

1   "Tape Don't Lie, and the Eagles Don't Want Manziel" by Mark Saltveit, *Bleeding Green Nation*, May 3, 2014.

OREGON BIAS

APRIL, 2014

Kelly has been frequently criticized for "Oregon Bias"—signing too many of his former Ducks to the Eagles' roster, from free agent safety Patrick Chung to bottom of the roster survivors like WR Jeff Maehl and off-season "camp bodies" such as lineman Isaac Remington, who was on the 2013 practice squad for less than a month, and WR Will Murphy, who replaced him and lasted almost two years but never made the team roster.

A longtime Oregon sportswriter told me that Murphy—a walk-on at Oregon who didn't play much there either—was a "great practice player," meaning that he hustled, helped organize other players and understood what the coaches were trying to do. Similarly, Chip hired five assistant coaches from Oregon, he told writer Patrick Wall from the Eagles website, because

> I have a meeting and have a tendency to talk really fast and I want things to be efficient. But I also know that I may forget to say something, and Pat Shurmur can go to Greg Austin and say, "What did he mean by that?" Or the same thing with Dave Fipp and Matt Harper for those young guys. Now I can put together guys with NFL experience coming here, and (the former Oregon assistants) can say, "This is what Coach means, this is how we operate." Kind of get in that fit that I talked about again. But it was integral.[1]

---

1   "The Oregon Five—Key to Kelly's Success" *Eagles Insider*, February 18, 2013.

Asked about Chip's taste for Oregon players, GM Howie Roseman told reporters that Kelly steps back from even evaluating his former players for the draft, to avoid any hint of bias.

> I know Coach got up here and he says he stays away from the [Oregon] evaluations, and it's the truth. He really does. I know when I started with Oregon in August, I don't ask for his opinion, I tell him mine, and then if we have a difference of opinion, we kind of talk about it and he tells me what he sees.
>
> Obviously [he] really liked [WR] Josh [Huff], but as an evaluator of the personnel staff, we really like Josh because it's easy to see what he does in our offense, so it's an easy transition for us.[1]

Of course, bias is not the only reason a coach might pick his ex-players. Oregon has been a top-five college team since 2009, and has produced a number of NFL stars such as Jairus Byrd, TJ Ward, Haloti Ngata, Max Unger, LeGarrette Blount, Mark Asper, Kiko Alonso and Kyle Long.

Another advantage was that Chip knew his former players so well. He recruited them, coached them, saw how they worked for years, and knew best whether they had the potential to grow at the pro level.

This was also true to a lesser degree for players that Oregon had scouted and played against. Chip has a tendency to draft players who did well against Oregon, from nose tackle Bennie Logan—who started at LSU for the first time in a non-conference game against Oregon—to USC QB Matt Barkley.

The knowledge works both ways. Sometimes it helps Kelly avoid flawed players such as Colt Lyerla and De'Anthony Thomas, a very fast kick returner, running back and track star, who's never again matched the production of his electric true-freshman year. Despite widespread rumors, Chip did not trade up to grab his star DE Dion Jordan at #3 in the 2013 draft; the Dolphins did, so a trade was clearly available. Jordan had an NFL body but underachieved at

---

1   "On the Roseman/Kelly Dynamic" by Sheil Kapadia, *Birds 24/7*, May 15, 2014.

Oregon and has proved a major bust in Miami.

Rick Gosselin of the *Dallas Morning News* argues that a successful college coach like Kelly has a major advantage against his NFL competition for a few years, citing the success of Pete Carroll, Jim Harbaugh and Dallas' own Jimmy Johnson, who won Super Bowls in his fourth and fifth years in the pros.

> The Eagles are coached by Chip Kelly, another successful college coach who recruited nationally at Oregon. He spent four years with the Ducks so he has a four-year window when he'll know the draft board better than the NFL lifers.[1]

I had predicted two dark horse Ducks for the Eagles in WR Josh Huff and DE Taylor Hart, a rare (in college) two-gapping 3-4 lineman. Huff did not have the 6'3" or better height that Kelly favors in wideouts, but he was unusually muscular, physical and fast, excelling at the WR blocking that Kelly emphasizes. He also overcame some very rough family dynamics[2]—his mother spent much of his college years in prison for assault and drug charges—and only blossomed in his senior year, indicating significant untapped potential.

---

1   "Gosselin: NFL coaches fresh from college ranks have big draft edge" by Rick Gosselin, *Dallas Morning News*, February 13, 2014.
2   "Oregon football: Ducks receiver Josh Huff finds the path to healing and success goes through Eugene" by Jason Quick, *The Oregonian*, September 24, 2013.

THE DRAFT

MAY 8-10, 2014

When the actual draft arrived, the Eagles tried to trade up (presumably for Brandin Cooks) but the price was too high.[1] There were six players the Eagles were targeting at #22[2] and all were gone by the time the Birds were on the board.

Johnny Manziel did in fact fall to pick #22, surprising almost everyone. But despite endless speculation about Chip's love for mobile quarterbacks, the Eagles ended up trading that pick (as I had predicted[3]) to a QB-hungry team drafting behind them, in return for a slightly lower pick and an extra third-round choice in a very deep draft.[4]

In the end, the Eagles selected a solid if unflashy group of players, including two Oregon Ducks.

- Louisville's Marcus Smith, an athletic, pass-rushing OLB, at the end of the first round;
- Vanderbilt's 6'3" WR Jordan Matthews in the second;

---

1   Les Bowen [@LesBowen]. March 8, 2014. Chip: offers to go up "were all too rich." Given depth of draft [Tweet]. Retrieved from www.twitter.com/LesBowen/status/464606580164800513

2   Les Bowen [@LesBowen]. May 8, 2014. Chip: there were 6 guys there at 22 we would have taken. Other people liked the same guys [Tweet]. Retrieved from www.twitter.com/LesBowen/status/464605816277196800

3   "Tape Don't Lie, and the Eagles Don't Want Manziel" by Mark Saltveit, *Bleeding Green Nation*, May 3, 2014.

4   The famously hard-partying Manziel played little during his rookie season, and went into rehab for unspecified substance abuse ("Johnny Manziel enters treatment" by Jeremy Fowler, ESPN.com, February 3, 2015).

- Oregon's muscular 5'11" WR/returner Josh Huff in the third;
- Florida CB/safety Jaylen Watkins in the fourth;
- Oregon DE Taylor Hart in the fifth;
- Stanford safety Ed Reynolds later in the fifth; and
- Wisconsin nose tackle Beau Allen in the seventh.

Kansas City picked De'Anthony Thomas in the fourth round. Colt Lyerla was not drafted by any team. He signed with Green Bay and was waived with an injury settlement on August 26th. On September 6th, he was arrested in Oregon[1] for non-alcohol DUI.[2]

The draft also marked the end of Chip's long silence, washed away in a flood of comments during seven separate press conferences. Kelly spelled out what he looks for in players: toughness, versatility, intelligence, athleticism and true NFL size (especially height, arm length and hand size).

The coach was wonderfully blunt about the limits of this crazy but crucial draft circus. Asked if he was happy with his draft picks, Kelly said,

> Honestly, I have no idea because literally... no one knows. Three, four years down the road, we're going to be, hey, that guy turned out to be a good player, there's going to be somebody that surprises everybody, us included. It's an inexact science, and if someone thinks they have a formula or a metric that can get you there, I haven't seen it yet.[3]

In retrospect, perhaps his comments should have triggered more concern.

At the time, though, it was refreshing to hear a coach or GM who didn't feel the need to be an expert on this highly speculative process. Kelly also admitted that he had wanted to draft Hart in the

---

1   "Ex-Packers TE Colt Lyerla arrested in Oregon for DUI," *Sports Illustrated*, September 7, 2014.
2   The charges were dismissed, without penalty, months later.
3   "Eagles coach Chip Kelly discusses drafting DT Beau Allen and more," Transcript of May 11, 2014 press conference, Philly.com, May 11, 2014.

third round, but Howie Roseman convinced him the DE would still be available in the fifth.

The Eagles drafted two wide receivers to replace Jackson and Avant. They traded up to grab all-time leading SEC receiver Jordan Matthews in the second round and selected the Ducks' clutch WR Josh Huff in the third round. Huff was a surprise for some, though an Arizona Cardinals writer told me later that he was a classic Bruce Arians-type receiver and also on the Cardinals' draft board in the third round.

In later rounds, the Birds picked two defensive backs—Stanford safety Ed Reynolds and Florida's Jaylen Watkins (who plays both cornerback and safety)—to fill the obvious gap there. The haul ended with huge (6'2", 330) nose tackle Beau Allen of Wisconsin.

The reaction to picking Marcus Smith in the first round can be summed up in one word: "Who?"

A few of the savviest draft watchers had flagged him—Mike Mayock of NFL Network, Tommy Lawlor of *Iggles Blitz* (who mentioned him in a trade-down scenario hours before the draft), and Mike Kaye of *Bleeding Green Nation* (who had called him months earlier)—but the fans at the Eagles' draft party were completely baffled.

Smith was a slightly undersized but highly productive outside linebacker from Louisville. He was versatile and a college graduate (only 50% of NFL players are). Like the Eagles' first pick in 2013—Lane Johnson—and Chip Kelly himself, Smith was a high school quarterback who converted to a less glamorous position.

As a football player, he had one outstanding item on his resume. Smith was second in the nation in sacks (with 14.5) and #1 in sacks per game (at 1.12).

He also played in one of the few 3-4 two-gap defensive alignments in college, and was probably the most complete 3-4 right OLB in the draft; he could rush, cover, defend the run and set the edge. On a conference call, he said he dropped into pass coverage about half the time in 2013.[1] The Eagles were finishing

1 Geoff Mosher [@GeoffMosherCSN]. May 8, 2014. On conference call,

a conversion to the 3-4 defense that Kelly installed at Oregon, and had a strong left OLB already in Connor Barwin, so Smith seemed like a perfect fit.

Even so, he was considered a reach by most analysts at #26. (NFL.com projected him as a third-fourth round pick.[1]) It wasn't clear whether Kelly or Howie Roseman wanted this pick, or both; and as the season developed, that became a politically charged question.

WR Jordan Matthews, on the other hand, seemed too good to be true. He was 6'3", fast, smart, and the SEC's all-time leading receiver (though that was partly because he stayed in college through his senior year, which few of the best talents do).

Matthews also had an upbeat, positive and studious approach that Chip Kelly clearly loved. When the Eagles asked about random individual plays in college, he remembered the down and distance, coverage and details of each. During practices, he made a point of running his catches out all the way into the end zone, just to go the extra mile.

Marcus Smith said he has played plenty of 3-4 OLB. Dropped 50% last year. [Tweet]. Retrieved from www.twitter.com/GeoffMosherCSN/status/464614987458412544

1 "Draft 2014 Prospects: OLB Marcus Smith" by Nolan Nawrocki, NFL.com.

MURDERLEG

MAY 10, 2014

The favorite addition of Philadelphia fans and writers wasn't drafted at all. He was signed as an undrafted free agent (UDFA) shortly after the seventh round ended.

Vanderbilt kicker Carey Spear was statistically a mediocre kicker (like Eagles incumbent Alex Henery, against whom he would compete in training camp). But he had two loveable traits:

1. his nickname was "Murderleg," and
2. that name understated his savagery as a tackler.

Usually, a kicker tackling the returner is a sign of desperation, but for the Vanderbilt Commodores, Spear was their kickoff return enforcer. There are lots of great video clips on YouTube if you search for "Murderleg;" thankfully, no non-football videos match that query. There's his body slam of Tennessee's Cordarrelle Patterson, for example.[1] Or flipping Wake Forest's Lovell Jackson completely upside down on another.[2] You get the idea.

Blogger Christian D'Andrea's favorite Murderleg hit came against Missouri in 2012. As he tells it, Spear got "clipped" by Mizzou's TJ Moe while kicking an extra point.[3] And Moe just happened to be

1   "Vanderbilt kicker Carey Spear levels Cordarrelle Patterson" by vucommodores, November 20, 2012. Retrieved from www.youtube.com/watch?v=OCmL4JvetG8

2   "Carey Spear's big hit on kickoff return" by vucommodores, September 2, 2011. Retrieved from www.youtube.com/watch?v=I1vp4IIfxwM

3   "Eagles Kicker Carey Spear Profile: Murderleg, She Wrote" by Brandon Lee Gowton, *Bleeding Green Nation*, May 20, 2014.

the guy who dropped back to return the subsequent kickoff.

According to D'Andreas, Murderleg then "spends the commercial break before the ensuing kickoff staring him down from 70 yards away, finishing his glare with a death point."

Spear pointed his outstretched arm directly at Moe for several seconds, like Babe Ruth calling his home run. And as Moe raced up field just inside the numbers, Murderleg flew in untouched to slam him so hard that Moe was knocked back in the air 3 yards. The YouTube clip of this incident is titled "Carey Spear Devours T.J. Moe's Soul."[1]

It was a shame he kicked even shorter and wilder than the Eagles' crumbling incumbent, Alex Henery.

In his five years as head coach, Chip Kelly had faced so much trouble with kickers that it felt like a curse. He is very methodical about getting great players and emphasizes special teams, yet his teams had lost big games in every year of his short coaching career because of short, missed field goals (from the Oregon-Stanford game in 2012 where it cost his Ducks a berth in the National Championship Game, to New Orleans in the 2014 playoffs). It was a peculiar blind spot, the one consistent flaw on his teams. As Spear proved increasingly unreliable in practices, it appeared that Kelly's kicker curse would continue.

1   "Carey Spear Devours T.J. Moe's Soul" by Anchor of Gold, October 6, 2012. Retrieved from www.youtube.com/watch?v=jHsAAhuowZg

PRACTICE GADGETS

MAY 27, 2014

Phase 3 of the off-season program—the organized team activities or OTAs—began on May 27, with actual offense-against-defense drills and all the famous Chip Kelly practice twists: blaring music, extreme speed, a robotic voice announcing each of the 26 short practice periods, and innovative, often goofy training devices.

They were using footballs with bungee cords attached; a running back holds on tight while another player tries to pull the ball out from his grasp. (This is designed to reduce fumbles.)

One new device was a stack of three garbage cans, with the top one slanted forward; quarterbacks try to throw into the slanted one from 30 yards away, though apparently few, if any, actually pulled it off when the press was allowed to watch.

The other new device was a sort of red metal "doorway" that running backs had to crouch down and run through, to simulate running into a small hole.

This device was new to the Eagles, but offensive line coach Jeff Stoutland used something similar back in 2011 with his linemen at Alabama.[1] Reporter Jeff McLane also credited running backs coach Duce Staley with a number of the innovative practice devices.

Kelly is always experimenting with new ways to help train players. In Kelly's first training camp, he introduced giant orange

---

1 "Alabama's new animated O-line coach Jeff Stoutland at spring practice" by Michael Casagrande, March 21, 2011. Retrieved from www.youtube.com/watch?v=vSZCE51o0dc

foam "football players" that the Eagles used to practice tackling.

Even more striking were the bug men, who date back to Kelly's Oregon days. In early practices, when rushers aren't allowed in seven-on-seven drills, QBs can develop the bad habit of throwing too low, since no lineman is there to knock the ball down.

So Kelly invented (and has refined) backpacks for assistants to wear, with a single giant fly's wing extending above their heads to the approximate height of rushers' raised arms. During seven-on-sevens, the bug men advance slowly toward the quarterback, like unusually muscular and clean-shaven zombies. In 2013, Michael Vick hit the bug wings several times, which foreshadowed difficulties he later had in throwing over linemen.

The bug men look funny but they work. According to *Pro Football Focus*, the combined Eagles quarterbacks had the fewest batted passes (two) of any NFL team in 2014. In contrast, Dallas had four, Seattle nine and Jacksonville twenty-one.[1]

Coach Kelly didn't exactly start using drones in his practices, but he came close. The restrictions on Phase 2 OTAs don't allow coaches on the field to direct players in drills. So Chip got a radio-controlled car and drove it onto the field so players could follow its sudden shifts left and right in agility drills.

All of this just shows how off-kilter Chip is; trying things that other people don't think of, or are afraid to try. It was easy to make fun of him with tired jokes about personalized smoothies, except that he kept winning (and having fun with his team while he did it). After a year in the NFL, Chip Kelly's lifetime record as a head coach was 57-14. That's not a bad start.

---

1 *Pro Football Focus*, 2014 Signature Stats: Accuracy in Passing.

MINI-CAMP

JUNE 17-19, 2014

In Year 2 of Chip's system, the players were much more comfortable, and practices accelerated. Kelly told reporters,

> We're going faster. We're getting more reps off, more plays off because the guys have a better understanding of the mechanics of it. But the basic structure of how we're doing things is the same.[1]

In 2013, the Eagles had the NFL's fastest tempo, with 32.1 seconds between plays by ESPN's count—the fastest yet recorded. (Dallas was more than 9 seconds per play slower, at 41.3)[2] In the 2014 spring practices, however, the Birds' offense was ripping off plays less than *10 seconds* after the previous one ended.

It's a mistake to think that the fast tempo is just a gimmick, a tactic that helps confuse and exhaust opponents (though it does that, too). Kelly is an efficiency lover, and running your plays off quickly is simply more productive. This is even truer in practice than in games, where Kelly will slow things down if he has a lead to protect.

The rapid pace of practice has a number of advantages, from getting players in shape without wasting time on conditioning drills to having more experience with the plays they'll run in games. But

---

1   Chip Kelly press conference at OTAs, May 29, 2014.

2   "Inside Slant: The Time Between Snaps" by Kevin Seifert, ESPN.com, December 13, 2013. The actual numbers were missing from the website at last check, as of 5/31/2015.

the real goal for Coach Kelly is to maximize reps, to run as many plays as possible whether it's a quick fake handoff and throw, or a full seven-on-seven scrimmage.

Time is a scarce resource, especially with the 2011 collective bargaining agreement rules that severely limit what you can do, and how much time you can spend, in practices. The Eagles want to complete all of their tasks in this limited time—install plays, decide which prospects will make the team, try players out at different positions, focus on key skills (such as not fumbling), experiment with new plays and formations, etc.

But they also realize that everyone else has the same limits. Every bit of efficiency they can wring out of the process is an advantage they have on their opponents in all of these areas.

That's why you see amazingly clever bits of organization, such as the passing drill where five quarterbacks throw simultaneously to five wide receivers. Drills are never stopped to explain something—teaching should be done in a meeting wherever possible, to get the most out of field time. If a coach needs to explain something right away, he will sub a player out of a drill—and put someone else in his place—so everyone else can keep going while he talks.

CULTURE

JUNE 18, 2014

During the three-day June minicamp, a reporter asked Chip about the team culture he was trying to build. The coach unloaded one of those expansive and unpredictable answers that makes a mockery of reporters who complain he isn't forthcoming.

> We want a bunch of guys that love playing football, not what football gets them... We had full attendance last year but that just depends on what model of organization you want. Do you want blind obedience or informed acquiescence or self-governance? If you have self-governance, I think the individuals have more invested in what's going on because they have a say and they have a stake in it and we are moving towards that model but I don't know if we are totally there right now.[1]

Reporters were left scrambling to figure out what he was talking about. It turns out that Chip was quoting a book called *How* by business ethicist Dov Seidman. Seidman distinguishes between

1. obedience enforced by the fear of punishment (which crumbles in its absence);
2. the kind where people learn the principles and try to follow them in return for rewards, and
3. workers sincerely agreeing with the leader's objectives and trying to adopt them for their own sake.

1   Chip Kelly's press conference after the second day of minicamp, June 18, 2014.

This was not the standard stuff of sports clichés. (When this author found and tweeted the source of Kelly's quote, Dov Seidman himself retweeted it.)

Kelly's principles may sound philosophical, but they are expressed in very practical terms. Jeff McLane of the *Inquirer* wrote an insightful mid-summer piece[1] about a seemingly picky rule: players are not allowed to take shortcuts across the small bit of lawn in front of the NovaCare Center. Why not? Josh Huff, who faced the same rule at Oregon under Kelly, explained the meaning behind this seemingly trivial regulation:

> Don't take any shortcuts in life, and always do the right thing even though the wrong thing might get you to the door quicker.

Jerry Azzinaro is Chip Kelly's Assistant Head Coach as well as the Defensive Line Coach, a position he also held at Oregon. Coach Azz elaborated on the meaning of this rule to McLane:

> Maybe you're not going to think about it as deeply and say somebody mowed that lawn, somebody spent hours preparing that thing, but I think as you're around really good people, good people don't do that.
>
> They clean up after themselves. They just try to do the right thing as much as they can. And no one needs to be looking. You just try to do the right thing.

That's what Kelly wants: players who understand what the team is trying to do, who buy in 100% and strive to make it happen whether any coaches are around or not.

McLane's article had the misleading headline "Walk Chip's Way: Eagles' Kelly a stickler for discipline," but the issue isn't discipline. "Buying in" is closer but still implies that obedience to Chip is the goal. It isn't. The culture Kelly is trying to build is based upon putting the team above your personal ego.

In this philosophy, the problem with a resentful or lazy player is

---

1   "Walk Chip's Way: Eagles' Kelly a stickler for discipline," by Jeff McLane, *Philadelphia Inquirer*, July 20, 2014. For some unknown reason the article is no longer available online, but McLane told me that he stands by it.

not their rebellion against the coach's authority. The coach shouldn't have that much ego invested, either. The problem is the missed opportunity. At that same press conference, Kelly explained:

> ...everybody has the same amount of time during the day and you can either spend your time or invest your time...
>
> We all have 24 hours in the same day and it's what you want to do. If you want to go play video games and watch TV and do all those other things, you're going to get beat out by the guy that is doing the little things that are going to make the difference between them making the team and not making the team.
>
> When we talk about investing in yourself we are challenging them to understand every action you have, has consequences to it.

These are very young guys, so constantly growing and (hopefully) maturing together is part of the job description. They're coming into their own amid very intense competition, and on a great team they all help each other develop—off the field as well as on.

Every day in training camp is an opportunity for growth, and a risk for dysfunction. A player who doesn't do his share hurts more than himself, especially if he is a veteran or team leader.

Offensive lineman Richie Incognito, suspended from the Miami Dolphins during the 2013 season for bullying teammate Jonathan Martin, was a good example. It's not just that he bragged about "breaking" a young player who had issues with depression. Incognito was the veteran and leader on that offensive line. He should have been helping the young rookie—and everyone else—get better.

Players and coaches should work hard, not because they're afraid of punishment or getting cut, but because they agree it's the best way to win. McLane identified a "a core group—led by Barwin, Kelce, wide receivers Jeremy Maclin and Riley Cooper, tight end Brent Celek, and guard Todd Herremans"—who had been coming in voluntarily to work out at the NovaCare Center during the off season.

New draft pick Jordan Matthews quickly established himself as just such a player. DeSean Jackson clearly was not, and LeSean McCoy needed to decide which side he was on.

McCoy had been the first player to defend Jackson back in April, saying he had bonded with him off the field, but even then he added:

> You know that nobody's safe in this game as far as being here forever. But then you feel like alright well I've established myself so much, I did so much. [But] anybody can go. So I think it just makes you straighten up a little bit more. Maybe things that you think that you can get away with, you can't. And that's how it is.[1]

How much McCoy really bought in was not clear. One source with the Eagles told me that

> There were two guys who were obviously just not as into [Chip's program]. There were days when [Shady] was just visibly not as happy, or not into it. He made a bigger effort than DeSean but ultimately he just got tired of it.

McCoy was known as a sort of class clown on the team. His position coach Duce Staley was a respected Eagles veteran, a former running back and the only assistant coach left from the Andy Reid era. Another source with the Eagles told me that, one day at practice after DeSean's release,

> He was just dicking around during a drill, LeSean was, and Duce got on him, got on him really hard, and I remember thinking, yeah this is the exact stuff that DeSean did, that forced him out of favor with Chip. It always seemed like this was going to be LeSean's last season. If you don't practice or comport yourself the way he demands, he's not going to put up with that.

---

1   "McCoy Voices Support For DeSean" by Sheil Kapadia, *Birds 24/7*, April 12, 2014.

Staley told attendees at the 2014 Eagles Academy for Men that Andy Reid had assigned McCoy to him as a "special project" when he first hired him as a coach, and publicly the two running backs had a great relationship.[1] If McCoy still had trouble focusing even for Duce, years later, then the lessons of Jackson's release must not have sunk in.

McCoy had just finished a season as the NFL's leading rusher (1,600 yards). He was clearly the biggest star on the team; as teammate NT Bennie Logan said, "He's got a lot of moves in his shoes."

At least publicly, Shady was making a show of fitting in. He was humbler in interviews, and said the team was better without DeSean (after earlier defending him). He wore sweat pants on a humid, above ninety-degree day—just to go the extra mile.

The question was whether this was self-governance, or enforced acquiescence.

If all of this makes life under Chip sound grueling and dreary, there are reasons to think it was more fun than that—at least for players and coaches. Kelly's wisecracking at press conferences gives a glimpse, but only those on the inside, the players and assistant coaches, really know for sure.

When Chip Kelly came to the NFL, he had to fill out a questionnaire. One of the questions was, "Who has the most important job in football?" Kelly's response was surprising for a typically obsessed, hard-working football coach.

Nobody. It's a game![2]

Kelly works very long hours, completely focused on winning football games, and demands just as much out of his players. But he also models having fun together in the process, from joyfully chasing players around the practice field with a yellow foam bat, to using a radio-controlled car to signal in practice, to teasing them and reporters after games.

---

1   "Eagles Academy for Men 2014 Recap" by Anthony DiBona, *Bleeding Green Nation,* April 28, 2014.
2   "It's game on for NFL's new coaches, especially Eagles' Chip Kelly," by Sam Farmer, *Los Angeles Times,* September 3, 2013.

This may not always be apparent to outsiders, because Kelly's humor is bone dry and straight-faced. His intelligence and experience also give him a confidence in his opinions that can be intimidating.

Shortly before Kelly took the Eagles' coaching job, Nick Aliotti (his defensive coordinator at Oregon) said:

> Chip puts on a tough exterior that's hard to get through or break through. But Chip is really a lot of fun to work for. He's funny, he's witty, he keeps things light in the office.

Of course, success always makes hard work more fun, but Kelly does not share the grimness of a Bill Walsh or Bill Belichick, two legendary coaches who have won constantly without risk of enjoying themselves.

After the Eagles won Kelly's first NFL game against Washington, he told reporters:

> It still is a game. And I think sometimes we take ourselves too seriously. I mean, we all love playing football, and there's a passion with it, but that's the way it should be played. I had a lot of fun with it, and I think our guys had a lot of fun, but you're always gonna say that when you win.[1]

And make no mistake about it, winning is a big part of the fun. That same press conference featured this exchange.

> Q: Is this what you thought it would feel like [to win an NFL game]?
> A: No, it's what I hoped it would feel like, and that's what makes it so special...

This spirit is contagious, and it helps rather than hurts the effort to win. Safety Malcolm Jenkins put it succinctly in October 2014:

> The most dangerous team is the one who has the most guys having fun playing for the man next to them!
> @MalcolmJenkins. 5:05 P.M. October 4, 2014.

---

1 Chip Kelly's Press Conference, Sept. 9, 2013.

DRIFTING

JUNE 20 - JULY 24, 2014

Through careful buildup of the NFL Combine, free agency, the draft and even OTAs, football has become a year-round sport—except for one month in mid-summer, when coaches and players take a month off. Diehard football fans are stuck in the doldrums, drifting with no wind in their sails, just waiting for the end of the endless break between mini-camp and training camp. Football writers struggle furiously to generate enough hot air to fill those sails.

Chip Kelly's Eagles finished their spring workouts rattled (after Hurricane DeSean) but speaking in positive terms. The team added a lot of depth (if no stars) in the off-season, and as a group they seemed to have bought in to Coach Kelly's concepts of hard work, egolessness, teamwork and healthy living.

Of course, the team would soon find out that many of the prospects were non-stars for a very good reason, or that they were simply unable to grow fast enough to reach NFL speed and talent levels. The NFL is a hyper-elite league, and no one has quite figured out the key to predicting who will succeed, even with the best "sports science" that money can buy.

THE COACHING FRATERNITY

JUNE 21, 2014

Just before the Eagles broke for their month-long summer break, a reporter asked Kelly if he had plans to visit any other coaches, something he has done since his earliest days at the University of New Hampshire (UNH). His answer was ambiguous.

I'm going to go catch up with a few dudes if I can.

It wasn't clear if he meant coaches or friends, but for Chip there isn't much of a difference.

Many if not most of his close friends are also football or basketball coaches, not so much of a "coaching tree" as a regional clique, with roots at Boston College, UNH and the New England Patriots. While at UNH, he was known for traveling all over the country during the off-season to pick the brains of spread offense coaches, even at the high school level. Paying his own way, despite his meager salary.

Kelly made his connection with the University of Oregon while he was on one of these trips, trying to find out how then-coach Mike Bellotti was implementing his version of the spread. A former UNH assistant, Gary Crowton, was Oregon's Offensive Coordinator at the time and suggested Kelly as his replacement, when he took the same job at Louisiana State.

Some of these guys remain at the high school or assistant coach level, while others have risen to the highest reaches of the profession, but that doesn't affect Kelly's friendship. He seems to treat them all with respect and affection. In 2012, he went to Pamplona, Spain to run with the bulls, joined by a mixed group of friends—coaches from New England, and coaches from Oregon.

Over the years, Chip has expanded his network to include a lot of the best current and former coaches, including Tony Dungy (two Super Bowl victories), Jon Gruden (only one), and Eric Spoelstra (who won the first of his two NBA championships at age forty-two). Since starting in Philadelphia, Kelly has compared notes with old lions like Dick Vermeil and Jimmy Johnson, and young hotshots such as Kliff Kingsbury.

Now, during his 2014 summer break, Kelly spent time with Ohio State's coach Urban Meyer (two national championships at the time, and another since then). They've been buddies since Meyer was at Utah (in 2003-4).[1] According to CSN Philly's John Gonzalez, Meyer was the one who suggested Billy Davis—the best man at Meyer's wedding—to Kelly for Philadelphia's defensive coordinator job.[2] He may have encouraged Kelly to sign his former quarterback Tim Tebow later on, as well.

Kelly also visited Washington State coach Mike Leach—known for helping develop the "Air Raid" variety of the spread offense—for a couple of days in Key West, Florida. On the Andy Staples podcast,[3] Leach said that Kelly tracked him down at the famous bar "Captain Tony's," celebrated by Jimmy Buffett in the song "Last Mango in Paris." While there, they ran into NASCAR driver Dale Earnhardt, Jr. Of course. But even with the renowned racecar driver in the mix, the focus stayed on football.

Other coaches now seek out Kelly's advice, too. When he was still at Oregon, renowned New England Patriots coach Bill Belichick brought him in to Foxboro three times to discuss his tempo offense techniques and one-word play calls.[4] (Belichick has four Super Bowl

---

1 "Mack Brown interviews Urban Meyer" By Zach Barnett, *Football Scoop*, August 12, 2014.

2 "Chip Kelly and Urban Meyer share secrets" by John Gonzalez, *CSN Philly*, August 1, 2014.

3 "The Andy Staples Podcast: Guset Mike Leach," *Sports Illustrated*, August 2014.

4 "Quick to the point(s): Just one word triggers the Patriots' potent no-huddle

victories as head coach, plus two more as an assistant.) The Patriots used these tactics to ramp up their already powerful offense, steamrolling Denver (led by QB Tim Tebow) in the divisional round of the 2011 playoffs, 45-10.

Kelly and Belichick held joint practices for their teams during each of Kelly's first two training camps. Asked how they got in touch, the Patriots' coach told WEEI radio that,

> Chip's a New England guy, so we crossed paths from time to time in New England. We kept in touch over the past few years…[1]

Belichick knows Kelly through Bill O'Brien, who is now the Houston Texans' head coach. O'Brien actually interviewed for the Eagles' job in 2013. From 2008 to 2011, he was the offensive play caller for the Patriots, as QB coach and later offensive coordinator. His connection to Kelly goes back much further, though, according to the *Boston Globe's* Greg Bedard:

> Kelly had become friendly with former Patriots offensive coordinator Bill O'Brien while both were rising in the college ranks. The UNH coaching staff would visit Brown, where O'Brien was coaching, for pickup basketball games and to talk X's and O's.[2]

O'Brien coached at Brown in 1993 and 1994, which gives you an idea of how far back these connections go.

offense" by Greg A. Bedard. *Boston Globe*, C.1, October 9, 2012.

1   "Cooper catches 2 TDs as Pats-Eagles skirmish" WEEI: *This Just In*, August 6, 2013.

2   "With 1 word, Patriots' no-huddle an NFL marvel" by Greg Bedard, *The Boston Globe*, October 9, 2012.

BUSTED

JUNE 30, 2014

The biggest mid-summer news of 2014 was the imminent suspension of starting right tackle Lane Johnson after he tested positive for PEDs.

The substance was never reported; the NFLPA contract doesn't allow official comment, though the Seattle Seahawks' positive PED tests in 2013 were said to be for Adderall (which also might mask other PEDs).

This was the second positive PED test for the Eagles in a year. Backup linebacker Jake Knott (who was already struggling to make the team) was unsuccessful in appealing his four-game suspension earlier in 2014. Not surprisingly, this led to a lot of jokes about "sports science" and smoothies, as well as comparisons to the Seattle Seahawks and their new-age, PAC-12 coach. But Lane Johnson was in no way a marginal player.

He was the #4 draft pick overall in 2013, and started at right tackle from day one. He had some trouble the first few games, especially in pass protection, but learned quickly and missed only one single snap all year. The Eagles' offensive line was remarkably healthy in 2013—every starter played every game—and that was a big reason for the team's late surge, where they went 7-1 to close out the regular season.

In a way, the team was almost too healthy, since the depth players weren't able to get any game experience. Journeyman Allen Barbre was first up to replace Johnson; he got some snaps against

Green Bay in 2013, and held his own against Clay Matthews (who, admittedly, has a cast on his arm). And of his seven lifetime NFL starts, all had been at right tackle—Johnson's position.[1]

Philadelphia's coaches were very positive about reserve lineman Matt Tobin, a twenty-four-year-old Iowa grad picked up as a UDFA in 2013, but he had never played a down outside of practice.

For better or worse, the "problem" of a too-healthy offensive line was solved in 2014, and the backup linemen were about to get all the snaps they could handle.

---

1 "Sources: Eagles' Lane Johnson suspended for PED use" by Paul Domowitch, *Philadelphia Daily News*, July 2, 2014.

THE NUMBER OF CRAPS GIVEN = 0

JULY, 2014

It's often said that Chip Kelly doesn't give a crap what anyone else thinks. A lot of people—especially politicians—claim that, because it sounds so confident and decisive, but it's rarely true. More often, they have carefully constructed a persona as someone who doesn't care what people think—because they desperately want people to think of them that way.

Chip truly does not care what the general public or the press thinks about him—but not in the resentful, proud way most people imagine. To be more precise, there's an important distinction here. Kelly is very interested in any *information* people can give him, including suggestions (if he respects their knowledge and intelligence). But he is not at all interested in the *judgments* other people have about what he is doing.

Unless you're part of the Eagles organization—on the team, or one of the coaches. Then he cares a lot about what you think. He's still not going to take a vote, but you automatically have a voice that he will listen to. And conversely, people on the team have a very special privilege—the right to an explanation of why Chip is doing what he does.

You know who does not have that right? Reporters. Writers. Pundits. Including me. We are left to work it out on our own, and he truly does not care what we think, or believe, or write.

This is an important philosophical principle for him. Asked about an allegation that he was racist, Kelly replied,

> I'm not governed by the fear of what other people say... You start chasing perception and you got a long life ahead of you, son... You can [only] control one thing. You can control yourself. I know how we run this organization, and it's not run that way.[1]

It might be more accurate to say, he is opposed to worrying about what other people think, as a marker of success or failure. He explained at some length in October of 2014:

> I say praise and blame is all the same. If you let outside noise affect you, then that means you value their opinion more than you value your own opinion. If that's the case, then your life is going to be just like this every single day: Someone said something good about me. I feel good about myself. Someone said something bad about me. I feel crappy about myself. If that's the way you want to live your life, then hang around with really good people because if not you're going to have a tough day.
>
> It's not easy. It's easier said than done, and everybody understands that. But you really, truly have to do that. You really, truly, I think when you put enough time and preparation in, then that's the confidence that you get. You don't get confidence because someone you don't even know said you had a good day or you look good or you feel good or whatever. I mean, that's really a tough thing to start to learn and develop over time. But I think our guys pretty much have a good amount of confidence in themselves as a group. You're going to have good days, you're going to have bad days. We had a really good day yesterday.

As for people's judgments, my sense is that Coach Kelly thinks that people will love him if his team wins, and they'll hate him if it loses, and no amount of talking or image manipulation will change

---

1   Chip Kelly's press conference at OTAs, May 28, 2015.

that. He's probably right.

Even with the press and public, though, he's usually willing to admit mistakes, which is always a good thing—the difference between confidence and arrogance. After his second game in the pros, against San Diego in 2013, he admitted that he hadn't known the rule governing injury time outs.[1] Following the 2014 draft, he volunteered to reporters that he would have drafted Taylor Hart in the third round, but that Howie Roseman convinced him he would still be there in the fifth (as he was).

I doubt many other NFL coaches would stand before a team meeting and say something like "Shady and I got into it, and I was wrong," as Kelly did after the Eagles' 2013 Tampa Bay game.[2]

While he's famously cagey with reporters, Kelly has a different attitude toward other coaches. He gave a series of talks to coaching clinics early in his Oregon career that spelled out exactly what he was trying to do with his program.[3] He listens to players' ideas, too. At New Hampshire, he even invited his team to suggest or create new plays.[4] That proved a bit unwieldy, but communication remains a two-way street.

The "Snow Bowl" game between Philadelphia and Detroit in 2013 was a beautiful mess, due to eight inches of fresh snow that fell on the field just as the game was starting. Not surprisingly, this disrupted the offenses of both teams and made kicking almost impossible.

Late in the third quarter, with the Eagles behind and struggling to move the chains, cornerback Cary Williams came to Coach Kelly and suggested that he change his whole offensive strategy. Williams noted that it was impossible for defensive backs to cut on the snow,

---

1 "Chip Kelly Admits He Didn't Know Injury Rule," *The Sporting News*, September 16, 2013.

2 "30 Yards and a Cloud of Dust" by Seth Wickersham, *ESPN The Magazine*, August 14, 2014.

3 For example, "Efficient use of practice time," in *2011 Coach of the Year Clinics Football Manual*, ed. Earl Browning (Monterey, CA: Coaches Choice), 2011, 138-45.

4 "Kelly is mastermind behind UNH football's potent offensive attack" by Mike Zhe, *The Portsmouth Herald*, August 25, 2002.

and suggested that long passes would be very hard to stop. Kelly followed Williams' advice, and the Eagles exploded for 28 points in the fourth quarter to win.

The problem is that, as Kelly's experience and knowledge keep growing, the range of people who can tell him something he doesn't know keeps shrinking. He already compares notes with many—if not most—of the living elite football coaches interested in spread offenses. The smaller his circle becomes though, the more risk he faces of getting stubborn or set in his ways. During the 2014 season, there were some reasons to think this might have already begun.

It's up to Chip to stay open-minded, to commit 100% to his ideas but also let go of them if real world experience proves that he didn't have it exactly right. There are a million traps of ego, stubbornness, even just exhaustion and frustration when things don't go as planned. A million ways for this coaching career to go wrong. And a real possibility of greatness if it doesn't.

TRAINING CAMP

JULY 25, 2014

In late July, the team began to solidify with the opening of training camp. The coaches installed the new plays they had worked up to fit the new players, but their work went much deeper than that.

Head coaches are usually compared primarily on the basis of their schemes and offensive play calling, or (in the case of the few defensively focused coaches) on their defensive alignments. But this is shallow and distorting in the case of Chip Kelly. He not simply an offense X's and O's wizard, as he's often made out to be. Not just because he also has a powerful defensive philosophy that isn't easily captured in statistics, but because the coach sees the battlefield entirely differently.

Plays are the tip of the pyramid, but Chip is all about the foundation. Below the plays, there are the mismatches between your players and opponents that your plays aim to exploit.

The mismatches are built through scheme and player selection—emphasizing size, speed and athleticism—and conditioning, which includes practicing, coaching and physical care.

That care, in turn, goes beyond stretching and treatment of injuries to include players' nutrition, hydration, attitude and sleep habits. Underlying everything is a code, a set of positive values in action, including integrity, hard work, humility, and sacrificing ego for the good of the team.

It's an audacious and extremely thorough approach that demands a lot from the players, and expects a lot of the coach.

There are more than a few who think it's unrealistic in the NFL, even naïve. Chip Kelly doesn't care.

• • •

No one was wowed by the Eagles' draft; it looked like Jordan Matthews would be the only starter in 2014. But the team had quietly built depth on both sides of the ball, which—given the reality of NFL injuries—wins games. In 2013, the dire thinness of the secondary was exposed with injuries to rookie safety Earl Wolff and cornerbacks Bradley Fletcher and Brandon Boykin. Subs Patrick Chung and Roc Carmichael were scorched by opponents, including in the playoff loss to New Orleans.

The top 2014 pick, OLB Marcus Smith, was surprisingly quiet in training camp. Most reporters had assumed that he was being groomed to replace veteran Trent Cole as the "Predator" (pass rushing OLB) in Billy Davis's 3-4 defense. Cole was a thirty-one-year-old converted 4-3 DE whose salary was scheduled to double from $5 million in 2014 to $10 million in 2015. In practices, though, Smith was backing up Connor Barwin at the "Jack" (of all trades) OLB, dropping into coverage as often as rushing.

What Davis (and Coach Kelly) really wanted were interchangeable linebackers equally good at coverage or rushing. Cole had eight sacks in 2013, but when he was on the field, he was going to rush, *period.*

It began to look like the Eagles might use Smith as their new Jack and slide Barwin over to Cole's Predator position on the right side. Barwin had 11.5 sacks in 2011 for Houston, so his rushing ability was clear, but he only managed five sacks in 2013 given his coverage duties opposite Cole.

The odd man out appeared to be Brandon Graham, another good 4-3 pass rusher who had had trouble adjusting to Davis's scheme. Many fans and writers predicted that the Eagles would try to trade him before the season started, as he hadn't seemed to improve much during Kelly's first season. Cole, on the other hand, had no sacks in the first eight games in 2013, then eight in the second half.

Kelly deflected questions on the subject with humor, as he often does. A reporter asked Chip if Brandon Graham was the ideal size for an outside linebacker in his scheme. Chip replied that, "Ideally I would want someone 6'11" that weighs 400 pounds. So he's a little bit under that."[1]

---

1   Chip Kelly's press conference during OTAs, May 19, 2014.

THE BOY KING DILEMMA

AUGUST, 2014

One player who did not need to battle for a roster slot was two-year veteran Brandon Boykin. Though he was stuck in the slot cornerback position playing barely half of the defensive snaps, the "Boy King" was one of the best playmakers in the NFL. His six interceptions were tied for second in the entire league—only superstar (and full time corner) Richard Sherman had more (eight). Boykin also had a slew of pass breakups to boot.

Every head coach promises to do better on turnovers, but Coach Kelly had delivered on that promise both at Oregon and in his first year at Philadelphia. Boykin was a big reason why.

At the same time, the Boy King had bigger ambitions, and the Eagles didn't want to fulfill them. He yearned to be a starting outside corner—with all the extra money and glory that position brings—rather than a slot CB, and that's understandable.

But Kelly sees NFL receivers and corners getting bigger and more physical all the time, and he furthered that trend by releasing DeSean Jackson—who is Boykin's size (5'10" maybe, if stretched out on the rack)—and replacing him with Jordan Matthews (6'3", 212) and Josh Huff (a very physical 6'0" and 205).

Chip loved having Boykin in the slot but wanted taller outside corners to deal with the Dez Bryants and Calvin Johnsons of the world. Philadelphia's beat reporters were constantly speculating that Boykin wouldn't accept that, hinting strongly that he would leave Philadelphia when his rookie contract expired at the end of the 2015 season. They hinted so consistently that you had to suspect that Boykin (or perhaps his agent) was telling them so, off the record.

In 2014, this dilemma got worse, not better, because a big factor in the Birds' playoff loss to New Orleans had been a bit of Kelly's own strategy turned back at him. The Saints used a spread concept, playing three wide receivers and forcing the Eagles into their nickel defense—only to run the ball against the Birds' smaller and quicker pass-defense sub-package. That was how they had ground out the final drive that iced the game.

Defensive Coordinator Billy Davis told reporters that with Malcolm Jenkins at safety now, instead of Patrick Chung or Roc Carmichael, the team was versatile enough to stay in its base defense in these situations. Unlike the woeful Chung, Jenkins could cover a TE or WR as well as stuff a runner, letting the team keep a bigger linebacker in to stop the run. That meant that Boykin would stay on the bench for even more snaps, despite his talent. Thus the dilemma.

So what were the options? The Eagles could try to groom Boykin for the outside corner position, bucking the trend of bigger receivers and corners, but it was clear that Chip didn't want to go that way, given Seattle's success with big DBs.

They could simply pay him outside corner money to play slot CB, which—given the importance they assign to the role, and the team's careful money management—might be worth it. Or they could actually try to trade him, even though he was one of their best players. The Eagles had already upgraded their secondary with CB Nolan Carroll, safety Jenkins and draft pick Jaylen Watkins, who plays both positions.

It seemed criminal to give up a player of the Boy King's talent, but with two years left on his rookie contract, he had high trade value. Coach Kelly's insistence on height in his cornerbacks was understandable, but it was a fair question whether his particular numbers were unrealistic, given the difficulty of finding shutdown cornerbacks of any height.

Kelly had been spoiled at Oregon, which had a phenomenal run of CB and safety talent, from Jairus Byrd and T.J. Ward to Walter

Thurmond, Cliff Harris and Ifo Ekpre-Olomu—all of whom played during Chip's six years there. Perhaps he thought All-Pro and All-American DBs were easy to come by.

His stubbornness on this issue came back to bedevil the Eagles at the most crucial part of the season.

PRESEASON GAMES

CHICAGO BEARS, AUGUST 8, 2014
NEW ENGLAND PATRIOTS, AUGUST 15, 2014
PITTSBURGH STEELERS, AUGUST 21, 2014
NEW YORK JETS, AUGUST 28, 2014

Preseason games don't matter one bit—for the standings. Chip Kelly told a press conference that the starters would probably only play 10-15 snaps of the opening game against Chicago, as long as they looked reasonably competent. (If they went three and out more than once, they'd have to stay in a bit longer.)

But preseason games are not unimportant. They go a long way toward deciding which of the ninety players on the training camp roster make the final fifty-three-man squad. Practice is fine and all, but in previous years, Kelly has made fun of reporters impressed with how his teams performed "against air." You can't see how players are doing for real until you're tackling to the ground.

These games can also reveal potential problems in the scheme or execution. In the opening 28-24 loss to the Chicago Bears, the engine of the offense was clearly sputtering, at least when the first team was driving. Nick Foles was just okay, with as many interceptions in the first quarter (two) as he had had in all of the 2013 regular season. He was surprisingly inaccurate as well.

Mark Sanchez, on the other hand, looked great as the backup quarterback, driving, scoring and protecting the ball. He was 25-31 for 281 yards, two TDs and one INT across the entire preseason.

Sanchez was wowing everyone with his positive attitude (after years of being mocked), as well as his short, sharp passes and the obvious chemistry he had with rookie wide receiver Jordan Matthews.

Chris Polk seemed to be a lock for the third RB position after great production in 2013; in only eleven snaps, he gained 98 yards with three touchdowns and another five first downs. *Plus* he caught four passes on five targets for 61 yards, and made four tackles on special teams. You would think that was enough to earn more playing time in 2014.

Over the summer, though, he was injured (partially torn hamstring) and unable to play or practice until late August. Kelly himself has said very directly that Polk needed to get back on the field if he wanted to make this team. As the saying goes, "You can't make the club in a tub."

The Eagles ended up keeping only three RBs on the roster, which surprised some. But that ignored the versatility of Trey Burton, who was listed as the fourth tight end. Burton was recruited to Florida as a QB but ended up playing running back, wide receiver, h-back and tight end.

Fully nine of ninety players on the Eagles' training camp roster were ex-Ducks, and some reporters (including Kempski) didn't like it. But at least three—Will Murphy, Josh Kaddu and Wade Keliikipi—were just camp bodies. Huff and Hart were almost guaranteed to make the roster as the team's third- and fifth-round draft picks. The Ducks on the bubble were WR Jeff Maehl and inside linebacker (ILB) Casey Matthews—marginal NFL talents who have stayed in the league for years with sharp special teams work—as well as DE Brandon Bair and RB Kenjon Barner.

Josh Huff struggled a bit against Chicago, catching only one of five passes for four total yards, though that one was a key reception down to the 1-yard line that set up a TD. Then again, he also ran back a kickoff 102 yards for a touchdown, providing the biggest highlight of the game. This made him the frontrunner for the team's kick return duties.

In the post-game press conference, Coach Kelly noted how

Huff used his physicality to finish the play, stiff-arming the kicker to the ground. He acted as if the defender was an annoying terrier pestering him.

In game two, though, Huff was injured trying to run back a very deep kick that he probably should have downed in the end zone. The team said he had an "AC sprain," which is essentially a separated shoulder. The rookie was out for the rest of the preseason at the very least; some Eagles beat writers speculated that, given his lackluster preseason, the team might put him on the injured reserve list for an unofficial redshirt year.

Aside from the TD return, Huff didn't show much as a receiver in the preseason. He had a lot of drops. Huff may have felt he could cruise into the NFL with the knowledge he gained playing for years under Kelly at Oregon; if so, he learned a lesson about the complexity and talent level of the pro game. Toughness doesn't help you if you get injured by disregarding danger. Arguably, this was one of Michael Vick's failings.

Rookie DE Taylor Hart played well in the preseason, too, impressing both Jeff McLane and Jimmy Kempski, but so did former Duck Brandon Bair, who was competing for the same position (backup defensive end). The twist is that Bair was Hart's mentor at Oregon, and they remain friends and collaborators, even though the odds were against both making the team.

Bair was an interesting case. You could call him the NFL's oldest rookie. At thirty, he hadn't played a single regular season snap in the pros, due to his Mormon mission and hanging around the bottom of NFL rosters at Kansas City, Oakland and Philadelphia the previous three years. He kept making teams but never getting into games. Meanwhile, he ran a few businesses, including a gym, and worked out religiously.

As it turned out, Bair simply played his way onto the squad with a great preseason. In one three-play series against Chicago, he fell on a fumble (ruled an incomplete pass) at the Bears' goal line, and nearly caught a tipped pass for an interception (it touched the turf before he could control it). Though the official scorecard disagrees, it looks like he may have been the one who blocked Chicago's field goal in the first period, too. Against Pittsburgh, Bair penetrated the pocket as part of a resurgent Eagles pass rush, and batted down a pass to force a punt. And in the final preseason game against the Jets, he recovered a fumble.

The entire defensive line looked good in the preseason, showing a strong pass rush against the Steelers that rattled Ben Roethlisberger and kept the Steelers out of their rhythm until the third quarter. Huge rookie nose tackle Beau Allen showed surprising mobility.

For the second year in a row, the Eagles had joint practices with the New England Patriots leading up to their preseason game. In 2013, the Pats had intimidated the heavily revamped Eagles, with physical play on defense and Brady picking apart the shaky Philly secondary. Brady had tormented CB Curtis Marsh in 2013 with pass after pass, play after play. 2014 was different. Led by Jenkins and, yes, a resurgent Marsh, the Eagles hit back punch for punch all week.

Post-draft, the Philadelphia Eagles had gone through the entire off-season with literally no roster changes at all. Then boom! Heading into preseason game three, Chip Kelly and GM Howie Roseman made a couple of roster moves that changed the entire season.

First, they waived undrafted free agent RB David Fluellen. Then, two hours later, they traded Fluellen for Colts kicker Cody Parkey.

Wait—they traded a guy they'd already waived? Yes. That's how smart Howie Roseman is. Waivers don't take effect for a number of hours, and Baltimore had already put Parkey in for waivers (since he hadn't beaten out Adam Vinatieri).

You would normally expect both to get waived again at the end of camp—and Fluellen was—but Parkey was the Eagles' only hope of breaking Chip Kelly's kicker curse.

CUT DOWN DAY

AUGUST 30TH, 2014

On the day that final roster decisions were due, Chip Kelly wasn't even in Philadelphia. He left GM Howie Roseman in charge and went to Baltimore with his buddy, Player Personnel Director Tom Gamble, to watch his other buddy Urban Meyer's Ohio State squad play Navy in nearby Baltimore.

In the most important final roster decision, Cody Parkey made the team and Alex Henery was released. There weren't too many other surprises. Ex-QB and multi-position player Trey Burton joined the final fifty-three, officially designated as the fourth tight end (but mostly a special teamer). Of the nine ex-Ducks, four were cut. Kaddu was released outright, and Barner, Murphy and Keliikipi made the practice squad. Bair joined Hart, Huff and WR Jeff Maehl on the squad.

There were some unfortunate injuries during the off-season including Josh Huff's shoulder separation. Travis Long (from the Washington State Cougars) had been set to be a key backup at both an inside and outside linebacker, so his ACL tear was a tough break. He had missed the 2013 season with an ACL tear on the other knee, leaving his NFL future in doubt. Long's injury cleared the way for Casey Matthews, the ultimate survivor, to hang on with the Eagles for one more year as a depth ILB (and the final ex-Duck).

Incumbent kicker Alex Henery had deteriorated rapidly—he was 1 for 3 in the preseason. The 47-yarder he muffed against New England was bad enough, but forgivable. But by the time he shanked an easy 31-yard field goal against the Steelers, the team had already released Carey "Murderleg" Spear—who missed several field goals in a row at one joint practice with the Patriots—and panic was setting in.

Special teams coach Dave Fipp was faced with a choice between the crumbling veteran kicker and a completely untested rookie (Cody Parkey) who had missed a 33-yard FG in the college national championship game that previous January.

The last preseason game against the Jets was Parkey's only chance to stake his claim, and he grabbed it. He scored 11 points, including field goals of 54 and 53 yards—both longer than Henery's career best of fifty-one. He also got touchbacks on his last two (of four) kickoffs, seemingly gaining strength with every kick.

Henery eventually signed with Detroit, and showed how close the Eagles had come to disaster. He missed three field goals in a single game against Buffalo. The kicker was cut and out of football the next day.

Finally, the preliminaries were over, and there was a lot of excitement. Football is America's most popular sport for a good reason: every game counts. All the action is crammed into a few months in the fall. Sure, it's all scrutinized and televised and argued over endlessly, but once the train starts moving it plows ahead until the season's over. There's always another big game in a few days, until there isn't.

Basketball and baseball have their long, dull buildup to the big show during actual regular games, which cost real money to attend and risk player injuries. January NBA games are terrible—sloppy, poorly executed, and no cheaper than the ones that matter.

Football's off-season is endless but it's free, and they've gradually marked it off with key milestones for the hard-core fans: free agency, the owners' meeting, OTAs, the draft, minicamp, and finally training camp in late July.

Now it was time. Eight months of waiting and preparation gave way to seventeen weeks of games—and hopefully, a few more after that. Just making the playoffs was no longer good enough.

Most pundits had placed the Eagles in the Top Ten of the NFL, and CBS's Cris Collinsworth pegged them for the Super Bowl. Anything short of the Divisional Round would be a disappointment.

GAME I.
JACKSONVILLE JAGUARS

SEPTEMBER 7, 2014
LINCOLN FINANCIAL FIELD, PHILADELPHIA

Jacksonville, up first, was a terrible team, and they shouldn't have given the Eagles the least bit of trouble. The fact that they did was a sign of the trouble to come. The Eagles were 10.5-point favorites at home against the Jaguars, led by quarterback Chad Henne who has a history with Chip Kelly. In Kelly's second game as Oregon's offensive coordinator, way back in 2007, the Ducks made a statement by crushing his Michigan Wolverines, 39-7. Since then, Henne has defined QB mediocrity as a pro with fifty-five touchdowns vs. sixty-two interceptions.

There were some interesting parallels between the 2014 versions of the Eagles and Chip Kelly's old college team, the Oregon Ducks.

Let's call the Oregon Ducks' football program the 'father' and the Philadelphia Eagles' version the 'son.' (Yes, Chip Kelly is the father of both, but don't over-think this metaphor into something creepy.) The programs were very similar, as Kelly's successor Mark Helfrich—Chip's offensive coordinator at Oregon—kept his program almost completely intact. Both teams had their first real test in the first weekend of September, and the family resemblance was striking.

Both teams were favored—Philly against woeful Jacksonville, and the Ducks in a much tougher battle against #7 Michigan State.

Both started out surprisingly shaky, trailing their opponents and seemingly unable to get their offenses moving at all. Both started their turnaround by stiffening on defense, then exploded offensively as their opponent tired and collapsed.

The Ducks looked like they were on the ropes against Michigan State's excellent defense, which *Grantland* described as a next-generation, improvisational defense equivalent to Kelly's offenses.[1]

Philadelphia looked a lot like they had found a way to lose a game no one could picture them fumbling away.

I say "fumbling" for good reason. Nick Foles' evil, incompetent twin re-emerged for the first time since the first Dallas game in 2013. He was terrible, fumbling on the first two drives on strip-sacks after holding the ball for roughly twenty minutes on each play. It was probably more like five or seven seconds, but that's what it felt like waiting for him to get hit.

Then, when it looked like the Eagles were on track again, he threw a terrible pick in the end zone. Beyond the turnovers, he looked indecisive and slow to react, missing multiple wide-open receivers.

On Twitter and online comment boards, many fans were ready to see Mark Sanchez take over the first time Foles limped after a sack. But Kelly wisely stood behind his starter—and it paid off in the second half.

As with Oregon, though, the turnaround began before the break with tougher first-half defense. On one particular drive, the Eagles gave a textbook example of the "Bend But Don't Break" philosophy Chip picked up from his former defensive coordinator at Oregon, Nick Aliotti.[2]

The Jags drove for twelve plays and 62 yards, burning up five-and-a-half minutes of clock against an increasingly stiff defense. The Birds held them on third down at Philadelphia's 18-yard line, and then ex-Duck Brandon Bair—playing his first pro game after

---

1   "A Defense to Match: Appreciating the Stingy Spartans in the Offensive Age" by Chris Brown, Grantland.com, September 2, 2014.
2   "Eagles Bent But Didn't Break" by Mark Saltveit, *Bleeding Green Nation*, September 8, 2014.

three years on the bottom of various NFL rosters—blocked the field goal attempt. (He also had a tackle-for-loss in an excellent debut that momentarily quieted the cries of "Oregon bias!")

Jacksonville had scored 17 points earlier in the first half, most of them after Foles' fumbles gave them short fields. Cary Williams had a poor game at cornerback, giving up two touchdowns to UDFA rookie receiver Allen Hurns. In fairness, Hurns played for Jacksonville's offensive coordinator Jedd Fisch at the University of Miami, so they were already on the same page. (*Miami bias!*)

After the blocked field goal, though, the Jags sagged. In the second half, they couldn't maintain the fierce pass rush that rattled Foles so much before the break. The same could be said in the Oregon game, except that it took until the fourth quarter for the Spartans to lose steam.

This was not a great start for Philadelphia on offense. In fact, it was ugly. But the defense looked great as Billy Davis' 3-4 scheme really took hold. It had already been better than anyone had reason to expect in 2013. Against Jacksonville, the concept of disguising who is going to rush really came into focus.

Everyone from Connor Barwin to Brandon Graham and Vinny Curry got in on the party. Curry and Graham looked much more comfortable dropping into pass coverage than they did in Davis' and Kelly's first year. Trent Cole got another sack, rookie Beau Allen rotated in at nose tackle without missing a beat and the entire unit displayed excellent teamwork and communication. It was a great sign for the year to come.

The offensive line, on the other hand, lost two players to long-term injuries. Top sub Allen Barbre (starting because of Lane Johnson's suspension) was knocked out for the year and Evan Mathis was lost for at least eight weeks with a torn medial collateral ligament (the little brother of the more famous ACL).

It worked out okay in this game; substitutes Andrew Gardner and David Molk looked great in relief, at least against the tiring Jaguars. But it was a worrisome development for a team that played all of 2013 with the same starting offensive line.

On defense, key backup ILB Najee Goode tore his pectoral muscle and was also out for the season. With Travis Long out earlier to an ACL, this left only Emmanuel Acho and Casey Matthews as bench ILBs, a dangerous situation.

Oregon fans recognized the pattern of the game. The heroes struggled in the first half, giving up points and struggling to get even a first down. After intermission, though, the defense ratcheted down and the offense exploded.

Against Michigan State, the Ducks scored 28 consecutive points in the second half; against Jacksonville, the Eagles ran up thirty-four in a row. This type of explosion has been called "The Oregon Ambush"[1] as far back as 2010.[2]

Against Chip Kelly's teams, you're juggling dynamite. You think you're pulling it off, juggle juggle juggle, almost done, oh crap, BOOM.

FINAL SCORE: EAGLES 34, JAGUARS 17

1   "Oregon Engages the Afterburners: Your Weekly College Football Wrap" by Matt Hinton, Grantland.com, September 8, 2014.
2   "The Oregon ambush claims its latest victim, and the Pac-10 title" by Matt Hinton, Yahoo! Sports, November 26, 2010.

GAME 2.
INDIANAPOLIS COLTS

SEPTEMBER 15, 2014
LUCAS OIL STADIUM, INDIANAPOLIS

Only three NFC teams won their first two games in 2014. The Eagles were one of them, but to everyone's surprise, the Seahawks and 49ers were not. Both teams lay ahead on Philadelphia's schedule, but early on the Birds were a game up on both.

Everyone likes to quote Chip Kelly's quip that "Bigger people beat up little people," but the heroes of game two were a 5'6" running back named Darren Sproles, and a 193-pound rookie kicker who looked way too young to drink legally.

Sproles was thirty-one, discarded by the New Orleans Saints because they thought he was old and declining. Chip Kelly nabbed him in return for a fifth-round draft pick and was barely able to contain his excitement over the summer.

Two games into the 2014 season, Sproles had shown everybody why. He already had 350 all-purpose yards, and the Eagles' offense led the league in both scoring and total offense—despite playing terribly.

Against Indianapolis, Sproles led the Eagles to a dramatic come-from-behind victory on a last-second field goal by Parkey (against the team that cut him in training camp). Just as impressively, the Eagles' defense shut down Andrew Luck—the best comeback QB in the NFL—with a crucial interception by Malcolm Jenkins and a three-and-out on his last two drives to lock it down.

None of which changed the fact that the Philadelphia Eagles were playing terrible football.

Nick Foles was blind to wide-open receivers and threw erratically when he did see them. He astonished analysts by throwing only two interceptions in all of 2013, vs. twenty-seven TDs, but he threw two in just the first two games of 2014 and got worse from there.

LeSean McCoy, 2013's leading rusher, didn't reach 80 yards by land in either of the first two games, and in this one, Foles—a notoriously slow runner—had more yards per carry (four runs, 22 yards for an average YPC of 5.5, vs. Shady's 4.2).

Chip Kelly likes to balance runs and passes—the Eagles threw 508 times and ran 500 in 2013—but the team was forced to throw eighty-two times in games one and two, vs. only fifty-nine runs.

The Eagles defense made Jacksonville's pass attack and the Colts' infamous run game look good—Trent Richardson, anybody?—and the Birds were terrible in the red zone on both sides of the ball. Even Cody Parkey, the young kicker who was one of the few bright spots for the team, missed a 38-yard field goal against Indianapolis for no good reason.

The thrilling comeback victory covered up a lot of doubts, and perhaps validated Coach Kelly's emphasis on teamwork and intangibles. Pulling together and staying strong is what a close-knit unit should be good at. But clearly this season was not going the way anyone anticipated, and most of the surprises were not good.

FINAL SCORE: EAGLES 30, COLTS 27

SPECIAL TEAMS

SEPTEMBER, 2014

Chip Kelly and the Eagles had done better in 2013 than anyone but the most biased hometown fan might have imagined.

One big disappointment, though, was special teams performance. This was puzzling because, by all accounts, Kelly put a lot more effort into special teams than Andy Reid ever did.[1] He added some players (such as Jason Phillips) to the roster primarily for their special teams skills, got more starters to contribute and made what he called "Teams" a big part of his practices.

And yet the results were uneven at best. Sportswriter Rick Gosselin of the *Dallas Morning News* produces an annual ranking of the NFL's ST units, assigning points to different aspects such as field goal kicking, returns and blocked kicks. The 2013 Eagles were just eighteenth, despite all the effort.

For no clear reason, Kelly had had weak kickers all through his years at Oregon as well as his first year in Philly. As a college coach, Chip picked up the nickname "Big Balls Chip" because he went for it on fourth down so often. A lot of that may have been desperation as much as guts. If you can't make a field goal from the 30, you're not going to punt.

In 2013, Henery's weak kicking had been directly involved in three of the Birds' seven losses, including the narrow playoff loss to New Orleans. You might say, "Well, you can't just go out and find a good NFL kicker any time, you know. They're rare."

---

1   "Not So Special" by Tommy Lawlor, *Iggles Blitz*, December 16, 2012.

Except that New Orleans did exactly that, signing Shayne Graham—a kicker who'd bumped all around the league for years, and hadn't played all year—seventeen days before the playoffs began. And Graham kicked the winning field goal as time expired.

I asked Gosselin what the crux of the Eagles' weakness was.

> Big problem was the return game. They finished twenty-sixth in kickoff returns and twenty-seventh in punt returns. If you have an elite returner, those are easy points to accrue.

Damaris Johnson and DeSean Jackson, the main returners in 2013, were not effective. Jackson was famous for his game-winning punt return against the Giants in 2010, but in 2013 he averaged only 5.1 yards a return. Damaris Johnson was only slightly better at 8.3 yards on punts and 25.9 on kickoffs. His longest kickoff return of the year was just 33 yards, so no team feared him.

Both were gone before the new season began. RB Chris Polk and new additions Darren Sproles and Josh Huff took over. Each of them had touchdown returns in 2014.

There were other improvements—Cody Parkey's excellent kicking, three free agents (Chris Maragos, Bryan Braman, and Nolan Carroll) acquired primarily for special teams, and a much-improved defensive line. The results would be spectacular. By the end of the 2014 season, the Birds would tie the NFL record for special teams touchdowns (seven) and lead the league in blocked kicks (six). New acquisitions Maragos, Braman and Carroll ended up having three of the four highest ST tackle totals. When Gosselin released his 2014 special teams rankings, the Eagles had jumped straight to #1.

Why did all the efforts of ST coach Dave Fipp and Coach Kelly fail to help in 2013 and succeed so dramatically in 2014? There's no clear explanation. It was a nice confirmation that they were on the right path, as well as a caution that you can't control everything, even when your approach is right.

DESEAN AGAIN

SEPTEMBER 18, 2014

The victory against Indianapolis set up the long-awaited showdown with Washington, a team with a new coach, a new twenty-seven-year-old offensive coordinator, and a new star wide receiver.

When DeSean signed with the bitter division rival, five days after the Eagles released him, reporters immediately circled the dates of the Eagles' two games against them. The first was on September 21st, and Jackson had promised a big game all summer.

Given that the wide receiver is a wildly talented player with suspect work habits, this was not good news for Philadelphia. "Professional" is not a word often used to describe Jackson. It's likely that playing for a division rival and having two chances to embarrass his old team every year motivated him to sign with the Skins.

Three days before the game, on September 18th, Jeff McLane of the *Inquirer* published a long article based on interviews with fully twenty-one Eagles players, nearly half the team.[1] The upshot was that all of the players were surprised that DeSean was released, that they didn't see it coming before it happened, and that they suspected more was involved than "football reasons," but they had no idea what that might be. No real surprises there. Players are going to be careful to avoid insulting either their coach or a former player.

But down near the bottom of the article, McLane included a couple of interesting nuggets. He revealed several details that hadn't

---

1   "Eagles players still unsure why DeSean was let go" by Jeff McLane, *Philadelphia Inquirer*, September 18, 2014.

been reported before about DeSean's nationally televised fight with his position coach Bob Bicknell during the 2013 season.

> The most notorious Jackson outburst came in last December's Vikings game. Avant, Cooper, Maehl, McCoy and quarterback Michael Vick all intervened at one point as he yelled at receivers coach Bob Bicknell. After the game, owner Jeffrey Lurie spoke with Jackson alone in one corner of the locker room.

Cary Williams—who admitted to being "a hothead" like Jackson—hinted at what the wide receiver's rebellion against Kelly's system may have looked like.

> We've got assessments every day. We've got a whole bunch of stuff that factor into whether you're buying into the organization. If you're not doing [your sports science] assessments every day. If you're not showing up on time every day. If you're not in meetings every day.
>
> I don't know if DeSean was or wasn't because I only see him in here [the locker room] and on the field on Sundays. But I do know he was a freaking great player.

Trent Cole theorized that the release was simply a matter of money and salary cap calculations. And then McLane almost imperceptibly slipped in a particularly ominous bit of speculation about the Eagles' biggest remaining star:

> Jackson was slated to earn approximately $10 million in 2014. McCoy, who has the highest salary-cap number on the team this season, speculated on whether the same fate could befall him.

LeSean "Shady" McCoy was the reigning NFL rushing leader, the offensive workhorse for a coach who emphasized the run. Even though there were rumors of friction with Chip Kelly, there was no way the Eagles could release Shady the next year, was there?

After DeSean's release, no one dismissed the possibility. Under McCoy's contract, he was going to cost the Eagles $12 million against their salary cap, second only to Adrian Peterson among NFL running backs.[1]

During a joint training camp session with the Patriots, McCoy battled a minor turf toe injury and said:

> Coach pushes me to the max more than any other coach I've been around. Coach Reid, he pushed me hard, but once I kind of got to a point, he let the veterans go a little bit. Chip is constantly on me.[2]

When Kelly was asked about the running back's work ethic in practice a few days later, he was less than enthusiastic:

> It's OK. Some days he's great out there. Other days, he's not so great.[3]

Under Kelly, the Eagles have an unusual workweek during the season. If they're playing a typical Sunday game, the Eagles take Monday off instead of the usual Tuesday, and they practice hard on Saturday. Most teams just have a walk-through on the day before the game. Kelly "learned from Olympic runners that the best way to maximize performance is to run hard the day before the race," according to *ESPN The Magazine's* Seth Wickersham. (The University of Oregon has a world-class track program.)

Reporter Ian Rapoport of the NFL Network later reported that Shady was unhappy with this unusual practice schedule.

> … McCoy told some friends he didn't always see eye-to-eye with Chip Kelly's ways, including working out extremely hard the Saturday before games. He complained several times that his legs did not have the burst that he wanted [as a result].[4]

In August of 2014, Wickersham had written a fascinating

---

1 "Sorting Out the LeSean McCoy–Kiko Alonso Trade" by Bill Barnwell, Grantland.com, March 4, 2015.

2 "LeSean McCoy's practices 'not so great'?" by Geoff Mosher, *CSN Philly*, August 19, 2014.

3 Ibid.

4 "LeSean McCoy's relationship with Chip Kelly had 'become strained,' LaDainian Tomlinson says" by Matt Lombardo, NJ.com, March 3, 2015.

portrait of LeSean's relationship with Coach Kelly after trailing the RB during training camp. The article painted a picture of McCoy's skepticism in 2013 turning to acceptance after the Eagles' 7-1 run to end that season.

When he tells me to do something, I just do it.[1]

But the article started out talking about how Kelly insisted that all players wear white socks, which McCoy resisted, and that they ride the bus together to games, in both cases to build team cohesion. Months later, when things went bad, McCoy brought up the socks in two separate interviews. Apparently it never stopped bothering him.

1   "30 Yards And A Cloud of Dust" by Seth Wickersham, *ESPN The Magazine*, August 14, 2014.

GAME 3.
WASHINGTON REDSKINS

SEPTEMBER 21, 2014
LINCOLN FINANCIAL FIELD, PHILADELPHIA

When the actual game against Washington finally arrived, it was even more dramatic (and nastier) than anyone could have imagined. Chris Polk ran a first-quarter kickoff back for a 102-yard touchdown, the first at Philadelphia's Lincoln Financial Field since it opened in 2003.

Nick Foles threw three TDs and zero INTs—his best game of the year and his only one without a turnover. LeSean McCoy had his worst game of the year, nineteen carries for just 22 yards and no receptions, no TDs, one fumble.

DeSean Jackson has been cocky and attitudinal since he played at Cal from 2005 to 2007. No one doubted that he wanted to get revenge against the team that cut him over the summer (and cost him millions of dollars a year in reduced salary). Not enough to postpone his summer vacation on a private island just so he could practice with his new teammates, but still, a lot.

Washington coach Jay Gruden actually mocked Jackson before the game on Gruden's local ESPN-affiliate radio show as his buddies whooped it up, laughing.[1] Jackson was coming back from a shoulder injury, the coach noted, and:

> I think he's going to be a game day type [decision]. He

---

1   "Washington Coach Jay Gruden Slams DeSean Amid Laughter" by Mark Saltveit, *Bleeding Green Nation*, Sep 19, 2014.

wants to go really bad obviously, he's going back to Philly, but if he's not 100%, if he's 60-70%, he's really not that [much] good to us. {laughter} He's already 160 pounds. If he's only... {laughter} He's already a very terrible blocker.[1]

Maybe this was a clever plan to anger Jackson and rile him up for the game, because Washington came out throwing to him on the second play from scrimmage (a 6-yard gain). And again, on the fifth play from scrimmage: 13 yards for another first down.

As cornerback Bradley Fletcher brought Jackson to the ground, safety Malcolm Jenkins (6'0", 204 lbs) added an exclamation point in the form of a driving tackle aimed directly into Jackson's injured left shoulder.

Jackson hopped up angrily and shoved Jenkins off, at which point Nate Allen (6'1", 210) shoved Jackson back harder and kept stepping up into the wide receiver's face as Jackson back-pedaled while he tried to look tough. (Jackson is 5'10" in platform shoes.)

That little exchange pretty much set the tone for the entire day. One play near the end of the first quarter was particularly frightening for the run-based Eagles offense. Skins cornerback David Amerson speared LeSean McCoy full speed, helmet to helmet, near the end of the first quarter, and it looked a lot like LeSean suffered a concussion.[2]

Shady lay on the turf for over a minute, dazed, before being helped to the sideline. He was seen yelling "I'm okay!" while trainers literally hid his helmet from him to prevent a quick return to play. He went into the locker room for a concussion protocol, but was apparently cleared. He returned five minutes later and played the rest of the game.

Center Jason Kelce was also injured during this game, suffering a sports hernia that required surgery. He was out until November,

1 "Washington Coach Jay Gruden Slams DeSean Amidst Laughter" by Mark Saltveit, *Bleeding Green Nation*, September 19, 2014.
2 "Did LeSean McCoy Have A Concussion? Eagles Star RB Takes Hit To Head, Fans Erupt" by Dan Diamond, *Forbes*, September 21, 2014.

and the offensive line was in serious trouble.

You knew that Jackson was going to get his long touchdown, and he did on the first play of a third-quarter drive: 81 yards, a post route where safety Nate Allen bit on a short in and CB Cary Williams had no chance of keeping up. Say what you want about DeSean Jackson, the guy is very, very fast.

Chip Kelly admitted after the game that Williams should have had help over the top from Allen,[1] but there was no excuse for Williams' failed tackle of DeSean at the 22. The 6'1", 190-pound cornerback just slid off the 160-pound receiver like Robin dropping down the Bat Pole. That was simply embarrassing.

For Jackson though, scoring is just the necessary condition for his favorite part of the game—a taunting victory dance with all eyes on him. He had clearly worked hard on this one and may have hired a choreographer.

First, he turned around and jogged backwards into the end zone, knees kicking high. Then he flapped his arms with exaggerated curviness in what was meant to be an eagle motion, except that eagles soar with straight wings, but whatever. Finally, he pivoted and kicked an invisible field goal, perhaps to symbolize the Eagles kicking away such a wonderful player.

Jackson even diagrammed his dance after the game for a CSN-Washington reporter.[2] And that wasn't the end of it. All game long, Jackson kept chirping at the Eagles' bench, talking smack despite a notable lack of production. Though he had a touchdown, two Eagles receivers had better games: Jeremy Maclin (154 yards) and rookie Jordan Matthews (two TDs).

Those were the undercards though. The title bout came two minutes into the fourth quarter. Nick Foles was apparently intercepted by Washington rookie CB Bashaud Breeland, though a review showed that the ball had hit the ground. As Breeland

1   "Chip & Cary: the Odd Couple" by Mark Saltveit, *Bleeding Green Nation*, September 24, 2014.
2   "DeSean Jackson breaks down 81-yard touchdown (VIDEO)," *CSN Washington*, September 23, 2014.

was being tackled and Nick Foles strolled toward the sideline, Washington's nose tackle Chris Baker blindsided the QB, knocking him up into the air and flat on his back. (Baker, coincidentally, was expelled from college after multiple off-campus fights.)

Baker tried to casually walk away but turned back to see something no man ever wants to see—the Eagles' Pro Bowl tackle Jason Peters bull-rushing him. Only the desperate strategy of grabbing Peters' facemask with both hands saved him from likely internal injuries.

There was a bench-clearing brawl while a team of trainers revived the quarterback after a couple of minutes. Baker (#92) and Peters (#71) were ejected, though only after the bumbling referees ejected Washington's Trent Williams (also #71) by accident first.

What happened next was almost too perfect for a heart-warming sports movie. Nick Foles rose strong and stoic and led the Eagles to a touchdown and a 34-27 lead. As Jeremy Maclin said after the game, "That's the guy you want, the guy who gets up play after play."

Then, after a Washington turnover, the Birds' rookie kicker Cody Parkey drilled a clinching 51-yard field goal. Washington put up a fight, scoring a late touchdown to draw close, but the Eagles' defense got strict and shut them down on two of their three final drives.

DeSean Jackson didn't catch any of his final three pass targets and the Eagles left the stadium with a gritty 37-34 victory, their third straight comeback from ten or more points down.

In the end, the final word went to the Eagles' backup linebacker Emmanuel Acho, who tweeted a meme picture that captured exactly why the Eagles were happy to see Jackson go. Acho found the telling bit of game film which showed that after inciting fights all game, Jackson backed away and just watched when everyone else was brawling.

FINAL SCORE: EAGLES 37, SKINS 34

GAME 4.
SAN FRANCISCO 49ERS

SEPTEMBER 28, 2014
LEVI'S STADIUM, SANTA CLARA, CA

The Eagles steamed into brand new Levi's Stadium, undefeated and hoping to kick the 1-2 San Francisco 49ers while they were down. San Francisco was in shambles with two key defenders out, a head coach fighting with management, and Colin Kaepernick displaying all of his flaws.

Instead, Philadelphia left California dismayed and perhaps exposed, with fans squabbling, coach Chip Kelly defensive and Nick Foles' big contract payday at the end of 2014 in doubt.

That's a lot of dismay for a team that came within 2 yards (on three consecutive plays) of a heroic, almost miraculous comeback that would have left them undefeated. But the way it happened was bizarre and troubling.

The Eagles' defense was strong, and their special teams were incredible. The punt return unit alone scored 14 points—a blocked punt for a touchdown, and a TD return by Darren Sproles.

The defense was impressive, too. The Eagles' much-maligned pass coverage was excellent for once, playing very tight and giving up only circus catches—plus one easy reception on a stupid rookie mistake. But that one mistake was a big one.

First round draft pick Marcus Smith II left his assigned man, RB Frank Gore, to chase Kaepernick as he scrambled. No one was there to cover for him, so Kaepernick threw a moon ball across his body to Gore—who had no one within 30 yards of him—for an easy touchdown.

Smith was in the doghouse for the rest of the season. Chip played him a bit in weeks five and six, but that was basically it. He finished the year with a grand total of 105 snaps, second lowest among 2014's first-round picks. Even more striking, Coach Kelly wouldn't use him on special teams, which the Eagles value highly, or in a blowout loss later in the year. Smith only had 34 snaps after the week 7 bye, and those were in dire injury situations after ILB DeMeco Ryans and rookie ST standout Trey Burton got hurt.

Aside from that one broken play touchdown to Gore, the Eagle defense was tight against the pass and sacked Kaep four times (with two more sacks wiped away by penalty). It was the first appearance of what would become a devastating pass rush throughout the year. The Eagles would finish the 2014 season with forty-nine sacks, tied for second behind only Buffalo.

The key was Billy Davis' deceptive fronts.[1] Instead of blitzing, he sent only four rushers on most downs, keeping coverage tight.[2] But whether he sent four, five or six men, the offense never knew which ones it was going to be.

Several players lined up for rushing, and one or two would drop into coverage after a stab step. The result was a number of plays where a blocker was standing around, looking for someone to impede, while an Eagle on the other side of the field had an open path to the quarterback.

Surprisingly, it was the offense that lost this game for Philadelphia. You know, Chip Kelly's specialty. The unit that was leading the league, and scoring 30 points a game? They failed to score against San Francisco. At all.

This was the game that the Eagles' offensive line finally

---

1   "All-22: Front Seven Brings the Pressure Against the Rams" by Larry Mitros, InsideTheEagles.net, October 8, 2014.
2   "Four-man pass rush adds up to sacks for Eagles" by Jeff McLane, *Philadelphia Inquirer*, October 9, 2014.

collapsed, with starting center Jason Kelce, starting guard Evan Mathis and top sub Allen Barbre out injured, and Lane Johnson in the last game of his suspension for PEDs. Todd Herremans, already the weakest link on the starting OL, moved to right tackle in Barbre's place. All told, left tackle Jason Peters was the only starter at his usual position.

Cheerful but undersized David Molk took over the Eagles' crucial center job, which includes reading the defense and calling OL alignments. Philadelphia's zone blocking scheme requires a lot of coordination between players, and with only one starter in his normal position, that just didn't happen. With seven minutes left in the second quarter, three Eagles linemen simply fell down on a sweep to the right, leaving McCoy trying to outrun six 49ers with only TE Brent Celek in front of him.

LeSean can juke most defenders one on one. But this was more like trying to outrun a pack of dogs, with similar results. They ran him out of bounds for a loss.

Even before Chip Kelly was hired in Philadelphia, a number of NFL pundits argued that his college-style football innovations would fail in the NFL. Defensive coordinators would quickly adjust to his plays, players would study tape and find tendencies, narrower hash marks would limit his ability to spread, and the faster defenders in the NFL would simply outrun attempts to catch them out of position.

There were no signs of this happening until Chip Kelly's twentieth game, against San Francisco. Give credit to the 49ers coaches for an excellent defensive game plan. Head coach Jim Harbaugh and defensive coordinator Vic Fangio knew Chip Kelly well, probably better than any other coaching pair in the NFL.

Harbaugh faced off against Kelly four times between 2007 and 2010 when they were at Stanford and Oregon, respectively. Chip was Offensive Coordinator the first two years, then head coach. Oregon won three times; the Cardinal prevailed in 2009.

Fangio was Stanford's defensive coordinator for the epic 2010 battle, when the #4 Ducks beat #9 Stanford. That Cardinal team was loaded with talent: quarterback Andrew Luck, tight ends Coby Fleener and Zach Ertz, and a cornerback/kick returner named Richard Sherman. Oregon, answering with the likes of QB Darron Thomas, WRs Josh Huff and Jeff Maehl, and RB LaMichael James, fell behind 21-3 in the first quarter.

A surprise onside kick by Oregon at the start of the second period reversed the momentum, and the Ducks poured it on for the rest of the game, winning 52-31.

After Harbaugh and Fangio went to the NFL, Chip visited them in San Francisco to compare notes on strategy. So the two were well acquainted with his offense, and they attacked it in the most basic way possible.

This game came down to a goal line stand by the 49ers with two minutes left and the Eagles behind by five. A touchdown would win, and on second down, LeSean McCoy ran down to the 2, where safety Antoine Bethea stopped him.

Fangio expected the Eagles to pass, and that's exactly what they did. McCoy is not a good weapon on short-and-goal, where his elusiveness is no use and his lack of raw power is a problem—even when the offensive line is fully healthy. And this one definitely was not.

The 49ers practiced this exact scenario during the week before the game and planned how to stop the Eagles' short passes. After the game, Fangio said:

> I don't know if you ever plan two plays from inside the 2 with the game on the line. But I will tell you this: The two calls we made on third down and fourth down, we practiced during the week on those situations.[1]

Cornerback Perrish Cox went even further.

> The two calls we had, I think they were actually the only two calls we went over at practice Friday. It worked out perfect.[2]

---

[1] "49ers rally past Eagles in second half" by Cam Inman, *San Jose Mercury News*, September 28, 2014.

[2] "Inside Voices: How the Eagles Tipped Their Hand" by Tim McManus, *Birds*

Bethea, who blitzed on third down and forced an incomplete pass, told the *San Jose Mercury News*:

> Obviously as you can see everyone was in the right place and we were able to get off the field.[1]

Bethea had an incredible game all around. He had seven tackles and forced a third-quarter fumble from Zach Ertz that led to an easy 23-yard touchdown drive. Then he intercepted Foles later in the same period before delivering his goal line stand heroics at the end of the game. Not surprisingly, he was named NFC Defensive Player of the Week.

Bethea also deciphered at least one of the Eagles' signals, which we know because he told his teammates on the sideline that when Foles said "Over" and waved his hand over his head, a run was coming.

Then, early in the fourth quarter, the Eagles had a 1st and ten at their own 20, down 2 points. Foles called that audible and Bethea spotted it, pointed toward the left side of the offense and shouted "Hey! Hey! Run! Run! Run! Run!"[2] Demarcus Dobbs stopped Shady for a 4-yard loss and, despite a 12-yard reception by Riley Cooper, the Eagles had to punt on 4th and two.

Beyond knowing what the Eagles were about to do, the 49ers also masked their defensive calls very effectively. This was ironic, because Fangio used the precise method that Kelly and DC Billy Davis favor: fielding interchangeable players to make it impossible to read the coverage.

Chip Kelly's schemes rely heavily on counting the number of defenders in the box, which usually boils down to "how many safeties do you have deep? One or two?" As Sheil Kapadia explained, San Francisco showed two safeties, but often moved one (Bethea) up into the box right at the snap, while the other (Eric Reid) shifted to

---

24/7, October 2, 2014.

1   "49ers rally past Eagles in second half" by Cam Inman, *San Jose Mercury News*, September 28, 2014.

2   "Player-of-the-week Bethea knew what Eagles had planned" by Eric Branch, *San Francisco Chronicle*, October 1, 2014.

single high safety coverage. Other times they both stayed back. This made it very hard for Foles to make the correct read.

Chip Kelly won't have to face Harbaugh again, at least not for a few years. The hard-driving coach quit the 49ers after the 2014 season and returned to the college game as Michigan's head coach. Vic Fangio took the job as Chicago's defensive coordinator, though. It will be fascinating to watch his chess match against Chip when the Eagles and Bears meet next—perhaps in the 2015 playoffs.

You might think that other coaches would have copied San Francisco's strategy against Philadelphia, but there was little sign of it during the rest of the 2014 season. Even assuming other DCs understood the strategy, the deceptive approach isn't as simple as ordering one of your safeties to hang out on the edge of the box.

You need two players with the flexibility to play both strong and free safety. In a league where competent safeties that can play even one of those positions are hard to find, this is a rare luxury.

The Eagles' offense had other problems that Fangio and Harbaugh couldn't take credit for. Riley Cooper had another terrible drop in the end zone—after one earlier against Indianapolis, and the big one in the 2013 playoffs. That pass attempt should have been the game-winning touchdown. He told reporters after the game:

> There was no excuses, I dropped the ball. It was a perfect throw, right on the money, couldn't have been a better throw from Nick [Foles] and that's definitely a ball that needs to be caught 10 out of 10 times.[1]

The rest of Philly's offense played poorly as well. LeSean McCoy—the NFL's leading rusher in 2013—picked up 17 yards on ten carries. He usually has a couple of individual runs that get more yardage than that in every game. Foles was 21-43 passing, with two interceptions kept company by two fumbles. Both players may have been suffering the effects of big hits (and likely undiagnosed concussions) they received in the previous game against Washington.

The Eagles may be too tough for their own good. Philadelphia

1   "Riley Cooper takes blame for dropped TD vs. Niners" by Geoff Mosher, *CSN Philly*, October 3, 2014.

has a blue-collar attitude, and the fans love big hits and tough guys who play through injuries.

This is a city where the most popular retired players are defenders like safety Brian Dawkins, lineman Reggie White and the late Chuck "Concrete Charlie" Bednarik, best known for knocking Frank Gifford out of football for a year and a half with a single sledgehammer tackle.

Chip Kelly is a perfect match for Philly in this way. He's a tough-minded former player, a "third-line grinder" on his high school hockey team, and a guy the players know asks nothing of them he wouldn't do (and hasn't done) himself.

The attitude he promotes of sacrificing for the good of the team extends to playing tough. Kelly has been rough on injured players, hinting publicly that certain ones (Earl Wolff, Mychal Kendricks) should play through or return faster from injuries. But his toughness might be a relic of an earlier era, a rare case where he favors tradition over science.

Brent Celek, Nick Foles, and LeSean McCoy all took brutal hits in the early part of the 2014 season, got right back up and kept playing. But maybe they shouldn't have. The effects of concussions are slowly becoming better known, and the results are not pretty. Retired players have wrestled with memory loss, erratic emotions, suicide, and brain damage that's visible at autopsy.

No concussions were officially diagnosed in these three cases, but each player saw their production suffer noticeably after getting their bell rung.

In the 2014 preseason, tight end Celek took two shots to the head so hard that they that literally knocked his helmet off. Following that, in the first four regular season games combined, he was three for eleven for a total of just 15 yards, after averaging 15.7 yards *per catch* in 2013. He would finish 2014 catching thirty-two of fifty-three passes for 340 yards, an average of only 10.6 YPC.

Foles took a lot of tough hits in 2014 with the injured offensive line, not least among them Chris Baker's cheap shot in the Washington game. The quarterback also looked like he was in a fog all year, not seeing open receivers and unable to judge distance on his long throws. To be fair though, he looked like that in the preseason as well, before any apparent blows to the head.

After McCoy's helmet-to-helmet shot against Washington, he managed only 12 yards on seventeen carries the rest of that game, plus a fumble and two dropped passes. Against San Francisco the following week, he wasn't much better: 17 yards on ten runs.

McCoy's pass-catching, which requires more subtle spatial judgment and coordination, deteriorated even more. In the first two games of 2014, LeSean caught ten passes for 64 yards. After his apparent concussion, he would manage only eighteen passes the rest of the year (in fourteen games) for a total of 91 more yards. His running yardage declined 18% in 2014, on about the same number of runs, but his receiving yards fell fully 71% from 2013.

After the 49ers game, reporters asked him if he was injured. "It doesn't matter," he replied. Asked the same question, Kelly said:

> He's healthy. He's not on the treatment list. He does normal maintenance like everybody else, but he hasn't had any injuries where we've done anything with him.[1]

Maybe the team "not doing anything with him" was the problem.

Clearly players can't count on the NFL as an organization to protect their brains from battering[2], or to police helmet-led tackles of the sort that Washington was routinely laying down in 2014. The league is a cooperative run by the owners, who might face a lot of legal liability and financial risk if they acknowledged and addressed the science over chronic traumatic encephalopathy (CTE). At best they will move slowly and steadily in the right direction, enough (they hope) to avoid punitive damages in lawsuits.

But fans and writers should at least think twice about cheering on the macho, "I didn't feel that" attitude among players and make

---

1 "Eagles Notes: LeSean McCoy is not injured, Chip Kelly says" by Zach Berman, *Philadelphia Inquirer*, October 1, 2014.
2 "League of Denial: The NFL's Concussion Crisis," *PBS Frontline*, October 8, 2013.

sure they're not getting brain damage that cripples their lives as well as their effectiveness on the field.

It's natural to cheer the toughness and self-sacrifice of players who "shake it off." But even if you accept the ethics of players trading future brain damage for fame and money—and I hope you don't—the strategy of playing tough was just not working for the Eagles. Their skill players were starting to look like characters in *The Walking Dead*.

FINAL SCORE: 49ERS 26, EAGLES 21

SPORTS SCIENCE

OCTOBER, 2014

Oregon and Philadelphia have gone farther than other football teams to get the most out of their players, using the methodical application of new discoveries in exercise physiology. The catchy term for this is "sports science," which sounds mysterious, but the goals are straightforward: preventing injury, building strength and making sure that players are at their physical and mental peak at game time.

Chip Kelly did not originate this—the US Navy SEALs, Nike Corporation and certain Australian Rules Football teams were involved earlier—but he quickly saw its value and applied it with full force, borrowing heavily (and hiring staff away) from those pioneers.

The Eagles have an entire Department of Sports Science with twelve employees. Several veteran players have said that they felt more energetic and less banged up, even at the end of the season, than they ever had in their careers.

After two Eagles failed tests for performance-enhancing drugs before the 2014 season, there was some suspicion that sports science might not be as wholesome as it sounds. But the program seems to be based in monitoring, not chemistry, and the focus is not strength but "recovery." That word doesn't get much notice, but it has come up spontaneously in interviews with players Jason Kelce, Marcus Smith, Nolan Carroll, DeMeco Ryans and Brandon Boykin.

That doesn't just mean recovery from injuries, or even from the normal strains and dings suffered during games. Recovery (from the previous day's training) has as much to do with preventing injuries, and maximizing the potential of today's practice and weight training. And it's part of the everyday routine in Philadelphia.

Coach Kelly told Ross Tucker and Bill Polian how it works:

> On an individualized basis we may back off. We may take [TE] Brent Celek out of a team period on a Tuesday afternoon and just say, 'because of the scientific data we have on him, we may need to give Brent a little bit of a rest.' We monitor them very closely.[1]

Nolan Carroll, who joined the Eagles after the 2013 season, told Tim McManus of *Philadelphia Magazine* that "We have a whole staff dedicated just to getting us to recover."

> Every single day when we come in here in the morning, we have assessments that we do to monitor how our body is feeling from the day before and I think that's something that no other team in the league is doing right now. It helps us as far as eliminating injuries that, [at] most other places you wouldn't be able to recognize until it's too late. They do a good job knowing when we're feeling bad and what injuries might occur and ways to prevent them.[2]

The Eagles measure players first thing each morning, using a combination of heart monitoring, hydration testing (by urinalysis), and a questionnaire (on an iPad, of course) asking their subjective perception of injuries, soreness and the like. That's followed by weight training "to activate their bodies," as McManus puts it, then a period of "Training Prep"—soft-tissue work—and finally on-field warm up.

That whole routine comes before practice even begins. Afterwards, players alternate hot and cold tubs and receive massages. And hopefully, they sleep a lot.

The Eagles' program has drawn heavily from discoveries at two

---

1   Ross Tucker Podcast, July 28, 2014.
2   "Inside Voices: How The Training Is Different" by Tim McManus, *Birds 24/7*, September 13, 2014.

leading centers for the development of sports science—the U.S. military special forces, and the University of Oregon football team.

James Hanisch, hired by the Eagles in Spring 2015 as a "High Performance Analyst," was previously Oregon's Sports Science Director, and started out working with teams in Australia, where much of modern sports science originated.

Shaun Huls, the Eagles sports science coordinator, was a strength coach at the Human Performance Research Laboratory, a collaboration between the Navy SEALs and the University of Pittsburgh[1] located at the U.S. Naval Amphibious Base Little Creek in Norfolk, Virginia. Anthony Zimmer, a "Sports Science Analyst" for the Eagles, worked there too.[2]

Huls cut his teeth as part of the Husker Power strength and conditioning program that helped the University of Nebraska football team win three national championships in the mid-1990s— along with Josh Hingst, the Birds' Strength and Conditioning Coach, and James Harris, Chip Kelly's chief of staff both at Oregon and Philadelphia.

It's easy to overemphasize the technology, though. When Hanisch was still at Oregon, he said that sleep and hydration were "the fundamentals" to recovery, "the biggest percentage chunks."[3] The team constantly monitored hydration, identifying players who sweat harder and feeding them extra fluids. They also had a darkened conference room where players could take a half-hour nap between two-a-day practices.

In Philadelphia, players are encouraged to sleep at least ten hours a night, make sure they are well-hydrated, and eat healthy foods. The Eagles banished Andy Reid's "Fat Boy Fridays"[4] (often mislabeled

1   "Navy's fittest of the fit team with UPMC" by Jack Kelly, *Pittsburgh Post-Gazette*, April 16, 2008.
2   Department of Defense Research Projects: Neuromuscular Research Laboratory, University of Pittsburgh, Volume 2, Issue 1, Spring 2010, p4
3   "How Oregon Stays Cool When Camp Heats Up" by Rob Moseley, GoDucks. com, August 14, 2014.
4   "What is Eagles coach Chip Kelly bringing to NFL?" By Ben Volin, *Boston Globe*, August 8, 2013.

as "Fast Food Fridays") and "Taco Tuesdays." The team cafeteria is now divided into sections for "Proteins," "Carbohydrates" and "Vegetables," and players are given customized protein shakes (the famous "smoothies") after practice. Center Jason Kelce prefers 2% milk, vanilla protein powder, avocados and blueberries. (Yum?)

A lot of this sounds more like grandma's good advice than science. Of course getting enough sleep is better. But how much is enough? Does one beer or glass of wine at night help or hurt your rest? Early to bed, or late? What about jet lag on west coast trips? Can study of circadian rhythms help teams maximize game time readiness?

These are the kinds of details that science can answer, and some of the results are dramatic. A study of varsity basketball players at Stanford found that increasing players' sleep to ten hours a night—the same amount Kelly recommends to his teams—improved both free throw percentage and three-point shot accuracy by more than nine percentage points.[1]

The Eagles are secretive about details of their sports science program, but Jenny Vrentas of *Sports Illustrated's* MMQB website described Huls and several of the high-tech machines the team uses in a July, 2013 article. One of the machines, she reported, is the Omegawave system, which "uses an electrocardiogram transmitter and a pair of electrodes that tap into the central nervous system to measure stress, fatigue and capacity for aerobic or anaerobic exercise."[2]

The Omegawave was developed in Eugene, Oregon—the home of the University of Oregon—in the 1990s by former Olympic trainers from Russia and the Ukraine who had left after the collapse of the Soviet Union. (The company has since moved to Finland.)

According to *Wired Magazine*,[3] the electrodes measure heart and

---

1   The Effects of Sleep Extension on the Athletic Performance of Collegiate Basketball Players, by Cheri D. Mah, MS, Kenneth E. Mah, MD, MS, Eric J. Kezirian, MD, MPH, and William C. Dement, MD, PhD. *Sleep*, 34(7): July 1, 2011 p943–950.

2   "Chip Kelly's Mystery Man" by Jenny Vrentas, *MMQB*, July 27, 2013.

3   "Taking VO$_2$ To The Max" by John Rochmis, *Wired Magazine*, July 17, 2000.

brain function, similar to ECG and EKG machines, but also track the brain's omega waves. Custom software interprets this data to create a report detailing an athlete's heart rate and capacity, liver and kidney function, reaction times, stress, VO_2 Max (the ability to use oxygen effectively), and capacity for intense workouts.

The machine was heavily promoted by Nike as far back as 2000. Dick Brown, who coached several Olympians including Mary Decker Slaney as director of Nike's Athletics West track and field club, reported that

> The recovery indicators it gives us are much more sophisticated than anything we've ever used before. I can immediately tell if somebody is ready to train or not, and I can tell whether we should modify that training.[1]

And yet, a source in Nike's research department (who asked not to be named) told me that the Omegawave—now nearly twenty years old—has never really caught on, in part because there isn't really any solid evidence that it works as advertised.

Bill Knowles is an expert in training and reconditioning for elite athletes, with the firm HPSports. (They do not work with the Eagles.) He told me that the Omegawave machine can be effective but requires years of accumulating data and acting on it before a team learns to use it effectively. It's such a personalized tool that it will always be hard to validate through studies.

Other teams may try the Omegawave and find it too fussy or hard to interpret, but Kelly has years of experience with it already.

There are other high-tech machines used by the Eagles. The EliteForm weight training system measures the force and speed with which a player lifts weights, as well as the total poundage. The OptimEye sensor by Catapult Sports is a highly detailed GPS tracker than players wear on the small of their back, allowing teams to track many details of their movements, including speed, acceleration and agility. Polar Systems' heart monitors also produce recovery reports.

---

1   "Taking VO_2 To The Max" by John Rochmis, *Wired Magazine*, July 17, 2000.

And those were just the ones Vrentas was able to find out about.

A more recent addition is NormaTec's "pulse gradient" compression pants, which players wear with their legs raised in front of them in what one player calls "full recovery mode."

All of this combines to help players reach peak performance—delivering 100% of your potential, not leaving reserves untapped or pushing yourself too hard.

None of these machines do anything to reduce the risk of torn ligaments and pectoral muscles, though, and the Eagles suffered several serious ACL and MCL injuries both in 2013 and 2014. But other injuries declined dramatically. The *Dallas Morning News* analyzed injuries among all NFL teams in 2013. Among projected starters, the Eagles missed only twenty-nine combined games all year, the fourth-lowest total in the league.[1] And sixteen of those twenty-nine were by Jeremy Maclin, as a result of his ACL tear.

In 2014, however, the team's record on preventing injuries was more mixed. By the end of game three against Washington, the Eagles had lost three of their top four inside linebackers, and four of seven offensive linemen to injuries.

Certainly the Eagles were lucky with injuries in 2013, and unlucky in 2014. But the whole point of sports science is getting more out of players, and it's worth asking whether the team is taking too much out of them, whether pushing players to the extremes of their ability is leading to injuries or shortening careers.

Chip Kelly's experience at the University of Oregon may not translate to the NFL, either, since college rosters are twice as big, and the Ducks used extensive rotation (especially on the defensive line) to keep players fresh.

College players are also younger. The Ducks didn't have any thirty-something veterans to keep healthy, but the Eagles had fourteen in 2014 (roughly one-fourth of the roster).[2] The average

---

1   "Eagles: Chip Kelly's sports science impact continues in Year 2" by Matt Lombardo, NJ.com, June 10, 2014.

2   That's counting Wade Smith. "2014 Philadelphia Eagles Roster" by Pro Football Reference. Retrieved from www.pro-football-reference.com/teams/phi/2014_roster.htm

age of the injured offensive linemen (Kelce, Mathis, Barbre and Tobin) was twenty-eight, and it's fair to wonder if Sports Science director Shaun Huls needs to dial down his program for the *viejos*. Then again, the injured ILBs were twenty-three, twenty-three, and twenty-five. So perhaps age wasn't the issue.

If the monitoring and other technology does work, why did so many Eagles get hurt in 2014? Actually, it's not clear that they did. The clusters of injuries at ILB, QB and on the offensive line obscured the fact that the Eagles were still unusually healthy at other positions. The website *Football Outsiders* has createed a statistic named "Adjusted Games Lost" to measure the impact of injuries; the 2014 Eagles were fifth best overall, with 48.6 (vs. a league average of 74.3).

> Philadelphia, noted for Chip Kelly's foray into sports science last year, had the best AGL in 2013 and ranked fifth this season. They are only the third team since 2002 to lead the league in AGL and finish in the top five the following season. Maybe this team is onto something with preventing soft tissue injuries.[1]

But it's also possible that the sports science program may lead to some injuries precisely because it works so well. I'll explain.

Much has been written about how stretching before exercise does *not* actually prevent injuries, in part because the increased flexibility allows athletes to extend themselves, and because stretching appears to mask muscle pain.[2]

In a similar way, sports science may be the victim of its own success. Players *can* do more, and with the excitement of the game and the rewards for elite performance, they may be pushing their bodies further than is wise, into dangerous territory.

Consider game three of the 2014 season, against Washington. A second-quarter screen pass to Jeremy Maclin turned into an 80-

---

1 "2014 Adjusted Games Lost" by Scott Kacsmar, *Football Outsiders*, March 4, 2015.

2 "Does Stretching Prevent Injuries?," by Amby Burfoot, *Runner's World*, August 26, 2004.

yard touchdown, which was called back to Washington's 40 yard line due to an illegal block in the back by Eagles center Jason Kelce. The penalty obscured an incredible sprint by Kelce. At 6'3", 295 pounds, he was running neck and neck with speedy WR Maclin (6'0", 198) 60 yards downfield from the line of scrimmage.

That is a phenomenal bit of athleticism, and I have no doubt that sports science helped make it possible. But Kelce left the game just after halftime with a sports hernia that ultimately kept him off the field for the next five games. The exuberance of an emotional game and his ability to run faster and longer than anyone else his size may have led him to literally bust a gut in the pursuit of victory.

Is sports science leading to injuries, or simply allowing players to push themselves further, into the red zone? We simply don't know. It's way too early to say. But as impressive as the results of Chip Kelly's programs have been, it's wise to remember that this is uncharted territory. We should keep an open mind and be alert to potential problems.

GAME 5.
ST. LOUIS RAMS

OCTOBER 5, 2014
LINCOLN FINANCIAL FIELD, PHILADELPHIA

After the tough loss to San Francisco, the Eagles came back home and jumped out to a 34-7 lead against the St. Louis Rams. Then it got rocky, as the Rams—with third string quarterback Austin Davis at the helm—scored three times in a row. St. Louis had the ball with 1:47 left, down 6 points and driving for a potentially game-winning touchdown. Austin connected with WR Brian Quick for 43 yards on the first play of that last drive, but the Eagles defense finally got stout and got a stop.

It was clear that the Eagles were a very confusing football team. They sucked in a lot of ways. And by some measures, they were the best team in the NFL.

The offense was completely misfiring. In 2013, Nick Foles had led the league in long throws (over 20 yards); by the end of this game, he had completed only four of thirty-one passes all season, with three interceptions.

The Rams game rivaled the previous week as Foles' personal low point in a miserable season, with just 207 yards passing, an interception and a ridiculous fumble. Scrambling for a fourth-quarter first down, he rolled forward to the ground instead of sliding, while holding the ball over his head with two hands. It came out, of course, an easy grab for St. Louis.

The offense had scored nothing against San Francisco and notched only 14 points against the woeful Rams. LeSean McCoy hadn't broken 100 yards in any of the five games, after doing so seven times in 2013. His eighty-four against St. Louis was his best so far, but during the Eagles' final late-game drive to preserve their lead, RB coach Duce Staley replaced Shady with Darren Sproles[1]— who hit the holes more decisively and promptly picked up 25 yards on his first snap. It was the Eagles' longest gain from scrimmage all game.

Foles threw a 9-yard touchdown to Riley Cooper at the end of the first half, but that was the Eagles' first offensive touchdown in the previous nineteen drives.

Despite all that, though, the Eagles were leading the NFL in scoring.[2]

What? In five games combined, the offense had generated a total of 66 points (just 13.2 per game), but the defense and special teams had combined for 90. In other words, special teams and defense were outscoring the guys who are supposed to score by 24 points—including five touchdowns on blocked kick and fumble recoveries. (They had one of each against St. Louis.) Add in those 90 points and the Eagles were tied with Indianapolis for the league lead with 156 total points.

Granted, that statistic was slanted by the fact that extra points and field goals are technically special teams points, but it shouldn't have even been close. The offense wouldn't be scoring a majority of the team's points until game eight (not coincidentally, the point when Sanchez would eventually take over as quarterback).

So the defense was great? Well, not exactly. The Birds delivered four sacks to the Rams but they surrendered most of a 34-7 lead at home. Cornerback Cary Williams had been giving up big plays all year, and against the Rams Nate Allen, Earl Wolff, and Bradley Fletcher joined him in pass porosity.

---

1   "Eagles' McCoy: It was Staley's decision to sit me" by Les Bowen, *Philadelphia Daily News*, September 8, 2014.
2   "Scoring" by Tommy Lawlor, *Iggles Blitz*, October 8, 2014.

Yet they kept winning. And it wasn't a fluke. Chip Kelly was methodically grabbing every advantage he could, and the little advantages added up to big plays. The defense gave up a lot of yards, but Kelly trains his defenders to go for forced fumbles and batted passes, and they got both against the Rams (forcing three fumbles and returning one for a TD after a strip sack). By the end of the 2014 season, the Eagles would lead the NFL in forced fumbles (twenty-six), fumbles recovered (sixteen) and fumble recovery touchdowns (two).

One weapon was the increasing use of a dime package, with Nolan Carroll as the sixth defensive back. Since he was adept at rushing or dropping back into coverage, he fit perfectly into Billy Davis' deceptive scheme. On one second-quarter play diagrammed by Geoff Mosher of CSN Philly,[1] Carroll lined up next to DeMeco Ryans showing A-gap blitz, but dropped into coverage. Vinny Curry blitzed from the outside instead, knocking the ball loose at the Philadelphia 15 where Fletcher Cox recovered. The play stopped a near-certain St. Louis score.

The Eagles scored on a blocked punt for the second game in a row. James Casey got credit for the block, but rookie tight end Trey Burton—who also blocked the punt against San Francisco—was just as important.

Burton not only got his hand on the same kick, but he pulled the ball back toward the center of the field so it wouldn't go out the back of the end zone. Chris Maragos, who the Eagles signed away from the Seahawks just for special teams, picked it up and ran it in 10 yards for a touchdown with a dramatic Russian kick-dance strut in the end zone—just twenty-three seconds into the game.

So yes, special teams were very special, but the main strength of this squad was its balance. There are eight ways to score a touchdown in the NFL,[2] and after five games the Eagles had nailed seven of them.[3] All they needed was a touchdown off a blocked field goal to

1   "All-22: Dime formation paying off for Eagles" by Geoff Mosher, CSN Philly, October 10, 2014.

2   Technically, there's a ninth—a team kicking off could pick up an untouched kick in the end zone. I'll bet anyone $20 this doesn't happen by the year 2020.

3   "Eagles are one touchdown away from setting an NFL record after their punt

be the first team in NFL history to hit all eight in a season.

That wouldn't end up happening in 2014, but the Eagles did finish the year with scores by rushing, receiving, kickoff return, punt return, blocked punt return, fumble return, and pick-six. In Chip's last game coaching at Oregon, his Ducks had scored the rarest way of all—a blocked extra-point-kick safety, for one point.[1]

Mix the good and bad together and the result was that the Eagles were 4-1, tied for the best record in the NFL.

Just to confuse matters further, the NFC East division had gone from a laughingstock to the best in football (by record, anyway). The New York Giants had won three straight, and Dallas was tied with Philadelphia (and San Diego) on top of the NFL at 4-1.

Only the continuous suckitude of Washington (1-4) had been true to form, and even they played very tough against the champion Seahawks. DeSean Jackson had a great individual game in a losing team effort, as he is prone to do.

After St. Louis, Philadelphia faced the Giants, with their bye week immediately after. If they could grind out a win at home against a suddenly tough New York team, they'd be 5-1 with two weeks for their wounded front line and inside linebackers to heal. That would be a result far better than they had any right to expect.

No one really believed that this was the best team in the NFL—the many NFL power rankings said so directly. (Not surprisingly, the consensus pick was Seattle.) But it was interesting to see the team-by-team comments, and where different writers thought the Eagles stood. Each power ranker went on and on about all the weaknesses of this team, but no one ranked them lower than eighth in the league, and many put them at third or fourth. (Their average ranking was 5.33.)

That was enough to give everyone a sense of how great this team could be if they healed up and put together a complete game.

FINAL SCORE: EAGLES 34. RAMS 28

block TD" by Charles Curtis, NJ.com, October 5, 2014.

1   "Blocked PAT ends in 1-point safety for Oregon (Yes, a 1-point safety)" by Matt Hinton, CBSSports.com, January 3, 2013.

GAME 6.
NEW YORK GIANTS

OCTOBER 12, 2014
LINCOLN FINANCIAL FIELD, PHILADELPHIA

It was a crazy week leading up to Philadelphia's big week-six NFC East showdown. The New York Giants talked trash all week and literally stomped on Philadelphia's midfield logo (a picture of an eagle) right before the game. Chip Kelly lost a shoe and jumped on Jason Peters' back. The Eagles released a silly cartoon of Eagles-linemen-as-ghosts haunting Eli Manning and giving him a wedgie, leading to even sillier complaints by the New York media about mean Eagles who encouraged bullying.[1] And a drunk Eagles fan stole a guy's leg.[2]

Oh yeah, there was a football game too. After the Giants symbolically stomped on the Eagles, the Eagles literally stomped back, shutting out New York 27-0, sacking Eli Manning and Ryan Nassib eight times, and destroying the Giants' hopes of a return to greatness.

The Eagles had been hinting at what they could do if they put together a complete game, four quarters with all three units contributing, and this was the answer: they were dominating, devastating, and very fun to watch.

---

1   "Eagles vs. Giants Cartoon featuring Little Eli Manning draws hilarious overreactions" by Brandon Lee Gowton, *Bleeding Green Nation*, Oct 11, 2014.
2   "After theft of prosthetic leg, man urges penalty other than jail" by Aubrey Whelan, *Philadelphia Inquirer*, October 15, 2014.

Better yet, NFL Films mic'ed up various Eagles players and coaches during the game for their shows "Inside the NFL" and "SoundFX." The results were fascinating.[1]

In 2013, SoundFX had captured an instant Chip Kelly classic, when Riley Cooper wandered over during a game and asked his coach "What's the plan?" Chip replied "Fuckin' score points. What's your plan?"

This year's edition started with one of the best Chip-isms ever—

Culture wins football. Culture will beat scheme, every time.

And the game bore it out.

The Giants came in on a winning streak based on their new offensive scheme, featuring quick, short passes to keep Eli Manning from getting rattled. Philadelphia responded by working hard together and sacrificing ego for the team. They shrugged off all of New York's petty provocations and beat the tar out of them.

The Eagles had a pretty good scheme answer, too, with tight press coverage, lots of nickel and dime packages and a fierce pass rush to re-rattle the lesser Manning.

It was the Eagles' first shutout of an opponent in eighteen years, despite the presence of rookie star Odell Beckham, Jr. The Birds had a bit of luck there—it was only ODB's second NFL game, after he missed the preseason and the first four regular season games with a hamstring injury. Philadelphia held him to his lowest number of yards (twenty-eight) and targets (four) for the year. Two weeks later he exploded against the Colts and never looked back, averaging 133 yards per game for the rest of the year.

The Eagles weren't perfect—Nick Foles threw two stupid interceptions, one without appearing to even look in the direction of the receiver—but they were pretty damned close. The pass rush was incredible, adding three forced fumbles to the eight sacks.

There are a lot of professional pessimists among Eagles fans,

---

1   "Inside the NFL: Giants vs Eagles Highlights (VIDEO)," NFL.com, October 2014 (at 0:07).

and one of their main complaints all summer and into the first two games of 2014 had been that the Eagles' pass rush was terrible. I think that overstated the situation—the Birds seemed to lead the league in near-misses when pressuring the passer, and did well with batted balls—but there was no doubt that they had very few sacks to show for it.

In 2013 they had had just thirty-seven sacks for the season, twentieth in the league and only six better than #32 Jacksonville. Fans and writers wanted a big sack monster in the draft, but somehow Jadeveon Clowney was not still available at #22. Philadelphia appeared to bow to pressure and took the best pass rush prospect remaining (after trading down once).

It did not work out well. Marcus Smith II was more of a project with a high upside than an immediate high-impact player. Or even a low-impact player. In fact, he barely touched the turf all season, and had given up a critical touchdown in the San Francisco game when he finally did.

Well, it turned out that they didn't need another player at all. They just needed to develop the ones they already had, and let everyone get more comfortable in Billy Davis' scheme. It's built around having almost every defender capable of rushing or dropping into coverage, which should make it hard for offenses to design protection schemes.

The problem is that the Eagles had a lot of one-dimensional players, mostly penetrating rushers (think Brandon Graham, Trent Cole, and Vinny Curry) without much ability to cover. That ruins the whole point of the deception; offenses could just look at these players and know they were going to rush. Many thought Graham was sure to be traded or even cut as a result.

Not anymore. All three of those players were vastly better at coverage after a year in the system, which let Connor Barwin rush and the defensive backs blitz and made Billy Davis' scheme a reality. After six games, the 2014 Eagles led the league in forced fumbles and solo tackles, and were second in sacks with nineteen (vs. Detroit's twenty). Barwin had three sacks in week six just by himself, en route to 14.5 on the year (fourth in the NFL).

Offensively, the recovering front line made all the difference, even if two starters remained out. Lane Johnson was back after completing his four game suspension. This was the first time in 2014 that Philly had played the same offensive line for two games in a row, and it showed.

They opened holes for LeSean, who responded with 145 yards and jumped from fifteenth to fourth in the league in just one game. The running attack opened up the pass game, and special teams remained strong. Sproles had a 43-yard punt return, and the Eagles blocked a punt for the third game in a row.

The return of rookie WR Josh Huff was a big boost for McCoy's run game, too. He wasn't targeted once on his twenty-three snaps, but Huff was superb blocking for RB McCoy and for other receivers. He expressed this quite succinctly:

> If you line up across from me, I'm gonna kick your ass.[1]

An animated GIF[2] posted to /r/Eagles by the Reddit user "slap_bet" illustrated that this was no idle boast. (Huff is #11 in the upper right corner, and backup center #63 David Molk looks pretty mobile too). Huff pushed back New York cornerbacks Prince Amukamara and Trumaine McBride 10 yards or more at a time, and McBride needed thumb surgery after the game, ending his season.

Later in the season, I asked Huff if blocking was harder in the NFL.

> Not at all, it's the same thing. I mean to me it's the same players that I lined up against in college, some of them just got a little bit bigger, some of them are a little bit faster and stronger.
>
> It's just having the correct position to block in and it's all up to you whether you make the block or not.

Questions of technique aside, the difference between Huff and

1   "Eagles rookie Josh Huff warns defenders if they line up across from him, he'll kick their butt" by Eliot Shorr-Parks, NJ.com, October 22, 2014.

2   "David Molk in space" at Imgur.com, October 13, 2014. Retrieved from www. imgur.com/9NvTx5z

DeSean Jackson is that Huff actually enjoys blocking. For Jackson, it's about as much fun as scrubbing the bathtub.

This was a big win and a fun game. Afterwards, Chip Kelly got a good running start and jumped up onto Jason Peters' back with a maniacal laugh as they left the field. Best of all, this victory was followed by the Eagles' bye week, offering them a much-needed chance to heal and rest. That vacation would be brief, leading into a brutal post-bye schedule.

The rest of the season involved traveling to Arizona and Green Bay, two of the toughest NFL venues in 2014, mixed in with home games against Carolina, Dallas, and reigning champion Seattle.

But in the glorious afterglow of the shutout, this team was starting to look like one that could go deep into the playoffs and maybe even have a bye in the first round. Schemes can change, but their culture wasn't going anywhere.

FINAL SCORE: EAGLES 27, GIANTS 0

BYE WEEK

OCTOBER 13-19, 2014

The Eagles' bye came in week seven, none too soon for the many injured Eagles needing to heal up before visiting the Arizona Cardinals on October 26th.

Both teams were 5-1 and apparently headed for the playoffs. This battle between two of the four remaining one-loss teams seemed likely to decide which one got a bye during the first (wild card) round of the playoffs.

Every Eagle practiced during bye week except fourth-string wide receiver/special teamer Brad Smith, though OG Evan Mathis was on the Injured Reserve list, ineligible to play until November 10th, and center Jason Kelce was almost certain to miss the game as well.

Two other injured players were uncertain to play, and they were crucial: inside linebacker Mychal Kendricks (healing from a calf injury) and running back/kick returner Darren Sproles, who sprained his MCL against the Giants.

Uncharacteristically, Kelly talked about Sproles' injury at a press conference, saying it wasn't too serious. A reporter asked if the team would sign a free agent to replace Sproles during bye week anyway, and the coach had some fun with the question.

> Q. As far as depth in that position, do you wait until the players come back or do you think he should make a move?
> COACH KELLY: Just said he's only out for like a week.
> Q. But you only have one healthy guy?

COACH KELLY: But we're not playing a game.

Q. That's the question.

COACH KELLY: No, we will not make any moves during our bye week to solidify our team for the bye.

The game was a rematch between the two hottest new coaches of the last two years, Bruce Arians and Chip Kelly. Both were 15-7 since the beginning of 2013, and their teams were tied for the NFL's best record going into week eight.

The two were an interesting contrast, iconic symbols of opposite paths. Arians had worked his way up the NFL chain of command as an assistant coach for twenty years, and Kelly did the same in the more innovative world of college football.

Not surprisingly then, Arians was an old-school, conservative, punt on fourth and one at midfield kind of guy (who improbably wore a beret), while Kelly was the newfangled deception-based spread coach (though he remained fundamentally sound with a run-first, take-what-they-give-you philosophy).

There was bad blood between them, too. In 2013, Arians mocked Kelly's approach with a confident prediction of injury to Philadelphia's quarterback.

It's a great college offense when you put a great athlete back there. But when you're facing great athletes, with the speed that's in the NFL who are chasing these guys, unless you're superhuman, you're going to get hurt sooner or later—not hurt, but beat up and bruised up.

Kelly's response was blunt. First, he corrected Arians' terminology by noting that the "read-option" Arians talked about is a play, not an offense. (Thus, he subtly implied that Arians didn't understand what he was talking about.) Then he added:

I don't care what other people think. It doesn't bother me. To spend time to think about what someone else thinks is counter to everything I've ever believed in my life. If I believe what other people think, that means I value their opinion more than I value my own. That's not the case.

In their first matchup, in 2013, the "gimmicky" college offense had dropped 24 points on the Cardinals before they scored a second time, and Philadelphia hung on for a tense 24-21 win that left Arians sputtering and bitching about the referees.[1] It's safe to say that both coaches wanted to win the rematch for personal as well as professional reasons.

---

1   "Williams To Cards: Let's Not Be Crybabies" by Tim McManus, *Birds 24/7*, December 3, 2013.

GAME 7.
ARIZONA CARDINALS

OCTOBER 26, 2014
UNIVERSITY OF PHOENIX STADIUM, GLENDALE

The Eagles were inches away from greatness in game seven, from a road win against one of the league's best teams, from dominating the NFC with an inside track to a first-round bye in the playoffs.

Not literally inches, as they were in the 49ers game, but they had driven to the Arizona 16 with thirteen seconds left, and had three shots into the end zone to win. Jordan Matthews actually caught a game-winning pass in the end zone as time ran out but was pushed out of bounds by safety Rashad Johnson before he could get his feet down.

The Eagles were without two of their great offensive linemen, without all-around weapon Darren Sproles, and without their best middle linebacker for all but twenty-two snaps. These players were all going to be back from injury in two more weeks; if they could have just held on a bit longer...

The team was not uniformly terrible, which made the loss that much more brutal. Cody Parkey made a 54-yard field goal, the longest for the Eagles in eleven years. Nick Foles threw for 411 yards, 187 to Maclin alone, and LeSean McCoy ran for a solid 83 yards on twenty-one carries.

Foles was not missing as many open receivers as he had been earlier in the year. In Glendale he connected on two 50+ yard passes, one of them a beautiful touchdown strike to Jeremy Maclin. But this did not in any way help Chip Kelly feel better about the outcome.

I asked the coach after the game if he was encouraged by the Eagles' success passing long, which had been a problem all year:

> No, I don't care about that. We lost the game, so I'm not concerned about that.

I'm pretty sure he does care about the long passing game, but my intuition told me it was not a good time for a follow-up question.

Despite that improvement, Foles was throwing a steady two interceptions a game, and not fluky tipped balls that someone grabs, either. One was eight feet behind his targeted receiver, directly into the arms of a cornerback, and Chip confirmed after the game that Riley Cooper ran the correct route. While Foles had not had the luxury of a full offensive line protecting him all year, the hope from 2013 that Foles might be a franchise quarterback was fading fast.

Philly played well except for five bad mistakes that handed Arizona the win. Two were Foles' interceptions and two were "X-plays" (explosion plays), long breakaway touchdowns that the defense gave up. The fifth mistake belonged to Josh Huff, who got his first significant minutes, often spelling Riley Cooper out wide at the #2 WR position.

Huff did some good things. On first and ten at the Arizona 19, he caught a short pass, and broke a tackle using his athleticism. As he raced for the end zone, though, he didn't tuck the ball in tight. Cardinals DE Frostee Rucker stripped it out from behind at the 7 and Arizona recovered, killing a crucial scoring drive.

After the game, Coach Kelly said that Huff ran the wrong route, too. A lot of coaches would have benched the rookie for the rest of the game. Chip went right back to him on the next drive, in the end zone. Huff had his man beat, with a lot of open end zone behind him, but Foles' pass was short, floaty and intercepted.

He went to Huff deep again on the next drive, incomplete. On the last drive of the first half, Huff made another rookie mistake, getting called for offensive pass interference on a pass aimed at

Jordan Matthews. And still he got back in on the game's final drive for two plays, out wide as the #2 receiver in place of the ineffective Riley Cooper. Huff was targeted deep left, but Foles had to throw it away under pass rush pressure.

Fans did not share Kelly's trust or patience. On talk radio and chat boards, they demanded that Huff be benched, said he sucked, repeated the tired charges of Oregon bias.

Yet Huff played well besides his one fumble and the OPI call, and when I interviewed him after the game, he seemed to have the right attitude—downcast, taking responsibility for his mistakes, and determined to go back Tuesday and work on fixing them.

I don't think Chip's second chances indicate some kind of stubbornness or Oregon Bias™. It has more to do with Kelly's approach toward developing young players.

Go back to Oregon, in the first game of the 2011 season. This was a huge non-conference game, #3 Oregon against #4 LSU (featuring Odell Beckham Jr. and a rookie nose guard named Bennie Logan, who had four tackles and a pass breakup in his first start).

Oregon had just landed its biggest recruiting coup of the Chip Kelly years, a flashy "athlete" named De'Anthony Thomas who ran and received equally well.

The game was tight until the third quarter, when DAT fumbled on two consecutive Oregon plays. He coughed it up at the Oregon 21 on a run, leading to an easy LSU scoring drive, and then fumbled the ensuing kickoff return at the Ducks' 41—leading to a second quick touchdown.

Oregon lost by thirteen, but Kelly refused to blame or bench the true freshman. After the game, as I relate in my book *The Tao of Chip Kelly*, he told reporters:

> Our players play from a desire to excel—not a fear of failure. I'm not yanking a kid when he puts the ball on the ground. As I learned from [basketball coach] Paul Westhead a long time ago, you may stop the bleeding, but you may kill the patient and that's not going to happen here.

The point is not to tolerate bad play or be a pushover. It's about developing players, especially newer ones. If they're learning and have room to grow, individual mistakes are less important than that bigger picture.

After the Arizona game, I asked a downcast Huff to explain his coach's approach. He said:

> He trusts his players. He knows that it's football and stuff happens. He trusts his players to go out and make the same play they would make in practice. [Chip doesn't] put his players in the tank where if they mess up he's not coming back to you, or anything like that. He wants to give his players confidence and keep their confidence high.

Kelly was implementing an old truth here: successful people learn from their errors. Huff continued:

> This is a learning curve for me... I want to be the best that I can be for this team. Unfortunately things didn't go my way this game, especially inside the red zone, but other than that, I'm just looking forward to getting back to it on Tuesday and fixing my mistakes.

Intel Corporation, the big computer chip manufacturer, has a personnel policy they call "up or out." Employees need to steadily move up the ladder every year or two, or go look for a new job at a different company. Kelly's approach is similar. Good NFL players are always learning and growing, whether from experience, video study, weight training or learning new skills. Any players who aren't—whether due to laziness, attitude or age—won't last long.

Chip isn't interested in finding out who has so much talent that they can skate by for a while. He'd rather try to find talented players who are also improving every day.

That doesn't mean that bad play has no consequences, but Kelly tends to stick with players until he gives up on them entirely—usually at the end of the year. The team released Jason Avant after the 2013 season, despite his tremendous team leadership and positive attitude, because he wasn't getting the job done on the field. But they waited until season's end.

Kelly did not bench Marcus Smith after he left Frank Gore open for an inexcusable touchdown in the five-point loss to San Francisco. The rookie got two more games with about the same number of snaps before Kelly threw in the towel at the bye. And even then, he later indicated that it was a lack of consistency in practices, not game errors, that kept the rookie seated.

You also need to have an alternative before you bench someone, which can be tough to find mid-season. Nose tackle Isaac Sopoaga was traded after eight games in 2013, but only because his backup, rookie Bennie Logan, had blossomed into a legitimate NFL starter.

Again, the key was building confidence. Clearly Logan would have had a rough time starting immediately as a rookie; it was shrewd to have him learn at the feet of a successful veteran, and shrewder yet to trade that vet away once the student was ready to take over.

All of this meant that Nick Foles probably had until year's end to makes his case as the franchise quarterback, unless he crumbled completely in a Geno-esque way. Nate Allen, who was older and had little upside at this point, probably had until the second the team found a better safety—but that could be a very long second, in a league with a dire shortage of decent backstops. It seemed pretty clear that the team hoped his replacement would be Earl Wolff, but that wasn't working out. If Howie Roseman couldn't find someone by the October 28th trading deadline, Allen's job was probably safe until the off-season.

Huff's fumble wouldn't have mattered except for the terrible defensive breakdown with 1:33 left, when Arizona's speedy rookie receiver John Brown caught a 75-yard bomb for the winning touchdown. Cornerback Cary Williams didn't play his man deep enough to handle his raw speed, and even worse, safety Nate Allen bit on a double move that took him out of the play.

It was inexcusable. Arizona was down 3 points on its own 25, with ninety seconds left in the game. That is the ultimate prevent defense situation, and no move should have been able to fake the safety out of deep coverage. The secondary had been the well-known weak point of the Eagles' defense since 2012; in a way it was surprising that teams didn't pick on it more often. Unfortunately, they seemed to figure this out as 2014 wore on.

On the other X-play, Larry Fitzgerald ran a short slant on an all-out blitz and took it 80 yards for a touchdown. The play was made possible by what was arguably a pick on safety Malcolm Jenkins by Cardinals WR Ted Ginn, Jr. Chip Kelly is not one to complain about referees, but earlier, rookie Josh Huff had been penalized for an illegal pick on a very similar play going the other way. Ginn's maneuver was ignored.

Here's what it looks like when Chip is upset about a call (and a loss). After the game, he says nothing. At the next day's press conference, he says measured things like this:

> Yeah, the penalties in that game were on both sides. They had 10, we had 11–that were accepted. I think it was just one of those games where we've got to understand how the officiating crew is officiating a game and play accordingly to it.

Then a reporter asks him directly about that apparent difference in calls between the two teams' pick plays. Watch the fireworks:

> Q. About the pick play, did you ever get an explanation on what the difference was between Cardinals WR Ted Ginn, Jr.'s and WR Josh Huff's?
> CHIP KELLY: We did not get an explanation, no.
> Q. You never got an explanation on the Ginn one?
> CHIP KELLY: No, did not get an explanation.
> Q. They were very similar type plays?
> CHIP KELLY: Seems like it when you look at the film.

Okay, that's not exactly Hoosier coach Bob Knight throwing chairs, but believe me, that was Chip being furious about a call. He was seething.

As Kelly himself often says, though, you're allowed twenty-four hours to celebrate or be upset about a game. Then it's on to the next one. This was a dinged up team that was on schedule to be healed up in two more weeks, though starting guard Todd Herremans tore his biceps muscle and was questionable. Since the next game was against Houston, with Jadeveon Clowney likely back to join J.J. Watt, that was scary.

FINAL SCORE: CARDINALS 24, EAGLES 20

GAME 8.
HOUSTON TEXANS

NOVEMBER 2, 2014
NRG STADIUM, HOUSTON

As it turned out, Jadeveon Clowney—the feared OLB and #1 overall draft pick—was still injured and did not play against the Eagles. The Birds beat Houston 31-21 and finished the day with the second-best record in the NFL at 6-2, but they also lost three more starters to injury—including QB Nick Foles—and continued to play poorly in many respects.

This led to lots of crazy statistics. For example, the Eagles had the second lowest red zone efficiency in the league[1], yet they were the fourth highest in per-game scoring.[2] This is probably the craziest: as Jimmy Kempski tweeted,

> Eagles have highest point differential and the worst turnover differential in the NFC.
> @JimmyKempski. 1:22 P.M. November 2, 2014.

That's right, the Birds were giving away a steady two to three possessions a game, weathering erratic quarterback play and a crippled offensive line, and still dominating opponents. It started to look like Chip Kelly's college boy system might work in the NFL after all.

---

1   "NFL Team Red Zone Scoring Percentage (TD only)" by TeamRankings.com, February 1, 2015.
2   "NFL Team Total Offense Statistics - 2014" by ESPN Stats and Info, ESPN. com. Undated.

Houston's most fearsome weapons were a ragged field that eats knees and a brutal pass rush led by the league's best defensive player, J.J. Watt, and his underrated teammate, linebacker Whitney Mercilus. (Yes, that's his real and very descriptive name. His parents, immigrants from Haiti, are Yvrose and Wilner Mercilus.)

Watt made his mark but was largely contained. Rookie receiver Jordan Matthews, who seems polite and soft-spoken off the field, even mocked the Defensive Player of the Year when he appeared winded late in the game. NFL Films caught Matthews yelling from the sideline:

Why you on a knee, 99? Why you on a knee?[1]

It was the aptly named Mercilus who did the real damage. He had had nine tackles, two sacks, three quarterback hits and one "cracked" collarbone, which belonged to Nick Foles. The Eagles' starting QB was out for the rest of the year.

Fortunately, backup QB Mark Sanchez played well coming in cold off the bench. Sanchez went 15-22 for 202 yards and two touchdowns, including a 52-yard bomb to Jeremy Maclin on Sanchez's very first play since 2012. (Maclin won the NFL Offensive Player of the Week award.)

The damage didn't stop there, though. The Eagles also lost *another* starting offensive lineman, right guard Todd Herremans, as well as veteran inside linebacker DeMeco Ryans, the quarterback of their defense. Both were lost for the rest of the year. Herremans had tried to play through his torn pectoral injury from the week before, but it proved impossible.

Ryans had actually intercepted a Ryan Fitzpatrick pass when he tore his right Achilles tendon untouched—likely because of that threadbare field—and fumbled the ball back to Houston. *Sports Illustrated's* Greg Bedard noted an eerie fact about the injury:

Four years ago Ryans ruptured his left Achilles tendon on nearly the same spot on the same field while playing for the Texans, the team that drafted him in 2006.[2]

---

1   "Inside the NFL: Eagles - Texans Highlights," NFL.com, November, 2014.
2   "In Sanchize We Trust" by Greg Bedard, *MMQB*, November 3, 2014,

Luckily, starting center Jason Kelce had just come back from injury, and All-Pro guard Evan Mathis was scheduled to return for the following Monday's game.

Coach Kelly works hard to plan for injuries. As Oregon fans know, he insists on rotating in bench players (especially on defense) and gives everyone significant snaps in practice, precisely so they'll be ready to be the "next man in" if needed. One reason for the fast pace of practices was simply to create more snaps to go around.

He makes a point of having two solid quarterbacks on his roster, noting correctly that it's almost statistically certain that your starter will miss one or more games each year.

The Eagles didn't make any splashy draft picks or free agent signings in the spring, but they quietly built up their depth and now it was paying off.

The off-season signing of Mark Sanchez launched a thousand "Butt Fumble" jokes, but it was looking pretty shrewd in November—especially compared to the rival Cowboys, who had signed Brandon Weeden and driven off solid backup Kyle Orton, who was winning games as the starter in Buffalo instead. The Cowboys' season was one big hit on Tony Romo's ailing back from falling apart.

Less noticed but just as important was the acquisition of cornerback Nolan Carroll, who had made a dime package (with six defensive backs) possible on passing downs. In 2013 the Eagles were vulnerable to runs when their nickel package was in, and they arguably lost the playoff game against New Orleans as a result. Carroll proved great at run stuffing, and was morphing into a sort of hybrid slot CB/linebacker. With Ryans out, the dime package—which only needs a single inside linebacker—looked to be a bigger part of the defense going forward.

Losing DeMeco was still a serious blow, especially given his leadership role. Ryans wore the headphone to receive plays from the sideline, and passed them on to his teammates. Coach Kelly put it this way:

He's the true leader. We talk about it all the time. Hes

Mufasa, you know, he's our guy.

In football terms, Ryans' loss should have been easier to weather than Mychal Kendricks' absence earlier in the year. DeMeco was great against the run, but his declining speed really hurt him on passing downs. For the second year in a row, the Eagles gave up a lot of first downs on third-and-long. Many of them were short passes over the middle such as slants, with lots of yards after catch.

The top two depth ILBs, Najee Goode and Travis Long, were out for the season with injuries. Chip Kelly was very blunt in noting that the two remaining backup ILBs, Emmanuel Acho and ex-Duck Casey Matthews, were weaker against the pass. In his October 2nd press conference, he said:

> They are obviously a lot better in the run game, and we have gotten into some more nickel and dime sets in passing situations to get them off the field.

Kendricks was the perfect ILB in those dime packages, and with his return, Matthews and Acho—who were improving weekly already—were likely to be much more effective replacing Ryans on running downs. Mufasa's leadership couldn't be replaced as easily, though. When he went down, both benches emptied as teammates (and his former Texan colleagues) gathered around to take a knee and pay respect.

There was a lot of talk after the game about whether Chip Kelly's offense was "quarterback-proof." Clearly it was not. Matt Barkley and, to some degree, Michael Vick did notably less well than Foles in 2013, and frankly Foles himself was a lot worse in 2014.

It seemed fair to say though that Kelly's system was quarterback-resistant. It doesn't depend on a hero QB to make things happen. As Sanchez told reporters this week,

> It feels like a fast break in basketball—you're the point guard, just dish it to the open guy. Don't hang on to it too long, try not to get hit.[1]

---

1   "The new, improved Mark Sanchez?" by Les Bowen, *Philadelphia Daily News*, November 6, 2014.

For a guy nicknamed "Big Balls Chip," Kelly spends a lot of time reducing risk—drafting versatile, big and fast players with good attitudes, reducing dependence on any one player, and relentlessly practicing his substitutes so that they're ready to fill in. Because special teams are an afterthought for most coaches, he'll happily grab the advantage there for the cost of a couple of inexpensive free agent specialists such as Maragos and Braman.

Similarly, Kelly would love to get an elite QB—it's probably the key to winning a Super Bowl—but there aren't enough for all thirty-two NFL teams, and Kelly's system is designed to get by okay without one.

He also tailors his offense to the players available. On the day after the game, he said:

> I don't have an offense–I've said that since day one. Our offense is directed around our quarterback. So tell me who is playing quarterback and I'll tell you what our offense is going to be...

That might be a bit overstated, but history backs him up. Kelly revamped his offense when Foles took over from Michael Vick, as he did when Oregon's dual threat QB Jeremiah Masoli gave way to pocket passer Darron Thomas—and again when another running QB named Marcus Mariota succeeded Thomas.

Kelly simply builds a team with a strong offensive line and as many weapons as he can muster, to give every QB a lot of different ways to succeed. The essential skill for the quarterback is reading the defense and making quick decisions. A strong arm or the ability to run is a great bonus, but it's not necessary as long as the QB is "fleet of mind," decisive and accurate. Sanchez was all of these things in training camp, and he had a great start against Houston. Being a faster runner than Foles didn't hurt.

FINAL SCORE: EAGLES 31, TEXANS 21

THE END OF FOLES?

NOVEMBER 3, 2014

For Foles, the injury completed a sudden and dramatic fall from grace. When the team had reassembled at the end of July for training camp, he was a hero with a bright future and a contract in the vicinity of $20 million a year for five years headed his way. Then came struggles in training camp and the preseason, and rough sledding in the regular season right up through his broken collarbone. His TD to TO ratio went from 2013's historic 27-2 to a very mediocre 13-10, even though the team was passing more.

Two days after his injury, NJ.com columnist Mark Eckel wrote that, according to an anonymous source inside the Eagles organization, Foles may have played his last game in Philadelphia. The source said:

> I think Howie is looking at quarterbacks. He's kind of soured on Foles, and I don't think he's alone. The organization isn't sold that he's the guy going forward.[1]

Some of this was optimism over Sanchez's success in finishing the Houston game, but Eckel quoted another source, interviewed before the injury:

> Let's just say the way things were going, he wasn't going to get a contract extension that's for sure. Now, if he has a big second half, that could change.

---

1 "Is Nick Foles done with Eagles? Team soured on quarterback before the injury, sources say" by Mark Eckel, NJ.com, November 4, 2014.

Foles' injury ended his chance for that comeback. Oddly, the report talked about Howie Roseman's opinion, but not Chip Kelly's. This may have just reflected the fact that Kelly and his confidants were harder to get quotes from, and it's true that Roseman as GM had the final say over player acquisition. But no one doubted that Chip Kelly had a big say in the matter, too.

In all his public comments, Chip had spoken very highly of Foles, not only in Philadelphia but years before at Oregon, too. The Ducks played Foles' Arizona team in the PAC-10 (later PAC-12), and Kelly singled him out for praise way back in 2011[1], when the QB took a big hit from future Eagles Kiko Alonso and Taylor Hart.[2] Foles managed to switch hands and throw a first down pass left handed as he was going down, then got up limping and went right back into the huddle.

> I catch myself watching him in awe sometimes… Nick is a hell of a football player. That kid's a warrior.

In the 2012 draft, however, Roseman wanted to pick Kirk Cousins over Foles, according to Eckel. Coach Andy Reid and Offensive Coordinator Marty Mornhinweg "insisted" and carried the day.

Roseman and Kelly had appeared to be on the same page before this report, but control over the team had never been fully resolved. Both men insisted that there was no problem since they never disagreed. That didn't answer the question of what would happen if they ever did disagree, though.

In 2013, Chip Kelly had interviewed for the Eagles job, then walked away, left Philadelphia and returned to Oregon. Days later he accepted the Eagles job, presumably after his offer was beefed up.

I doubt that the extra beef was more money. Kelly has never been a money guy. As late as 2007, he was making a reported

---

1   "Oregon coach Chip Kelly on Nick Foles: 'I watch in awe sometimes'" by Anthony Gimino, *Tucson Citizen*, September 25, 2011.

2   "Nick Foles takes big hit from Kiko Alonso and Taylor Hart 9/24/2011" by madmike1951. September 26, 2011. Retreived from www.youtube.com/ watch?v=cULz2SdcxfE

$60,000 a year as the offensive coordinator at the University of New Hampshire. This is purely conjecture, but I've always suspected that he was holding out for more control over the team, something most owners would be naturally reluctant to give to a guy with four total years of head coaching experience, all in college.

In an interview right before Kelly's first game as coach in 2013, owner Jeffrey Lurie told the *Inquirer's* Zach Berman that he had given Chip final say over the fifty-three-man roster, which is unusual.[1] In other words, Roseman could sign or draft or trade for anybody he wanted, but Chip could just cut them at the end of training camp. Lurie explained:

> It made sense to balance the player personnel and head coaching, and empower them both, and force a complete collaboration.

The comments about "souring on Foles" sparked the first public disagreement between the two. When a reporter asked the coach on November 6th about the anonymous comments, he wasted no time making clear who was boss:

> I don't know where that stuff comes from, I know this, I know I control the roster. And I think you guys can say first-hand, I don't talk to anybody. So whoever says they have a source in terms of what's gonna go on with roster maneuvers or people going up and people going down, they never talked to the right person because that comes from me, and that never was the case.[2]

Kelly was throwing a couple of sharp elbows in Roseman's direction. He made it clear that these leaks about "souring" on Foles came from Roseman or his scouting staff, not Chip. He was also warning Roseman not to oppose him on player choices. Sure, he was saying, Roseman could sign or draft anybody he wanted, but Chip

---

1   "Lurie: Kelly won't be judged on wins and losses" by Zach Berman, *Philadelphia Inquirer*, September 9, 2013.
2   "Inside Voices: Kelly And the Balance Of Power" by Tim McManus, *Birds 24/7*, November 22, 2014.

didn't have to play them, or even put them on the final roster. This put the disappointing rookie class of 2014 in a new light.

They were disappointing mostly because they weren't playing. Could it be because Kelly didn't want them in the first place?

We know that wasn't true for Josh Huff or Taylor Hart, because Chip told reporters that he not only wanted these guys, but that Roseman talked him into waiting and not drafting them higher than necessary. Huff's troubles have been discussed already. Hart's absence was the result of a good problem to have; the surprising strength of the defensive line. He was competing against Brandon Bair, his old mentor from Oregon, and if they were even close, it made sense to redshirt the rookie and play the thirty-year-year old Bair, who also showed a knack for making plays.

But OLB Marcus Smith II only played sixty-four defensive snaps all year, which was stunning because Smith was a first round pick. In fact, Kelly later told reporters flat out that Roseman chose Marcus Smith II.[1] Meanwhile, safety Ed Reynolds barely made the practice squad despite playing a position of extreme need. Yet mid-season, the Birds signed two new safeties—Jerome "The Osprey" Couplin, and Chris Prosinski—instead of moving Reynolds up from the practice squad.

Tim McManus of *Birds 24/7* wrote about Kelly's comments a couple of weeks later, and added a vague but ominous bit of inside information without naming or describing his source(s):

> There have been persistent rumblings about shifting dynamics behind the scenes: Namely, that Kelly and Roseman's relationship has cooled and that the collaborative process between coach and general manager is not where it once was (Kelly and Gamble remain tight, per sources).
>
> Kelly's clout within the organization is growing as his methods continue to bear fruit... While many are contributing to the ongoing building process, there is

---

1   "Kelly said Roseman drafted Marcus Smith" by Jeff McLane, *Philadelphia Inquirer*, March 11, 2015.

little doubt where the bulk of the power lies. And that seems like a departure from Lurie's intended design.[1]

This was the first skirmish of a battle that would soon erupt into open warfare. In the short run, though, the question was "How would Sanchez as quarterback affect the offense?"

If the preseason had been an accurate guide, rookie WR Jordan Matthews and TE Zach Ertz could be expected to do more. Despite dropping a pass that Houston intercepted, Josh Huff continued to show that potent mix of speed, elusiveness, and physicality that he was drafted for, fighting for a couple of first downs by putting his shoulder into defenders.

And the Eagles' running game could be expected to explode over the next few games with a mostly healthy front line and the return of RBs Darren Sproles and Chris Polk, who pummeled his way to 50 yards and a touchdown on eight carries. Backup OG/OT Tobin was much stronger on runs than passes, and a strong run game is a great boost for any quarterback, much less an often-mocked substitute QB rebuilding his confidence.

Halfway through the season, it was very hard to figure out this team. They were sputtering while showing tremendous power—like an out-of-tune Maserati engine—and somehow they seemed to be a legitimate Super Bowl contender. Despite the three new big injuries, the various NFL power rankings almost unanimously rated this team as the fourth best in the league. And outside of the New York Giants game, they hadn't even played well yet.

---

1   "Inside Voices: Kelly And the Balance Of Power" by Tim McManus, *Birds 24/7*, November 22, 2014.

GAME 9.
CAROLINA PANTHERS

NOVEMBER 10, 2014
LINCOLN FINANCIAL FIELD, PHILADELPHIA

Mark Sanchez started his first game in two years against Carolina, and led the Philadelphia Eagles to a 45-21 win that was far more dominating than the score suggests.

This is the same Mark Sanchez who was run out of New York as a failure, who went from leading the Jets to the AFC Championship Game in his first two seasons to having Tim Tebow and Geno Smith brought in as competitors, then getting injured and eventually cut. The guy who came to Philadelphia known best for his "Butt Fumble."

Sanchez was by no means perfect at home against the Panthers. On his first possession, having been handed the ball on Carolina's 22 yard line after a fumble, he drove the Eagles for 0 yards on three plays and settled for a field goal. Several of his passes were off-target. He made wrong calls on zone-read plays, and threw one dumb interception that luckily was ruled out of bounds.

Overall, though, he was excellent—20/37 for 332 yards with two TDs, no interceptions and a quarterback rating of 102.5. Sanchez ran the tempo offense better than Nick Foles did in 2014, hitting open receivers and getting the ball out much faster (an average of 2.42 seconds vs. 2.73 for Foles).[1]

---

1   Brandon Lee Gowton [@BrandonGowton]. November 13, 2014. Small sample

Most importantly, he avoided the two biggest problems the Eagles had had under Foles—turnovers and red zone failures. Before the Houston game, the Birds were last in red zone TD percentage at 34.8%, and only one of eleven on red zone third downs.[1] In the first game and a half under Sanchez, the Eagles were a perfect seven for seven in the red zone.

Why? "Turnovers," Chip Kelly had said bluntly after the Arizona game. "I think the turnovers are really the biggest part that's killing us in the red zone right now." Philadelphia had seventeen turnovers in its first seven games, including nine Foles interceptions (vs. two for all of 2013).[2] Sanchez threw two more after coming in for Foles in Houston; the Texans excel in takeaways.

But against Carolina, the Birds had no giveaways while forcing five: two forced fumbles and three interceptions. One was a pick six. Philadelphia set the tone with two takeaways on the Panthers' first three plays, starting with a fumble punched out by Casey Matthews (who did the same thing for Chip Kelly against Carolina's Cam Newton—then at Auburn—back in the 2010 season's National Championship Game).

Carolina did its best to put pressure on Sanchez, too. They sold out to stop the run, packing the box and switching to man coverage with a single high safety.[3] The idea was to force a rusty Sanchez to beat them with his arm, and he did—wielding a cartoonish pump fake and smoothly avoiding pressure by moving up in the pocket.

It was a mystery why Nick Foles had been so much worse in 2014, but one obvious factor is that he was uncomfortable behind the Eagles' tattered offensive line. He seemed to have lost his nerve, routinely backpedaling in the face of any pressure and throwing off

size, but Mark Sanchez's average time of 2.42 seconds to attempt a pass is significantly faster than Foles' 2.73 time. [Tweet]. Retrieved from www.twitter.com/BrandonGowton/status/533000750079967233

1   "Eagles' inconsistency in the red zone persists" by John Gonzalez, *CSN Philly*, October 30, 2014.
2   "This time, turnovers finally catch up with Eagles" by Reuben Frank, *CSN Philly*, October 26, 2014.
3   "All-22: How Sanchez Moved In the Pocket" by Sheil Kapadia, *Birds 24/7*, November 13, 2014.

his back foot.

Sanchez had some lucky timing here—starting left guard Evan Mathis returned for his first start, and center Jason Kelce (still inaccurate on some snaps) had come back one game earlier. But it takes a lot of guts for anyone to stand tall against NFL pass rushers, and Sanchez's experience—sixty-eight pro games, as Coach Kelly pointed out—paid off. As star left tackle Jason Peters told Sheil Kapadia,

> They were taking away the run and playing man, so we were running man-beater routes. We started getting the pass going, and they couldn't stop it.[1]

During the preseason, Sanchez loved throwing to rookie wide receiver Jordan Matthews, and that continued against the Panthers. Sanchez threw to him four times on a single drive, culminating in a 13-yard touchdown, and Matthews finished the day with seven catches on nine targets for 138 yards and two touchdowns.

This was not the first time Chip Kelly had made the most of a quarterback no one else valued. Duck fans may remember his first year as offensive coordinator, 2007, when the team went through four quarterbacks due to injury (Dennis Dixon, Brady Leaf, Cody Kempt and Justin Roper). Though the team dropped from its #2 ranking after Dixon's injury, it won the Sun Bowl in an upset as Roper threw four touchdowns.

After Kelly's first year as head coach (2009), he kicked starting QB Jeremiah Masoli off the team following his second arrest of the off-season. Chip handed the reins to a converted sophomore wide receiver named Darron Thomas. Thomas had none of Masoli's dual-threat ability, and his post-college pro career peaked at Arena League substitute. But Kelly rebuilt his offense around him and took the team to the National Championship Game against Auburn.

Clearly, Kelly has skill at bringing the most out of undervalued players (Darren Sproles, anyone?) and this is most evident with quarterbacks. Nick Foles was a marginal backup at the beginning

---

1   Ibid.

of the 2013 season, a guy who was 1-5 as a starter during his rookie year and had clearly lost a QB competition against thirty-three-year-old Michael Vick. After Vick's injury, Foles had a spectacular year with the third highest quarterback rating in NFL history.

But Kelly does not transform quarterbacks. He transforms his flexible offense to fit their strengths and minimize their weaknesses. As long as they are good at reading defenses and choose among their many options quickly and decisively, it doesn't matter if they are fast or slow, rocket-armed or marginal, lightning-footed or—Foles.

Kelly has emphatically rejected the idea that his offense can be run by anyone, correctly noting that this disrespects the skill and athleticism needed to play in the NFL. But he has developed a program that can adapt to a wider range of skill sets than most offenses, and does not require the most highly valued (and hard to find) skills.

He's also building a team that can win in many different ways, belying his reputation as a coach who only cares about offense and play calling. In August, no one would have predicted that this Eagles team would struggle offensively and be saved by superior defensive and special teams play, but that is exactly what has happened. Philadelphia started its first two drives on Carolina's 22 and 43 after turnovers, and picked up touchdowns on a punt return and an interception later in the first half.

The Eagles' pass rush continued to improve at a frightening pace, racking up nine sacks against Carolina on top of the three interceptions. It was tempting to think that Chip had gotten revenge against Cam Newton for that loss in the National Championship Game, leaving him limping, but that would imply that the team didn't pass-rush as hard as it could have in other games. And that's ridiculous.

Connor Barwin spied Cam Newton to take away his scrambling ability, and still got 3.5 sacks. Clearly defensive coordinator Billy Davis learned from the San Francisco game, where Colin Kaepernick burned the Eagles again and again by scrambling on passing downs.

After the game—his first start at home—Sanchez drove

down to Philadelphia's two most famous cheese steak sub shops, Geno's and Pat's, which sit across the street from each other, and diplomatically ate one from each place. The visit was a publicity coup. The next day, a reporter asked Chip Kelly what this visit said about Sanchez.

> COACH KELLY: The fact that he was hungry after a game?

All of this success made it look like the Eagles big showdown at Green Bay's Lambeau Field was shaping up to be a classic battle. But that's not how it worked out.

FINAL SCORE: EAGLES 45, PANTHERS 21

GAME 10.
GREEN BAY PACKERS

NOVEMBER 16, 2014
LAMBEAU FIELD, GREEN BAY

Going into week eleven's showdown between NFC division-leading teams, optimism about the Eagles was soaring like Icarus right before his wings melted. This game against Green Bay would define how great the Eagles really were. Talk of Philadelphia as a legitimate Super Bowl contender abounded, and one moron—this author—wrote that the tiff might be a preview of the NFC Championship Game.[1]

That would all be hilarious now if the Eagles' severe beating hadn't been so painful. The Packers scored early, often, and without mercy while smothering Philadelphia's faltering attack. With two minutes left in the first quarter, it was 17-0 Green Bay. At the two-minute warning for the first half, it was 30-3. With three minutes left in the third, 39-6. And then it got ugly.

Actually, 39-6 was the low point. The Birds kept pace for the rest of this drubbing, but mostly because the Packers were exhausted from scoring and bored with kicking the Eagles' butts. There were no silver linings here. Everyone played poorly, including the recently recovered front line (with four of 2013's five starters back in the lineup). WR Jordy Nelson repeatedly torched CB Bradley Fletcher,

---

1   "Chip Kelly Update: The Quarterback Whisperer?" by Mark Saltveit, FishDuck. com, November 14, 2014.

and Philadelphia couldn't figure out how to stop it.

The recently dominant pass rush disappeared, Mark Sanchez was in a New York (Jets) state of mind, and even the vaunted special teams unit gave up a punt return touchdown (though they blocked two kicks and got a hand on a third). Josh Huff, playing gunner on a punt return, ran up in front of returner Micah Hyde and shimmied without actually tackling him. He later said he had been coached to do that, a misconception that Chip was quick to correct. (He had been told not to overrun the runner, as gunners often do.)

Huff later clarified his comments and seemed back on track with the good attitude he more commonly shows.

> I just haven't been myself to be quite frank. I haven't been myself at all. I've been trying to force everything, force my routes. I've been thinking too much about messing up, I haven't just let it loose. The way I can fix that is just play balls out, play balls to the wall and just compete for myself and compete for my teammates and compete for the city of Philadelphia.
>
> I know what I can do and I'm just so impatient to show that and it's caused me to drop balls, it's caused me to not protect the ball that I know how to protect and just trying to do too much instead of letting the game come to me. I don't know what else to say about how piss-poorly I've played so far this season.[1]

What he really needed to do, though, was add good playing to his good attitude. Huff had another terrible drop, one that popped up in the air off his hands and could easily have been intercepted. This was the point in the season that Chip Kelly stopped targeting Huff, due to his drops and other mistakes. It took him a couple more games to get back into the rotation.

Another ex-Duck, Brandon Bair, continued his strong season with a blocked extra point. This held the score to 39-6 late in the third quarter, instead of 40-6, but that wasn't quite enough to swing

---

1   "Frustrated Huff Opens Up" by Tim McManus, *Birds 24/7*, November 18, 2014.

momentum Philly's way.

Unsurprisingly, doom and gloom quickly replaced Super Bowl talk among Eagles fans, but the team seemed surprisingly resilient.

Green Bay was a very good team that became great at home, and had—as of mid-November, 2014—the NFL quarterback playing at the highest level.

It was hard to wrap your head around how well Aaron Rodgers had been playing. He was twenty-two for thirty-six against Philly for 341 yards with two TDs and no interceptions for a QB rating of 120.3. Here's the amazing thing: that performance actually *brought down* his QB rating for home games over the previous two years. The Packers were scoring nearly twice as many points at home (41.5) as on the road (22.2).

Given that, losing to Green Bay at Lambeau Field was not a reason to despair. Losing to the woeful Tennessee Titans in week twelve? That would have been an excellent reason to despair.

FINAL SCORE: PACKERS 53, EAGLES 20

GAME II.
TENNESSEE TITANS

NOVEMBER 23, 2014
LINCOLN FINANCIAL FIELD, PHILADELPHIA

Four days before the big Thanksgiving battle with Dallas, Philadelphia dispatched the Tennessee Titans methodically. It all started with Josh Huff's redemption. After a very tough rookie year marked by four drops and a fumble that limited his playing time, and some unfortunate remarks to reporters, Huff ran back the opening kickoff 107 yards—an Eagles record—to crush any upset hopes the Titans might have had.

There were some hopeful developments—the offensive line looked much better, especially in pass protection; LeSean McCoy had a big game with 130 yards including one run for fifty-three all by itself—and some continued worries.[1] Mark Sanchez's early red zone success (seven for seven in his first two games) collapsed as he scored TDs in only three out of seven tries against Tennessee, and one of four in Green Bay. And no matter how well a team does against the Titans, it's worth remembering that all you did was beat the Titans.

FINAL SCORE: EAGLES 43, TITANS 24

---

1   "Eagles vs. Titans: 5 Good Things, and 5 Bad" By Mark Saltveit, *Bleeding Green Nation*, November 23, 2014.

GAME 12.
DALLAS COWBOYS

NOVEMBER 27, 2014
AT&T STADIUM, ARLINGTON, TEXAS

On Thanksgiving Day, 2012, in front of twenty million TV viewers nationwide, Mark Sanchez had a game, in fact a single play, so humiliating that it has its own Wikipedia article: The Butt Fumble.

Exactly two years later, on Thanksgiving of 2014, he carved up the Dallas Cowboys like a slow-cooked turkey and rebuilt his legacy in front of thirty-two million people, the largest regular season audience in seven years.[1] Sanchez was nine for eleven for 99 yards passing and ran for a touchdown—just in the first quarter.

But his most important statistic was zero—the number of interceptions he threw that Thursday, after clocking in at a steady two INTs per game since taking over for injured Nick Foles.

And finally, he started keeping the ball on some of the read-option plays and running himself, starting with his touchdown on the first drive, and ending with a perfectly executed read-keeper for 13 yards that he finished with a beautiful baseball slide. Nick Foles' attempts to slide range between hilarious and kind of sad, so that was a wonderful thing to watch.

The rest of the offense played well against Dallas, too. LeSean McCoy ripped off a 36-yard run on the fourth play from scrimmage

---

1   "NFL Week 13 TV Ratings: Eagles/Cowboys Top Reg. Season Game Since '07" by Paulsen, *Sports Media Watch*, December 6, 2015.

and finished with his biggest game of the year, 159 yards on twenty-five carries. Riley Cooper caught pass after pass, Sproles and Maclin and Matthews picked apart the Cowboy's suspect secondary, and Josh Huff ran(!) for 7 yards and a first down late in the fourth quarter.

But let's not forget the defense, which played a complete and dominating game. The Eagles started by shutting down Dallas' run game, holding league-leading rusher DeMarco Murray to 73 yards on twenty carries, with one TD and a long of only nine. The pass defense was physical and disruptive, too, with two interceptions to join one post-reception fumble recovery.

The Birds did give up some long passes, as per usual, but they held Romo without a passing touchdown for the first time in thirty-eight games, and pressured him relentlessly.

Even without the bitter rivalry between these two teams, or the huge Thanksgiving Day national TV audience, the stakes were very high.

After all the turmoil and injuries that Philadelphia had suffered in 2014, the season boiled down to games #12 (on Thanksgiving), #13, and #14: two against Dallas with Seattle at home in between.

The Eagles and Cowboys entered the game tied, though Philadelphia owned the tiebreaker (thanks to a better division record). Winning two of these three games would give the Birds a great chance at a bye in the first round of the playoffs, but losing twice would probably keep them out of the playoffs entirely.

Both teams played a game four days earlier, but Philadelphia's sports science, conditioning and blitz-tempo practices gave them a clear advantage in the short week. Dallas' defense was sucking wind even on the second drive (another Philly TD), and by game's end they had no strength with which to muster a comeback.

Romo was blindly heaving up long passes, leading to three second-half interceptions for the Eagles (one called off on a holding penalty).

The only down note for the Birds was that their red zone troubles continued; they were only one for five inside the twenty. But in a bitter rivalry delayed until week twelve, that was a very minor thing to complain about.

FINAL SCORE: EAGLES 33, COWBOYS 10

GAME 13.
SEATTLE SEAHAWKS

DECEMBER 7, 2014
LINCOLN FINANCIAL FIELD, PHILADELPHIA

The Seahawks and Eagles are similar in a lot of ways, with dominant running attacks, strong defensive front lines and innovative West Coast college coaches who run a lot of read option plays. Coming into the game, Philadelphia's D (which held high-scoring Dallas to 10 points at home) seemed underrated, though Connor Barwin had been named the NFL's defensive player of the month for November. Seattle's defense wasn't *over*-rated—it was still the NFL's best—but it was at least fully rated.

Pete Carroll and Chip Kelly had faced each other as head coaches only once, on Halloween night in 2009. #10 Oregon destroyed #4 USC, 47-20, which was the Trojans' worst loss in twelve years. But the coaches had matched wits the two previous years as well, when Kelly was the Ducks' offensive coordinator.

In 2007, Oregon (with QB Dennis Dixon at his peak) beat Mark Sanchez and the Trojans 24-17. The victory was sealed by two Matthew Harper interceptions of Sanchez, who was starting just his third game as QB.[1]

The next year, though, Sanchez was the star, passing for 349 yards and three touchdowns, as #9 USC crushed #23 Oregon 44-10.

---

1   "2007 - OREGON -v- usc [Q1]" by mrrustyduck. June 22, 2008. Retrieved from www.youtube.com/watch?v=yqv5vPh5xq0

The Trojans stuffed Oregon's powerful run game, holding it to just 60 yards. This was only the second start for Oregon QB Jeremiah Masoli, after injuries to starters Nate Costa and Justin Roper, and he couldn't hold on to an early 10-3 lead.

It was interesting how many ex-PAC 10/12 players were in this game. Sanchez threw against CB Richard Sherman (Stanford) in college, too, and FB/DL Will Tukuafu played defensive end at Oregon. Doug Baldwin, Jermaine Kearse, Marshawn Lynch, Max Unger, Zach Ertz, Josh Huff, etc. etc.

The Eagles had won every home game so far this season, but the world champions beat them in Philadelphia, 24-14.

The Eagles' offense actually did well, in one sense. Philadelphia scored 14 points, with two touchdown passes against the league's best secondary. San Francisco and Arizona had managed only 3 points each against the 'Hawks.

It wasn't nearly enough. And it boils down to talent. For all the talk of Chip Kelly's offensive genius, he doesn't design plays that beat a defense's schemes. He designs plays that create one-on-one matchups against defenders, so that he can get the ball to the most favorable face-off.

There's one big flaw. It only works if there's a matchup you can win, and if you can get the ball to that skill player. Seattle runs a very simple defense on every down, mixing Cover 1 and Cover 3 from the same formation, and they have the talent to win every one of those matchups. Which is exactly what they did. Since they don't change their defense, it's impossible to deceive them.

Philadelphia also executed poorly. LeSean McCoy was grieving the death of a very close cousin and missed practice on Friday. His running on Sunday (50 yards and a costly fumble) reflected it.

The offensive line—especially reserve Andrew Gardner—did not sustain or even make their blocks consistently, as Sheil Kapadia broke down in his All-22 review.[1]

The primary failure was by Mark Sanchez at quarterback,

---

1 "All-22: Why the Eagles' Offense Got Shut Down" by Sheil Kapadia, *Birds 24/7*, December 10, 2014.

though. He's the "point guard" who's supposed to be distributing the ball and shooting the occasional three-pointer to keep the defense honest. The "three-pointer" in this case means keeping the ball on a read-option and running or throwing a quick screen when the defense overplays the run.

Sanchez broke open the game against Dallas in week thirteen by doing exactly that, but he froze up against the admittedly scarier front line of Seattle. He also missed some big opportunities, none bigger than with 9:07 left in the fourth quarter, down 24-14, after Mychal Kendricks stripped Marshawn Lynch and the Eagles recovered the fumble.

Chip Kelly had been calling aggressive plays all game, starting with a pass right at Richard Sherman on the first play from scrimmage (which he nearly intercepted). Zach Ertz scored a 35-yard TD early in the third quarter on the "All Go Switch" concept, which Villanova WR coach Brian Flinn describes as "a classic single high safety beater." (It was even in the 1990s era "Tecmo Bowl" video game.) Ertz ran a wheel route from tight end, criss-crossing Riley Cooper's seam route from wide left, with another switch on the right side. The ball was underthrown but Ertz won a jump ball and broke another tackle to score.

After Kendricks forced the fumble, Kelly ran that same play again, and Jordan Matthews—running a wheel route from the slot—couldn't have been more wide open, in the same spot down field where Ertz caught his touchdown. The closest defender was 10 yards behind him. Imagine the change in game momentum if Philadelphia had converted that easy touchdown, and trailed by only 3 points with nine minutes left in the game.

But Riley Cooper was also open in a much smaller window over the middle. Sanchez threw a good eight feet behind him, creating an easy interception for Tharold Simon. And with that, the Eagles' hopes evaporated.

The misfires obscured a lot of good developments. The Birds' front seven was fantastic with seven tackles for loss, stuffing Marshawn Lynch himself on play after play and containing Russell

Wilson better and better as the game went on. Unfortunately, their careful "contain" rush gave Wilson more time to throw, and he mercilessly exploited the Eagles' Achilles heel—third-and-long. Seattle converted two 3rd-and-fifteens and a 3rd-and-thirteen in the game, morale killers in a mostly excellent defensive outing.

The Eagles scored on their only red zone visit, had a 46-yard kick return from ex-Duck Josh Huff (leading to Ertz's touchdown), and got outstanding games from Fletcher Cox and Mychal Kendricks (with eleven tackles each). They played the world champs tough, led by a free agent backup quarterback that everyone else had scoffed at, and had some solid opportunities that they missed.

The Birds also got a sense of what they need to work on. This team was not at the top tier yet, with a need to upgrade at cornerback, inside linebacker, safety and—unless the 2013 Nick Foles returned from injury, instead of 2014's poor imitation—at quarterback.

FINAL SCORE: SEAHAWKS 24, EAGLES 14

GAME 14.
DALLAS COWBOYS

DECEMBER 14, 2014
LINCOLN FINANCIAL FIELD, PHILADELPHIA

In the most crucial game of the season, the Eagles got off to a bad start by muffing the kickoff, and then things got worse.

It was no secret that the Eagles were vulnerable to the deep throw. Cary Williams and Bradley Fletcher had the size Chip Kelly and Billy Davis wanted at cornerback, but they lacked ball-hawking skills and the ability to jam receivers at the line. As 2014 progressed, opponents began to figure out how to get the CBs on an island without safety help and beat them over the top.

And so they did, over and over. Arizona. Green Bay. Seattle. You often hear that a good secondary will help your pass rush, giving them more time to reach the quarterback. For the Eagles, the reverse appeared to be true as well. The strong pass rush had masked the secondary's problems. But when the front line came back down to earth, getting two or three sacks instead of eight or nine, opponents started picking the Eagles apart. As radio producer James Seltzer told me, "Dez Bryant just punked Bradley Fletcher."

Specifically, Bryant scored three touchdowns over Bradley Fletcher.

The big question was, why didn't the coaches adjust? Fans certainly had all the answers, and on talk radio, the answers started with Brandon Boykin moving outside. Never mind that Boykin wasn't having nearly as good a year as he did in 2013. As Seltzer told me, "You couldn't convince a single person in Philly, on Philly talk radio, that Boykin couldn't have done a better job."

Of course, Bryant is also tall (6'2") and very good at using his size. He could have used his height against Boykin in ways he couldn't against Fletcher. But it would have been hard for Boykin to do worse.

Josh Huff had an epic 44-yard catch and run, showing the potential he was drafted for, but it was hard to get excited about that when even making the playoffs was very much in doubt.

Defensive Coordinator Billy Davis was criticized for not doubling Bryant all game. (He did on about half of the passing downs.) The problem is, when they did double him, TE Jason Witten ran rampant. The veteran tight end converted three third-down plays *on a single drive* in the first quarter against Nate Allen and Malcolm Jenkins, forcing Davis to compensate.

He could have switched Fletcher with another CB, but which one? Brandon Boykin and Nolan Carroll already had CB jobs in the nickel and dime packages, respectively. While they could play outside, Fletcher hadn't been trained to cover their roles inside, and he wasn't quick enough anyway.

If Fletcher came out, either raw fourth-round pick Jaylen Watkins would have had to replace him against elite wide receivers, or Watkins would have had to learn a new position on the fly to replace Boykin or Carroll in the sub-packages.

The reality was that the Eagles still had major holes in their talent, especially at DB and ILB. No matter what scheme the coaches installed, that wasn't going to change until the off-season.

Chip Kelly invites fans to expect miracles. He does things like taking the Oregon Ducks to the national championship game even after kicking the starting quarterback off the team—in his second year ever as head coach. In 2013, he turned Nick Foles—a struggling rookie third-rounder—into a Hall of Fame quarterback.

But Kelly isn't magic, and sometimes the results he gets are exactly what you'd expect. Foles regresses to the mean for a young third-round pick. A bad secondary gets abused by an elite QB and WR combo. A waived and much-mocked backup quarterback plays unevenly and can't deliver in a big clutch game with everything on the line.

That's all normal. And normal's not bad, not when you could be Tampa Bay or Tennessee or Oakland. Washington, a very successful franchise headed for its second season of double-digit losses in a row, was showing how much worse than normal things can get. Fans have grown to expect miracles from Chip, and sometimes they just get normal football. The good news is that normal is his floor, and his ceiling is miracles.

FINAL SCORE: COWBOYS 38. EAGLES 27

GAME 15.
WASHINGTON REDSKINS

DECEMBER 20, 2014
FEDEX FIELD, LANDOVER

Any division team is difficult to sweep, since teams know each other so well. Washington had a ton of talent, despite the colorful dysfunction that saw coach Jay Gruden openly mocking various players on his squad.

In 2014, Gruden managed to ridicule (and bench) all three of his quarterbacks, starting with Kirk Cousins. By mid-December, Colt McCoy had gone from being signed as a free agent third-stringer to starting to a season-ending injury, and his coach was stuck with RGIII again. Though no longer the star he was in his rookie season, the young QB had the potential to be dangerous if the Eagles' pass rush didn't recover from its poor showing against Dallas.

Some people were speculating that Philadelphia might pick up Griffin from Washington's recycling pile after the season, so the game functioned as a sort of long-form tryout with the Eagles for him.

So how did Gruden try to motivate his current QB? By insulting him, of course. A month earlier, just before benching Griffin, Gruden had said:

> His biggest thing, he's been coddled for so long...
> Some adversity is striking hard at him now, and how
> he reacts to that off the field, his mental state of mind,

how it affects his confidence, hopefully it's not in a negative way.

No, why would his confidence be hurt by those comments? Wait, there was more. Griffin was still young, right? Just a second-year quarterback? Gruden wasn't buying it.

> He's auditioned long enough. Clock's ticking. He's got to play. We want Robert to excel, we really do. But the last two games, it hasn't been very good, anywhere… His footwork was below average. He took three-step drops when he should have taken five. He took a one-step drop when he should have taken three, on a couple occasions, and that can't happen. He stepped up when he didn't have to step up, and he stepped into pressure. He read the wrong side of the field a couple times. So, from his basic performance, just critiquing Robert, it's not even close to being good enough to what we expect from the quarterback position.

And then Gruden had benched him four days later. As they prepared for their game with Philadelphia, though, with McCoy injured and Cousins—who had lit up the Eagles earlier in the season—even deeper in the doghouse, Gruden was stuck with RGIII. So was he going to make nice? No. He told NFL.com that they had to make sure Griffin never needed to drop back and pass, if they wanted to win.

> It's important for us to have success on first and second down so we don't have to drop back and throw it thirty times a game, have a lead so we don't have to worry about it. [Otherwise] the drop-back reads, progressions have to be accomplished, and that's something we're fighting through right now.[1]

Maybe this was some kind of genius motivational reverse psychology, though Washington's 3-11 record up to that point suggested it wasn't. What was odd was that Griffin's passing numbers

---

1 "Gruden: We need lead so RGIII won't have to drop back" by Conor Orr, NFL.com, December 16, 2014.

weren't bad at all—69.3% completion rate and 7.59 YPC, compared to only 65.6% and 8.14 YPC in his rookie (of the year) season.

So all of that drama seemed like good news for the Eagles, especially since Washington had given up the second-most sacks in the NFL to that point in the 2014 season (fifty-three, compared to Philadelphia's twenty-five).

The bad news was that Philadelphia remained weak at both cornerback positions and one of two safeties, which wasn't going to change until the season was over. It had become apparent you could break this defense by forcing Fletcher to cover your best receiver man-to-man, without safety help.

By this point, talk radio was on fire with criticism of defensive coordinator Billy Davis for stubbornly refusing to bench Fletcher. The team was reluctant to even put in the nickel package against eleven personnel, for fear that Washington would run on them (as New Orleans had done in the 2013 playoffs).

A simpler solution would have been having a linebacker jam tougher receivers at the line of scrimmage before handing them off to Fletcher, which the Eagles did against tough WRs in 2013. Fletcher was theoretically playing press coverage but he had simply not been able to disrupt routes—even against the slight DeSean Jackson.

When the game was actually played, the Eagles made no changes in the secondary, and Washington predictably took advantage. The Eagles' offense performed well. Mark Sanchez passed for 374 yards (while Washington only threw for 220, of which Jackson had 126), and Philadelphia outran the Skins as well. Zach Ertz set an Eagles record with fifteen receptions, the breakout game observers had been expecting all year, for 115 yards just by himself.

But turnovers and bad pass defense killed the Eagles again, as had been the case all year long. Mark Sanchez fumbled one drive away, and threw an interception with 1:31 left and the score tied. Washington then drove to the Eagles' 26 and kicked the game-winning FG with five seconds remaining.

During the game, Bradley Fletcher gave up two passes of over 50 yards to DeSean Jackson. The second one set up Washington's third touchdown, which gave them a 24-14 lead at the end of the third quarter. That was the final straw, and the Eagles finally benched Fletcher in favor of Nolan Carroll.

Fletcher may have been injured; he was inactive for the final game of the season with a reported hip injury. Or maybe it was the coaches' disgust at his inability to play press coverage. But after the game, Coach Kelly and defensive coordinator Billy Davis said nothing about that. They stood by their decision to leave Fletcher in until the moment they didn't.

Davis told reporters:

> I don't regret anything... Like all players, you have to give him a shot to get out of a slump when you're in a slump or you just end up bailing on everybody every time one play goes bad. You can't play ball that way or build confidence that way. I made the decision to switch when I thought it was time to make a switch. Unfortunately, it didn't work out.[1]

Chip Kelly just said what everyone had been thinking for a while: "We just needed to get someone else in there and see what he could do." He did note that Fletcher came back in with the dime package, replacing Carroll in the quasi-linebacker role.

There were two new causes of failure as well: a rash of penalties (thirteen to Washington's three), and Cody Parkey's collapse. The rookie kicker, fighting a groin injury in his kicking leg, missed two of three field goal attempts wide right in the three-point loss after missing only two of thirty-one attempts the entire season.

The defeat completed a late season collapse that was particularly devastating. The Eagles had been openly discussed as a Super Bowl contender and ranked in the NFL's top four after thrashing Dallas on Thanksgiving Day. Then came three consecutive losses that destroyed the high hopes of Eagles fans and put a chink in Chip Kelly's aura of invincibility.

Kelly had never lost three games in a row at Oregon. Heck, his

---

1 "Defense Hurt By Big-Play Passing Game" by Dave Spadaro, PhiladelphiaEagles. com, December 20, 2014.

Ducks never lost two in a row unless you count the 2010 season's National Championship Game and the first game of the following year, against #5 ranked LSU.

The Seattle loss was tough, though hardly a surprise. The loss to Dallas (also at home) was a backbreaker, though. And the road loss to the 3-11 Washington Deadskins was soul-crushing. DeSean Jackson only had three big games all season, and two were against his former teammates.

To no one's surprise, Jackson handled his success with all the class and professionalism of *Here Comes Honey Boo Boo's* Mama June. First, he reprised his bird-flap-and-kick celebration dance from game three (which, as you'll remember, Washington lost), and even added a little wanking motion at the end as a bonus.[1] Then, he graciously said,

> Get the f-ing Birds out of here... They're going home. Tell them goodnight. Toodaloo. Bye bye. The bird's chirpin'.

Recognizing a Philadelphia reporter he knew, he shouted,

> Whatcha doin' here? I bet you they're over there crying. You should go back over there with them.[2]

Jackson, who had told reporters he wasn't bitter over his release by the Eagles and had "moved on," then said that a lot of Eagles players miss him and "constantly tell me how much they miss me..."

I'm guessing those friends must play on the offense, because Jackson went on to insult all of the Eagles defenders who had been his teammates:

> They're very naive and they play how they play. They could care less who is out there or who is at wide receiver, they're going to play their defense the way they play it. That's the Philadelphia Eagle defense.

---

1   "DeSean Jackson flaps wings, mocks Eagles after Washington's win" by Rodger Sherman, *SB Nation*, December 20, 2014.
2   "DeSean: Eagles Are 'Very Naive'" by Tim McManus, *Birds 24/7*, December 20, 2015.

I've been there a lot of years and witnessed a lot of players—wide receivers, tight ends—get off on some huge games on them, and I'm just happy to be on this side and be able to send them home with a loss.[1]

Basically though, Jackson was on the right track. The Eagles offense performed well in the game (aside from Parkey's missed field goals), and the defense let the team down.

The loss to the Skins was terrible, and it called into question the very foundation of Chip Kelly's approach. He has bet the farm on a certain vision of what wins football games—one that you could ridicule as a "good guys finish first" approach. It's a great story if teamwork, selflessness and hard work result in victories, and most people want that to be the reality. Is it though?

One reason that the DeSean Jackson waiver was so controversial was that it symbolized this approach so neatly. For all the logical "football reasons" you can list to cut DeSean—and they really are there—you also know that he is the antithesis of every value Kelly stands for. He is selfish, chronically late, disruptive, immature, and puts himself before the team, time after time.

A lot of teams would say, "Whatever, he's talented. We'll happily take him off your hands." Washington did, and after the 2014 season ended they also grabbed Chris Culliver despite his offensive comments about gays and women, and his arrests for hit and run and possession of brass knuckles.

Then again, Washington was a 3-13 team in 2013, and after adding DeSean they only improved to 4-12.

The game against Washington was precisely the kind of game that Kelly's system was supposed to help win. Everyone understood losing to the defending world champion Seahawks, and to a rival as strong as Dallas.

Washington was different. They were not a good team, and suffered from a lack of cohesion. But at least in this one game, inglorious damaged talent and the cheap ego boost of revenge

---

1   Ibid.

prevailed over all the solid virtues Chip Kelly is promoting. And that's a reason to wonder if his coaching method is based on the way he wants the world to be, rather than the way it actually is.

The bottom line was that, as a result of this loss, the Eagles were not going to the playoffs. They had been 9-3, with a playoff berth all but locked up. And then they choked, hard. As Kyle Scott of *Crossing Broad* told me:

> I'm surprised how it was not a bigger story how big that collapse was, that they were headed for a bye in the wild card round and didn't even make the playoffs. The fact that DeSean put the exclamation point on it like that (with all of his posturing after the game)—why are we not angrier?

Certainly Kelly wasn't too happy. After the game, a reporter asked him what his thoughts were about the team's slide.

> My thoughts are it's gut-wrenching. That's what I was just trying to explain. Whether we lose in the playoff game or whether we lost in this fashion, they're both gut-wrenching situations. We're extremely disappointed. We're frustrated.

FINAL SCORE: SKINS 27, EAGLES 24

GAME 16.
NEW YORK GIANTS

DECEMBER 28, 2014
METLIFE STADIUM, EAST RUTHERFORD

Now only one game remained. It would be an easy one to lose with nothing to play for, better draft position to gain by losing, and the Giants at home seeking revenge for their 27-0 shutout in Philly earlier in the year.

Eagles Nation was losing perspective. People were talking about shaking up the roster, trying different combinations on defense, or starting Matt Barkley at quarterback Sunday to see what he could do.

That's not Chip's approach, as Tommy Lawlor pointed out at the time. Kelly believes in a very particular process, starting with lots of reps in practice.[1] How you perform there (and in games) determines how much playing time you get. He's not going to throw out that process to test out someone doing poorly in practice—such as Marcus Smith II. Kelly had said openly during press conferences that Smith needed to play better, more consistently, in practice to get time on the field.

As bad as the Washington loss was, this Eagles team had gotten to 9-3 despite bad quarterback play all year long, despite leading the league in turnovers, despite relying on a rookie kicker and defending horribly on 3rd and long. These were flaws in scheme and talent, there on tape for all to see, and it finally caught up with Philadelphia

1   "Weird Time" by Tommy Lawlor, *Iggles Blitz*, December 22, 2014.

in week fourteen.

The surprise wasn't that they collapsed, but that they had stayed aloft for so long. Before the season, I had predicted that the Eagles would go 10-6, which was an improvement over 2013's identical record given the tougher schedule. That was exactly where they would end up if they could gut out this last game, against the odds. (Vegas called the Giants a 2.5- or 3- point favorite.)

There was more than just pride at stake. If the Eagles pulled together and won, they would go a long way toward affirming that Chip Kelly's long-term rebuilding program was on the right track. (As long as they got a CB or two during the off-season.)

Nolan Carroll started in place of Fletcher, who was inactive with a "hip injury." Odell Beckham had another big game—185 yards on twelve receptions, including a 63-yard touchdown—to cap one of the best rookie years ever for a wide receiver. But he didn't score three touchdowns despite the Giants' best efforts, and Nate Allen intercepted a pass to stop another drive.

The Eagles returned to form with solid passing by Sanchez (23-36 for 292 yards, two TDs and one interception) and another blocked punt (by James Casey) for another touchdown (by Trey Burton). Jordan Matthews and Zach Ertz had big receiving games, Shady ran for 99 yards, and Cody Parkey kicked two field goals to shake off his rough game against Washington.

It wasn't glorious but it was a win. And it was the end of the season.

FINAL SCORE: EAGLES 34, GIANTS 26

POSTMORTEM

DECEMBER 29, 2014

The disappointing end to the year raised a lot of questions, many difficult to answer. What happened to the intangible benefits of the ego-less team spirit Coach Kelly worked so hard to build? Shouldn't it have prevented the late-season collapse?

Did the magic dissolve as the season wore on, or did Kelly's tricks sneak some wins early in the year that masked this team's flaws? Center Jason Kelce figured it was the latter when he talked to reporters in the late spring.

> I've said this before, and this might piss off a few people, but in all honesty, we started off 9-3, we started off really, really good. And we got lucky quite a few times early in the year to win games that we probably shouldn't have been in. And I think the fact that we ended the season the way we did, didn't make the playoffs, in hindsight, it's almost a good thing because it forces the coaches, it forces the organization to reevaluate what we had.[1]

Were all the injuries a sign that the frenetic pace of practice and games couldn't be sustained in the NFL, even with all the sports science Jeffrey Lurie could buy?

Were Chip Kelly's physical requirements for defensive backs unrealistic? Bradley Fletcher and Cary Williams were just the size and

---

1   "Three Eagles Leftovers From OTAs" by Sheil Kapadia, *Birds 24/7*, May 31, 2015.

type of cornerback he wanted, but they were a glaring vulnerability that other teams exploited over and over.

Meanwhile, even with increased use of nickel and dime packages, Brandon Boykin played just 42.7% of defensive snaps, and was not allowed to move outside.[1] Sure, he was not ideal size against someone like Dez Bryant, but Fletcher was already giving up touchdowns to Dez. How much worse could he have been? And why not play him against DeSean Jackson (also 5'10") or Odell Beckham, Jr. (5'11")?

Safety depth was a problem as well. For all his problems, Nate Allen played 89% of downs, twenty-eighth out of some 900 defensive players, and Malcolm Jenkins had the highest percentage of snaps of all NFL defenders, at 99.6%. The Eagles just didn't have anyone they trusted to spell these two.

What had happened to Nick Foles?

The Eagles passed a lot in 2014, with 256 more yards than 2013, thirty-one more first downs—and twelve more interceptions. They probably passed too much. The real offensive decline was in the run game, and Chip Kelly's tempo offense works best with balance between runs and passes. Any incomplete throw stops the clock and allows opponents to substitute.

Foles threw deep often (and inaccurately) in 2014. He led the league in long pass percentage, according to *Pro Football Focus*. Sanchez threw deep much less, about the league average; just thirty-seven attempts over 20 yards to Foles's 59. They both were pretty bad at it, making only 35%, which ranked them twenty-sixth and twenty-seventh respectively out of thirty-eight qualifying QBs. That's Matthew Stafford/Eli Manning territory.

There are good reasons to be skeptical of the advanced statistics generated by *Pro Football Focus*, a website that reviews each play to generate "signature statistics" such as the percentage of deep passes (over 20 yards) that were catchable. Furthermore, this particular number is linked to the wide receiver, not quarterback, so throws by

---

1 "Defensive Player Snap Count Stats: 2014 NFL Season," SportingCharts.com, undated..

Sanchez and Foles in 2014 (combined) are compared against Foles and Vick (combined) in 2013.

Nonetheless, the results are striking. For all Philly wide receivers and quarterbacks in 2013, 43% of deep passes (twenty-nine of sixty-seven) were catchable. That was seventh best in the NFL. In 2014, even though there were more deep throws, the catchable percentage dropped to 32% (twenty-one of seventy-three). Only six teams were worse.

Diehard fans will remember two bad drops in the end zone by Riley Cooper in 2014, against Indianapolis and San Francisco. Those were the Eagles' only deep drops all year, however, according to PFF (which counted one in 2013). Jeremy Maclin completed all nine catchable bombs thrown his way, scoring five touchdowns—but the other twenty-five of his thirty-four deep throws were uncatchable.

Despite his manly return after getting suplexed in the Washington game—or perhaps because of it—Nick Foles seemed to feel pressure more and flee it. There was a lot of talk before the season about how he would likely regress from his historic 27-2 TD to INT performance in 2013. As it turned out, he literally regressed, moving farther and farther back in the face of pressure until it was often a long throw just to get back to the line of scrimmage.

Foles took twenty-eight sacks over thirteen games in 2013. In 2014, he only suffered nine sacks in eight games, but he often threw off his back foot, with bad results. On November 2nd, when the Eagles played Houston, the team's great retired safety Brian Dawkins tweeted:

> take the sack dog. We (defense) got u if we punt!
> @BrianDawkins. 10:33A.M. November 2, 2014.

Of course it's not as easy as that. Foles took two sacks on a single set of downs against Houston—and was knocked out for the rest of the year with his broken collarbone on the second one.

When Mercilus delivered that injury, Foles was leading the league in turnovers (seven INTs, three fumbles). A favorable turnover ratio is a big element of Chip Kelly's strategy, and he wasn't going to let that continue.

Unfortunately, Sanchez had just as many interceptions, though his accuracy and release time were better. He wasn't great at deep or sideline throws. The other thing that really limited his game was his reluctance to run, which makes the read option play worthless.

Of the two rookie receivers, Jordan Matthews was a huge success. According to Eliot Shorr-Parks, he rated as the NFL's second-best slot receiver.[1] Huff was harder to evaluate. His outstanding blocking doesn't show up in statistics, but will be even more valuable as the team shifts back to balance between run and pass. Huff's fumble against Arizona was disastrous, though, and he had way too many drops; by PFF's count, he dropped fully one-third of his catchable throws (four of twelve).

On the positive side, he showed the physicality and elusiveness that make him potentially dangerous. Huff caused six missed tackles in 210 snaps in 2014[2]; Riley Cooper caused only two in 980 snaps, and even Maclin had only eight in 1,043 snaps. The rookie also showed an ability to move the sticks, often by putting his head down and pounding out the extra yards needed. Huff had four first downs on just eight receptions.

His special teams work was also impressive, and it wasn't just his two kick return touchdowns; the wide receiver had four tackles as well.

1   "Phillip Dorsett, Devin Smith would best complement Eagles receivers Jordan Matthews, Josh Huff" by Eliot Shorr-Park, NJ.com, April 15, 2015 .

2   Ibid.

MISSING DESEAN?

DECEMBER 31, 2014

One big question loomed over the others. Was DeSean Jackson's absence responsible for the team's offensive struggles? Had Chip Kelly's decision to cut him been as devastating as many predicted?

It makes a lot of sense that Riley Cooper suffered without a dangerous deep threat to draw safeties over to the other side of the field. Perhaps his big year in 2013 was purely a result of that defensive strategy, in which case his multiyear contract with lots of guaranteed money was a disaster. Going into 2015, it would actually cost the team more money to cut Cooper than to leave him on roster. It may have been the only thing keeping him on the squad after his weak 2014 season.

It's harder to link Foles' regression to the loss of his top receiver. Statistics just don't support that theory. Jeremy Maclin ended the year with numbers eerily similar to Jackson's the year before—eighty-five receptions for 1,318 yards and ten TDs, compared to eighty-two for 1,332 and nine. Both Jackson and Maclin had career years in their sixth NFL seasons, when they first played for Kelly.

Jackson, meanwhile, regressed to fifty-six catches for 1,169 yards and six TDs playing for Washington, almost identical to his best year under Andy Reid (in 2009). He did more damage deep, but that was the result of better deep passing (especially when Kirk Cousins was their quarterback).

In other words, it looked like Chip Kelly helped DeSean more than DeSean helped the coach.

The main problem for the Eagles was that Foles and Sanchez couldn't connect on long throws with anybody (which made Maclin's production all the more impressive). Either they didn't see wide open receivers, or they missed them with errant throws. It's hard to see how adding another open receiver to miss would have helped.

In another way, though, the loss of DeSean probably hurt Kelly's squad a lot by setting back the rebuilding of talent a year. The Eagles' roster decisions in 2014 were dominated by the need to replace Jackson, and the cost of that project was high.

Knowing they were going to ditch DeSean, the team agreed to unfavorable deals with Maclin and Cooper that came back to bite them, forcing them to keep Cooper and let Maclin walk. And Howie Roseman was forced to use two of his three top draft picks in 2014 on wide receivers when they desperately needed defensive backs, offensive line depth and possibly a project quarterback. The Eagles paid heavily for that DB weakness.

FRONT OFFICE THUNDERDOME

JANUARY 2, 2015

For the first time ever in his head coaching career, Chip Kelly's season ended when the regular season did. It had to kill him, as proud as he no doubt was that his Ducks destroyed Florida State in the Rose Bowl and headed into the National Championship Game favored by a touchdown. He was Moses, unable to enter the Promised Land and watching his people go on without him. Bittersweet.

Asked if he would attend the Rose Bowl game against Florida State, Kelly told reporters he had work to do but would try to make the big show at AT&T Stadium. Within a couple of days, we learned what he meant by "work to do."

There was a Byzantine power struggle in the Eagles' front office that week. It began late in the afternoon on New Year's Eve, when GM Howie Roseman fired Kelly's ally, Player Personnel Director Tom Gamble. No reason was given, but the purge was immediately understood in the context of the power struggle between Roseman and Chip Kelly, which had burst into public view in November with the leaks that Roseman was unhappy with Nick Foles.

Gamble was Kelly's man in Howie's scouting department, a highly respected NFL veteran who Roseman had tried (but failed) to recruit before Kelly arrived. He joined the Eagles in 2013 when Chip asked him, but the bigger reason was that Gamble's father—the former GM and President of the Eagles—lived in the Philadelphia area and was very ill. (He died on January 28, 2014.) Gamble was re-hired by the San Francisco 49ers within a month of his firing.

The Philadelphia beat writers took Gamble's firing to be yet another in a long line of bureaucratic victories for Roseman. *Inquirer* columnist Mike Sielski wrote:

> What Howie wants, Howie gets. There is no other conclusion to draw from the Eagles' dismissal of Tom Gamble... There's a long list of executives who have left the Eagles because they were in some measure of conflict with Roseman... Chip Kelly's now on notice: That's a tenacious general manager you're working with, Coach, and if you expected your authority to be complete and unquestioned, you've come to the wrong place.[1]

Geoff Mosher added:

> Roseman has since seized control of the front office and has altered the personnel and scouting staff to fit his vision of a mainstreamed process, but the drama persists and continued with Gamble's departure.[2]

In an article titled "Roseman gains edge in Eagles power struggle," Jeff McLane listed Roseman's victims:

> GM Tom Heckert left in 2010. Ryan Grigson, Gamble's predecessor, left in 2012. Longtime team president Joe Banner stepped down a few months later. In 2013, director of pro personnel Lou Riddick did not have his contract renewed. And now Gamble is out.[3]

More simply, McLane tweeted the score:

> Howie 1, Chip 0.
> @Jeff_McLane. 11:22A.M. December 31, 2014.

---

1   "Gamble's dismissal shows that Kelly does not have complete authority" by Mike Sielski, *Philadelphia Inquirer*, January 3, 2015.

2   "Gamble's ouster signals Eagles' front-office turmoil—again" by Geoff Mosher, *CSN Philly*, December 31, 2014.

3   "Roseman gains edge in Eagles power struggle" by Jeff McLane, *Philadelphia Inquirer*, January 2, 2015.

CSN Philly's Reuben Frank went even further. He quoted "a one-time Eagles front-office exec" (likely Joe Banner) as saying that

> Jeffrey sees Howie as a messiah. Howie can do no wrong in his eyes.[1]

There was only one problem with this interpretation. Two days after Gamble's dismissal, Howie Roseman was stripped of his GM responsibilities and kicked upstairs with a raise, after Chip met with owner Jeffrey Lurie and presented his vision of a better future for the team. Roseman was now the "executive vice president of football operations," according to the team's official statement, and his responsibilities included:

> ...directing contract negotiations, salary cap management, and NFL strategic matters, while overseeing the team's medical staff, equipment staff and more.

McLane pumped out an updated tweet:

> My bad: Chip 1, Howie 0.
>   @Jeff_McLane. 3:38 P.M. January 2, 2015.[2]

Howie remained in charge of contracts, free agent re-signings, and the salary cap, though, and that was a big concern going forward. It's dangerous to have someone in such a key role with lots of reason to resent, and possibly undercut, the coach.

The details of everything that went down may never be known, but three of the Eagles' beat writers presented powerful (if somewhat speculative) visions that are worth reading if you like this kind of manly soap opera.

Geoff Mosher of CSN Philly painted a dark and compelling portrait that rang true but suggested future conflict between Kelly and Roseman, whom former staff paint as shrewd but paranoid.

---

1   "Front-office discord creates concern about Chip Kelly's future" by Reuben Frank, *CSN Philly*, January 1, 2014.
2   Jeff McLane [@Jeff_McLane]. January 2, 2015. Retrieved from https://twitter.com/Jeff_McLane/status/551160511325569025

The idea that Kelly and Roseman are out of each other's way now is absurd. They still have to work together when it comes to player retention, free-agent signings and other areas where money and personnel blend.

What happens when Kelly wants to keep a player Roseman believes is overvalued?[1]

On a lighter but no less shrewd note, the *Inquirer's* Bob Ford had great fun ridiculing the idea that Roseman was "promoted."

As his parting gift from the world of real power in the organization, Roseman got a shiny new title, a contract extension, and as much tinsel as the team could publicly layer onto his demotion.

The announcement read like a come-on for a gas station opening, the kind that promises "prizes, balloons, and more." Roseman will continue to handle contract negotiations; salary-cap management; and NFL strategic matters; as well as overseeing "the team's medical staff, equipment staff, and more."

And more! Not that sorting out a pesky hip-pad issue in the equipment room wouldn't be enough to satisfy any eager executive on a job well done, but Roseman will get to do *even more*.[2]

And finally, a recap by the *Inquirer's* Zach Berman confirmed the paranoia part of Mosher's portrait. He quotes an ex-employee as saying that "Howie is motivated by fear" (of missing great prospects, of not being the best) and offers a concise summary of Roseman's talents and limits:

"He could tell you that a guy would go in the second round—he couldn't tell you if that player would be good," a former team employee said.[3]

---

1 "Eagles' shake-up revisited: Why was Roseman pushed aside?" by Geoff Mosher, *CSN Philly*, January 6, 2015.

2 "Kelly's move against Roseman was as quick as his offense" by Bob Ford, *Philadelphia Inquirer*, January 5, 2015.

3 "The rise and fall of Howie Roseman as Eagles GM" by Zach Berman, *Philadelphia Inquirer*, January 10, 2015.

Knowing the draft value of a player you want is incredibly helpful. But would Roseman be willing to help Kelly look good, after the coach pushed him out of his dream job? It would be impossible to know until the last draft pick was submitted on May 2nd. And maybe not even then.

The 2014 draft was widely considered to be a bust, with Josh Huff struggling, Jaylen Watkins barely visibly, Taylor Hart inactive all year, Ed Reynolds on the practice squad and Marcus Smith II hardly able to get on the field.

Amidst the turmoil, recriminations leaked out. Kelly told reporters that the Marcus Smith II pick was ultimately Howie's decision, which is true from an organization chart point of view, but didn't tell us who really wanted him chosen.

Meanwhile, the *Daily News's* Les Bowen reported that some scouts had been upset because Kelly changed their draft board after it had been set. They did not say which players or potential picks were involved, though, and it was not clear which side of this tiff Tom Gamble had been on.

COACHING HIRES

JANUARY 22, 2015

For the second year in a row, Philadelphia's quarterbacks coach got promoted to offensive coordinator for another NFL team. After the 2013 season it was Bill Lazor becoming the OC in Miami, where he promptly installed an imitation-Chip-Kelly offense.

In 2014 it was Bill Musgrave—Oregon's Hall of Fame QB, second only to Marcus Mariota among Ducks in career passing yards—who got poached. For all his hard work (or maybe as punishment for Foles' retrenchment and Mark Sanchez's same-trenchment), he was sentenced to several years as offensive coordinator of the Oakland Raiders. Musgrave promised to bring some of Kelly's plays to Oakland, which was the victim of Nick Foles' record-setting seven-touchdown game in 2013.[1]

His replacement as Eagles QB coach was Ryan Day, the offensive coordinator and QB coach at Boston College.

As a player, Day was also Chip Kelly's first great quarterback at the University of New Hampshire, and no doubt some will criticize Kelly for "New Hampshire bias" on top of his much-discussed "Oregon bias." But the hiring impressed some of the more notable national football analysts, starting with Chris Brown of *Smart Football* and *Grantland.*

Bruce Feldman of ESPN, who had just published "The QB: The Making of Modern Quarterbacks", added this on Twitter:

---

1   "Raiders offensive coordinator Bill Musgrave will use some of Chip Kelly's plays" by Jerry McDonald, *San Jose Mercury News,* January 20, 2015.

> Tough loss for #BC. Ryan Day is considered by his peers as one of the rising stars in coaching. Now goes to work w/ his old buddy Chip Kelly
> @BruceFeldmanCFB. 4:01 P.M. January 22, 2015.

Kelly then rebuilt the Eagles' personnel staff around thirty-year-old wunderkind Ed Marynowitz, who has worked for the Eagles for years. Despite his youth, Marynowitz was Alabama's head of recruiting from 2008 to 2011 and met with many of the NFL's personnel managers during that stretch.

He apparently impressed them, too; no one seemed to have a bad word to say about him. And yes, he's a "football guy"—Marynowitz was a star quarterback for LaSalle, a Philadelphia-area college where he still holds many passing records.

Marynowitz did not replace Howie Roseman as general manager. His new title was vice president of player personnel, allowing Roseman to keep as big a role in contracts and renegotiations as owner Jeffery Lurie thought was wise.

Marynowitz had reportedly clashed with Roseman, and this shakeup implies that Kelly's move to take control over personnel was really about getting the Eagles' existing "football guys" back in charge of player selection, and giving this impressive young talent room to grow. Marynowitz looked to be a good fit for Chip.[1]

After the draft, Marynowitz replaced Roseman's three top scouts as well, and Kelly talked about the advantages of integrating coaches and scouts. Clearly, it had not worked well for the two camps to be fighting each other the previous year.

Not surprisingly, the Birds also replaced their defensive backs coach, John Lovett, with Denver's highly regarded Cory Undlin, who was released when Broncos head coach John Fox got canned.

Bradley Fletcher and Cary Williams were tall, strong cornerbacks who generally stayed with receivers, but never could figure out how to jam them at the line or when to turn their heads around to play the ball on long passes. This resulted in a lot of penalties as well as

---

1 "More on the Front Office" by Tommy Lawlor, *Iggles Blitz*, February 5, 2015.

deep completions, and the coaches should've been able to improve their technique.

On the other hand, the coverage schemes and the decision where to play Boykin were more likely the responsibility of Defensive Coordinator Billy Davis, or perhaps Chip Kelly himself. Neither was going anywhere.

EVALUATING THE PLAYERS

FEBRUARY, 2015

With the coaching staff settled, it was time to look at roster needs.

Everyone knew that safety Nate Allen and cornerbacks Cary Williams and Bradley Fletcher were marginal—including other teams' offensive coordinators. By the end of the season they were picking on Fletcher so relentlessly it would constitute illegal bullying in most schools.

The coaches wouldn't replace Fletcher with free agent CB pickup Nolan Carroll until the last quarter of game fifteen, and we have no way to know whether that was due to Carroll doing poorly in practice, coaching stubbornness, reluctance to change the roster mid-season, or a desire to keep Carroll focused on the dime package he specialized in.

Furthermore, the retrenchment of safety Earl Wolff and slot CB Brandon Boykin was a surprise. After six interceptions in 2013, Boykin should have feasted behind a DL that jumped from thirty-seven sacks to forty-nine (second in the NFL). Instead, he faded into obscurity.

Wolff looked very promising in 2013, but came nowhere near beating out Nate Allen for the strong safety job the following season. He was never really the same after getting injured in the Green Bay game in mid-November, 2013, and his 2014 season ended on November 18th with some "mini micro-fracture surgery."

The hope was that he had unresolved knee problems all year, and would be healed from the surgery in time for the 2015 training camp. But there was a skeptical note in the coaches' comments about Wolff this year that was not encouraging. They appeared to feel that he should have toughed it out through his injury better or played harder; it wasn't clear.

It's possible that the sports science monitoring may give the coaches a sense of when a player isn't pushing themselves as hard as possible to return. This is just speculation, but Coach Kelly's comments about Wolff and Mychal Kendricks fit that theory.

The injuries on the front line highlighted the need for more young offensive linemen; three of the team's five starters were over thirty. But the most discussed need for an upgrade was at quarterback. Nick Foles started the year as one of the most promising young quarterbacks in the league, one strong season away from a big payday. He ended it injured, with his reputation in tatters and the Eagles content to let his rookie contract play out.

Chip Kelly's best college quarterback, Marcus Mariota, went pro after winning the Heisman Trophy and taking the Ducks to the National Championship Game (which they lost). Everyone assumed that Chip wanted Mariota to replace Foles, and Chip did nothing to change their minds. He reportedly told multiple other GMs that the Hawaiian QB would bring multiple Super Bowl trophies to whoever drafted him.

The Eagles drafted #20, though, and Mariota was widely pegged to be the second pick overall, behind rival QB James Winston (who Mariota defeated in the first national college semifinal game on New Year's Day). The price to move up that far would be astronomical, and Kelly "dispelled" the notion that he would do so, though it didn't stop Eagles fans from imagining every possible scenario that might make it possible.

There were many positives for the team in 2014. Cody Parkey went to the Pro Bowl and broke the NFL rookie record for scoring with 150 points. He made every one of his 54 extra points and thirty-two of thirty-six field goals (including four of four from over 50 yards). In 2013, Alex Henery had made just twenty-three of twenty-eight.

Darren Sproles, Chris Maragos, Josh Huff and Bryan Braman turned the Eagles' special teams unit into the NFL's best. Jordan Matthews was the second-best slot receiver in the NFL as a rookie, behind only Randall Cobb, with 484 yards and eight touchdowns.[1] Brandon Graham grew into a great OLB, capable of dropping into coverage without giving up any of his rushing ability; in turn, his newfound versatility freed up Connor Barwin to rush more, and he responded with a career best 14.5 sacks.

In fact, much of the perceived failure of the 2014 draft class was a result of the strength of the linebackers and defensive front line. DE Taylor Hart and OLB Marcus Smith weren't able to outplay veterans to earn snaps as depth players, but the veterans were kicking ass. It was too early to describe the rookies as failures.

At OLB, Smith would have had to outplay Trent Cole and Brandon Graham, two superb players. Hart was beaten out by his mentor and fellow ex-Duck, Brandon Bair. If Hart and Bair were even close in skill, it only made sense to play the thirty-year-old veteran now and let the twenty-four-year old lift weights and acclimatize. (He reported to the 2015 OTAs twenty-five pounds heavier than he had been a year earlier.)

College Coach Kelly is committed to player competitions deciding who gets on the field, and is very used to the idea of a redshirt year from his college coaching days. He certainly wasn't going to play a rookie who did worse in practice, just because he was a first (or fifth) round draft pick. On December 22, a reporter asked the coach if he would play some of the rookies in week seventeen, since the Eagles were out of the playoffs. Kelly was direct:

> If they warrant playing time, and we've been with these guys since preseason camp, then they'll play. But we are not going to turn around now and say, "Because you haven't beaten anybody out in the last 15 weeks, we're going to let you play this week."…
> Let's get this straight, we're going to win the

1   "Phillip Dorsett, Devin Smith would best complement Eagles receivers Jordan Matthews, Josh Huff" by Eliot Shorr-Parks, NJ.com, April 15, 2015.

football game, so there's no, "Hey, let's go see what [the young guys] can do." Our job is to go play the New York Giants and we're going to do everything we can to beat the New York Giants.

Kelly also has a principle of not attacking his players, even after they do poorly. To this day, he has not criticized DeSean Jackson for either his on-field play or off-field behavior. And at that same December press conference, he declined an easy opportunity to criticize Bradley Fletcher, even though the CB had just been benched for the fourth quarter.

A team source put it to me this way:

Whether Chip likes a guy or not, he's not going to throw his players under the bus. Chip just doesn't work that way. On talk radio, he gets killed for a lot of stuff. But here's the thing, I just don't think he cares.

I don't think he gives a shit, not one iota, what anyone in the media or fandom or talk radio thinks. I think he only cares about the guys in his locker room, the guys on his staff, and winning football games.

HANG-GLIDING
IN A HURRICANE

MARCH 10, 2015

In Chip Kelly's first two years, the Eagles were very conservative in free agency, signing inexpensive deals with undervalued, mid-range players who had room to grow.

Apparently that was Howie Roseman's idea, because Chip as GM immediately started chasing the big-ticket star FAs. The Birds signed Byron Maxwell, whose $63 million contract was the third-largest behind only Ndamukong Suh's monstrous $114 million pact and Darrelle Revis' relatively modest $70 million handshake.[1]

The Eagles also chased Patriots safety Devin McCourty hard, offering him more than the $47.5 million he accepted to stay home in New England. Even that lower amount was fifth-largest in the NFL, while Jeremy Maclin's deal with Kansas City—which the Eagles wouldn't match—was fourth at $55 million.

Kelly began his first stint as an NFL general manager the same way he coaches—fast, decisive, and not giving a damn with what anybody thinks. In the first three days of the official NFL year, when free agency and trading first become possible again, he outmaneuvered the entire rest of the league put together by adding seven players, letting eight go, and re-signing two (including emerging stud OLB Brandon Graham). Everyone was left staring, confused and awed.

---

1   "2015 Free Agents," Spotrac.com, 2015..

I won't even try to get into all of the crazy turns, from the NFL Network falsely reporting that the Rams were giving Philly the #10 pick *and* Sam Bradford for Foles, to 49ers RB Frank Gore agreeing to a deal before changing his mind. It wasn't for the faint of heart.

Forget the "emotional rollercoaster" cliché. This was hang-gliding in a hurricane, soaring toward the sun on a thermal one minute, then plummeting to the cliffs the next. Roller coasters only offer the illusion of danger. This was the real thing. Chip had the confidence to jump off the cliff and either soar through the sky or crash to death on the rocks.

Here is one thing that happened, in early March according to MMQB's Jenny Vrentas.[1] Terry Pegula, the new owner of the Buffalo Bills, was relaxing on his yacht "Top Five" in West Palm Beach with a few friends—coach Rex Ryan and some key assistants, team president Russ Brandon, and GM Doug Whaley. Wine and cigars were enjoyed.

Suddenly, Whaley's phone rang. It was someone with the Eagles. "Any interest in LeSean McCoy?" Rex Ryan loves to "ground it and pound it" and had no good QB prospects; of course there was interest in the NFL's third-best rusher.

The only problem was that the Eagles wanted draft picks, and the Bills had already traded away their 2015 first round pick to move up for WR Sammy Watkins in 2014. So Whaley, according to Vrentas, told the Eagles representative to "Just do me a favor and look at our roster."

They hung up, and called back quickly with a simple request— give us Kiko Alonso, a star linebacker for Chip Kelly at Oregon and the NFL's 2013 Defensive Rookie of the Year. Straight up, no picks, no money. Done. The whole thing went down in less than a half hour.

Like almost every player Kelly acquired in 2015, Alonso was recovering from a major injury—in this case, a torn ACL that cost Kiko his second pro season.

The deals came fast and furious. Veterans Trent Cole, Todd

1 "The Rex Effect" by Jenny Vrentas, *MMQB*, April 14, 2015.

Herremans and Cary Williams were released. CB Walter Thurmond was signed. Starting quarter back Nick Foles was traded, along with a second round pick, for St. Louis Rams QB Sam Bradford, a former #1 overall pick. By the third day of free agency, both DeMarco Murray and Ryan Mathews had signed on to form the NFL's best backfield while crippling the hated Cowboys, and stunned fans either cheered or struggled fiercely to maintain their habitual grumpiness.

The Eagles made too many transactions to list. Here are a few highlights:

- They added two much-needed cornerbacks, Seattle's excellent Byron Maxwell and a potential steal in the oft-injured Walter Thurmond III, who was Chip's first defensive star as Oregon's rookie coach in 2009.
- For about the same amount of cap money, Philly replaced LeSean McCoy, the #3 NFL rusher, with DeMarco Murray, the #1 rusher, PLUS stud inside linebacker Kiko Alonso (plugging a major defensive hole) AND Ryan Mathews, another great if often-injured RB. Both backs are quick and powerful north-south runners more suited to Kelly's scheme than McCoy, who was admittedly great but declined in 2013 at twenty-seven, as most RBs do.
- The combination of Murray, Mathews and Darren Sproles resembled Chip's great Oregon backfields, with two quick, tough RBs and a "TAZR"[1], like De'Anthony Thomas, who can line up as a tailback, wide out or slot receiver. The Eagles even had Jeff Maehl and Josh Huff to block and catch the occasional pass, as they did for the Ducks.
- The overdeveloped running game looked set to fix the Eagles' red zone woes and offer QB insurance in case Sam Bradford flops or gets hurt. Backup Mark Sanchez threw a lot of picks in 2014 and lacks a good deep ball, but he hands off with the best of them.

---

1   "Introducing the 'Tazer' position" by Rob Moseley, *The Eugene Register Guard*, April 14, 2009.

- Jeremy Maclin, the team's best WR, signed with Kansas City. That stung, but the Chiefs vastly overpaid him at $11 million a year, and the Eagles let him walk.
- Since WRs are overpaid and RBs are undervalued, it was smart to get runners in free agency and draft receivers at low rookie pay rates.
- Releasing Trent Cole and re-signing Brandon Graham to start in his place gave the team a young, ascending OLB in place of a fading lion who cost $4 million a year more. The starting linebackers (Barwin, Kendricks, Alonso and Graham) were now rock-solid, though depth remained a question at OLB.
- Signing RB DeMarco Murray—the core of the Cowboys' impressive 2014 offense—and WR Miles Austin hurt the Cowboys as much as it helped Philadelphia. It was something like psychological warfare. Dallas actually released Austin before the 2014 season, but under the ridiculous $54 million contract they gave him in 2010, he will eat up $5.1 million of the Cowboys' salary cap—seventh most on the team—in 2015 while he catches passes against them.

The Eagles still needed an elite QB, whose name was not yet known. Fans had hoped Bradford was just trade bait to finagle Mariota; Cleveland confirmed that they had offered the Eagles a first round pick for him. Chip Kelly held two press conferences during the week free agency opened up and "dispelled" the notion that he would trade the farm for Mariota. Kelly never said he wouldn't trade for Mariota, though; he just said he wouldn't "mortgage the team's future."

FEELING A DRAFT

APRIL 30 - MAY 2

With Chip Kelly's first draft as general manager approaching, fans were riveted, with a mounting certainty (and excitement) that Chip would engineer some massive, improbable deal and land Marcus Mariota as his franchise quarterback. For a vocal minority, this was precisely what they feared; that Kelly would get robbed by wily veteran GMs who knew how badly Kelly wanted to reunite with his best college quarterback.

The coach's denials dissuaded no one, and of course pre-draft statements are full of smokescreens and misdirection with any coach.

Meanwhile, the team quietly began Phase 1 of OTAs, voluntary workouts not directed by the coaches. There were some absences in 2015 after 100% attendance the year before; notably guard Evan Mathis (who was asking for more money for the second year in a row) and ILB Mychal Kendricks (who instead worked out with his brother, another ILB who had just graduated from college, amid signs that Mychal had fallen out of Coach Kelly's favor.)

Tampa Bay had the first pick and selected Jameis Winston, as everyone expected. NFL insiders were reporting that Chip Kelly had offered absurd packages of picks and players for Mariota, confirming the worst fears of his doubters. Ian Rapoport tweeted:

> What package are #Eagles talking about to go to No.
> 1 or No. 2? Two first rounders, a third rounder, Fletcher
> Cox, Boykin, Kendricks, more. Wow.
> @Rapsheet. 4:57 P.M. April 30, 2015.

If there was such a discussion, it's much more likely that the offer was those draft picks and any one of those players, not all three. In any case, it doesn't matter, because the rookie GM walked away from the deal. As Kelly told reporters later:

> It was just a really steep price. It was like driving into a nice neighborhood and looking at a house, and they tell you the price and you walk away. We didn't walk in the front door and take a look around.

In the end, the Eagles drafted a bunch of players that fit Kelly's parameters, though he disproved a couple of stereotypes (such as "Oregon Bias"). Kelly did select two more PAC-12 players who had performed well against the Ducks, but he did not over-draft his favorite prospects or take wild gambles.

The coach's first round choice was Nelson Agholor, a WR from USC with measurables very similar to Jeremy Maclin's. The remaining five were all defensive players, and three were defensive backs.

Kelly traded up in the second round to get the very athletic DB Eric Rowe (6'1", 205 lbs) who played both safety and cornerback at Utah. That move cost him one of his two fifth round picks, and a swap of the other for a sixth round pick. At the same time, Kelly made the most conservative trade possible—giving up his fourth round pick in the current draft for a third round pick in 2016.

His picks were high character players as well. Four of the six were on their all-conference academic teams, and five of six were scheduled to graduate by the summer. JaCorey Shepherd was about to finish at the University of Kansas Business School with a degree in Management and Leadership; he worked with Big Brothers/Big Sisters and won KU's community service award. Nelson Agholor moved to the U.S. from Nigeria at age five and radiates the intense positivity that the Eagles loved in his fellow WR Jordan Matthews. At his first press conference in Philadelphia, the USC WR was already throwing out his own version of Coach Kelly's Chipisms, those catchy nuggets of football wisdom. You might call the rookie's version "Agholorithms":

"My high school coach always told me 'maintaining is just a form of regression.' You try to get better every day."

"I think I understand the way life works. I don't feel like I'm entitled to anything… Work like a peasant. That's the mindset."

"I control the controllable. Want to be judged on things I can control, like preparation."

There were no Oregon Ducks acquired, even among the sixteen undrafted free agents that the Eagles signed immediately after the draft ended. Kelly's window of insight from his days coaching the Ducks was closing after two years in the NFL. Since many top prospects go pro after three years playing in college, this was the last group at Oregon that Kelly was sure to have coached, and he didn't draft any of them.

Oregon's star cornerback Ifo Ekpre-Olomu, an All American, was a highly skilled, 5'10" ballhawk who suffered a very bad knee injury in December of 2014. The Eagles passed him over twice in the sixth round, opting for cornerbacks JaCorey Shepherd of Kansas and Randall Evans of Kansas State. Shepherd, a shutdown corner who converted from wide receiver, may have dropped in the draft because he was only an inch taller than Ekpre-Olomu and ran a slow (4.65) 40-yard dash due to a hamstring injury. The Eagles saw good value based on his elite ball skills and character.

The acquisition of Shepherd and free agent Walter Thurmond (5'11"), along with Kelly's comment that Brandon Boykin would be considered as an outside corner in the 2015 training camp, indicated that the team's rigid height standards for cornerbacks might be softening. Then again, when OTAs opened in late May, Thurmond had converted to safety, and Nolan Carroll was lined up alongside Byron Maxwell as the other first team outside CB.

Kelly obviously was determined to end the Eagles' secondary problems by any means necessary, acquiring six DBs between free agency and the draft. This heavy focus—and trading away one of the team's seven picks for future considerations—left some gaps however.

The biggest was on the offensive line. With injuries healed, the Eagles had three excellent starters back, but both starting guards were cut. Thirty-year-old Alan Barbre was penciled in to replace Evan Mathis at left guard, and three marginal depth linemen were going to compete on the right side. The Eagles had not drafted a lineman since 2013. They brought in four UDFA offensive linemen among the sixteen they signed, but the team remained vulnerable to another rash of injuries like that one that disrupted the 2014 season.

Likewise, the starting linebackers were very strong and there was a logjam at ILB, but outside linebacker depth was very thin. The only returning players were Travis Long, returning from his second ACL tear in two years, and Marcus Smith II, the draft bust from 2014. Short of a trade or a surprise UDFA success, Smith would have no problem getting on the field in 2015. The team could only hope that whatever shortcomings kept him off of it in his rookie year had been addressed.

The biggest concern, though, was at quarterback. Sam Bradford was a skilled passer with spread offense experience, who would be playing with a talented front line and receiver corps for the first time in the NFL. His knee was a major worry; two ACL tears in two years on the same knee are much more of a concern that the same injuries on different knees. Behind him, the Eagles had only Mark Sanchez, with the weak arm and penchant for turnovers, Matt Barkley and Tim Tebow.

The team's strength in the run game was a form of quarterback insurance, and Kelly was probably wise not to make an RGIII-priced trade for Mariota, but the most important position in football was this team's weakest. That's not good, no matter how great your program or scheme might be.

Kelly's program really needs a catchy name like "Air Raid" or "Gang Green." After the ups and downs of 2014, "Controlled Chaos" seems as fitting as any.

STARS, OR CORPS?

APRIL 8, 2015

LeSean McCoy had grown up in Pennsylvania, gone to college at Pittsburgh and played his whole career in Philadelphia, so he was not happy about being traded to the Buffalo Bills. Jeff McLane flew up to Buffalo for new Bills coach Rex Ryan's first official workout, and got some exclusive saltiness from LeSean, and it expanded from there.

By June, he had made so many bitter comments that some Philadelphia fans were calling him "Salty" McCoy instead of Shady.

> [Chip Kelly is] not the bad dude everybody makes him out to be. He's just different. But I don't really have any hate for him. I really don't. In the beginning I did, but I don't. If I see him I'll speak to him, respectfully–"How are you doing, coach? Good luck."[1]

"I used to hate him but now I really don't" is not an especially convincing stance. Much of LeSean's criticism was seen as a somewhat immature expression of hurt feelings, but one point may have contained an important kernel of truth.

He told McLane that:

> I don't think he likes or respects the stars. I'm being honest. I think he likes the fact that it's "Chip Kelly and the Eagles." ... It was "DeSean Jackson–a high-flying, take-off-the-top-of-the-defense receiver." Or "the

---

1   "LeSean McCoy says Chip Kelly doesn't respect stars" by Jeff McLane, *Philadelphia Inquirer*, April 8, 2015.

quick, elusive LeSean McCoy." I don't think [Kelly] likes that.

The concept that Kelly wants to make himself the marquee name for his team is ludicrous, but there is something to idea that Chip doesn't like stars—in the sense of "ego-driven celebrities."

Of course he wants the biggest talents possible, which is why he signed DeMarco Murray and pursued Mariota, but both men are team players. Clearly, team cohesion is a priority for the coach, and any behavior that promotes a player's individual interests at the expense of that collective bond offends him.

There is also a strategic element. A single star, especially at wide receiver, can be more easily schemed against and perhaps shut down by a star CB such as Darrelle Revis or Richard Sherman. He also makes your team vulnerable to injury; if the star gets hurt, then what? There is no avoiding the need for an elite quarterback, but at the other skill positions, a corps of talented receivers or running backs may be a better weapon. Given the limits imposed by salary caps, it's an increasingly practical alternative, too.

Eagles rookie WR Jordan Matthews had the second-most yards of any slot receiver in 2014, but most NFL fans probably wouldn't even recognize his name. That's fine with him. When the *Inquirer's* Zach Berman asked him if he would be the team's #1 receiver in Maclin's absence, he rejected the whole concept and pointed to the two teams in the Super Bowl, New England and Seattle, neither of which had a receiver with 1,000 yards.

> People ask me about being the No. 1 wide receiver; Forget it. I want us to be a receiving corps... I don't think one "No. 1 wide receiver" was in the Super Bowl this year, but they're two Super Bowl-winning teams that have receiving corps that work their butts off, that block in the run game, that catch the ball when they have to.[1]

---

1 "Eagles' Matthews downplays notion of No. 1 receiver" By Zach Berman, *Philadelphia Inquirer*, April 4, 2015.

This attitude fits what Kelly is doing with his team—replacing single, high-paid, self-centered stars with a corps of versatile players. DeMarco Murray is the league's leading rusher, but he's also an excellent pass catcher and pass protection blocker. Getting Murray did not stop Coach Kelly from signing Ryan Mathews, and together with Darren Sproles it may be the deepest running back unit in the league.

DeSean Jackson has been supplanted by three young and interchangeable wide receivers with positive, humble attitudes in Matthews, Huff and Nelson Agholor. Each can block or sprint, play slot or outside, run a screen or an end around. Many teams have one great cornerback, and a couple have two, but no one has three shutdown corners, and this corps will always leave Kelly with a favorable matchup.

RACISM?

MAY 6, 2015

A month after his first criticisms of Chip Kelly, McCoy was asked to elaborate. This time he went much further and called Kelly racist for cutting him and DeSean.

> You see how fast he got rid of all the good players. Especially all the good Black players. He got rid of them the fastest. That's the truth. There's a reason... It's hard to explain with him. But there's a reason he got rid of all the Black players—the good ones—like that.[1]

The facts don't really support McCoy's claim, given that Kelly replaced him with two Black running backs, one of whom was clearly better than McCoy last year. In his first year as GM, Kelly drafted six players and all of them were Black except the last one—seventh round pick Brian Mihalik, an athletic 6'9" DE.

If there is any position in football where racism has favored white players, it has been at quarterback. Yet few coaches have a better record for diversity at that position. Kelly has started six different quarterbacks in his head coaching career, and five are people of color: Mark Sanchez, Michael Vick, Marcus Mariota, Darron Thomas and Jeremiah Masoli. Sam Bradford, a Native American, is likely to make that six of seven. And he just got rid of the only exception, Nick Foles.

Kelly responded to McCoy's charge directly:

---

1   "LeSean McCoy basically calls Chip Kelly a racist" by Jimmy Kempski, *Philly Voice*, May 6, 2015.

I have great respect for LeSean; however, in that situation, I think he's wrong. We put a lot of time in looking at the characters and factors that go into selection and retention of players and color has never been one of them.[1]

---

1   Chip Kelly's press conference at OTAs, May 28, 2015.

RECONDITIONING

MAY 9, 2015

Because the Eagles are so tight-lipped, reporters and avid fans are reduced to measures as desperate as scanning the website for unannounced changes in staff titles. Diehard fan Greg Richards (@igglesnut on Twitter) spotted one on May 9, 2015 and tweeted:

> From Eagles' website, Shaun Huls' title has changed from 'Sports Science Coordinator' to 'Director of Sports Science and Reconditioning'.[1]
> @igglesnut. 11:47 A.M. May 9, 2015.

That's not a word most fans are familiar with, but it's a common and longstanding term in the field of exercise physiology. Reconditioning is the process of restoring injured athletes directly to their elite athletic levels.

Recently, in the science-forward circles where "high performance" is the term of art for scientifically maximized elite athleticism, the concept has deepened. I spoke with Bill Knowles, an expert in the field who does not work with the Eagles.[2] He's the "Director of Reconditioning and Athletic Development" for HPSports, in Wayne, PA, and works with a number of European pro soccer and rugby players. (The HP in the firm's name stands for "high performance.")

---

1 The Eagles organization made no announcement about this change, and declined an opportunity to comment for this book.

2 Shortly after this interview, the Eagles hired Knowles to rehabilitate Sam Bradford's knee injury, but this was not known publicly until several months later.

Knowles told me that

> ... a serious joint/tendon/muscle injury should be
> looked upon as a neurophysiologic dysfunction, not
> just a basic peripheral musculoskeletal injury. With this
> in mind we must train movements, not muscles during
> all stages of post-injury care.

In the traditional model, an injured player is in rehabilitation—specialized training focused on repairing the injured limb, usually a knee—until the therapist "releases" them to the team's conditioning coach, so they can resume regular training.

Reconditioning begins with appropriate full body training immediately, instead of waiting until the knee is biologically healed or "fixed." Asked at a press conference about the change in Huls' title, Kelly explained that

> when guys get injured, you spend a lot of time
> concentrating on just rehabbing the knee, but it
> also means that you've got to take care of the arms,
> you've got to take care of the cardiovascular, you've
> got to take care of a lot of other things besides just
> that specific rehab for that particular injury. Not only
> do you rehab the injury, you also have to recondition
> the body.[1]

The Birds also hired two more sports science guys out of Oregon: James Hanisch, who ran the Ducks' Sports Science program, as the Eagles' "High Performance Analyst," and J.P. Crowley Hanlon, a recent graduate who majored in advertising, as "Logistics Coordinator."

The team does not share information about sports science willingly, even thought it promotes that phrase as part of the Eagles' "brand"—in part to attract free agents to the team.

But the Eagles picked up a lot of injured athletes over the off-season. From QB Sam Bradford to CB Walter Thurmond, ILBs Kiko Alonso and Jordan Hicks and RBs Ryan Mathews and DeMarco,

---

1   Chip Kelly's press conference for OTAs, May 28, 2015.

you hear the same criticism over and over. "Sure, he's talented and high character, but he has had a lot of injury problems."

At the March, 2015 Owners' Meeting, Kelly talked about his team's ability to bring players back from injury.

> ... you look at, I think, the history right now in terms of sports science and what doctors are doing now, it's unbelievable. Look at the year Jeremy Maclin had coming off of two ACLs. Look at our center. Jason Kelce came off an ACL when I first got there. He had a sports hernia surgery in the middle of the season and still made the Pro Bowl. Our left tackle, who is arguably a Hall of Famer, is coming off two Achilles [injuries] and has played at an outstanding level.

In 2013, Kelce and Peters anchored an offensive line where nearly every player was coming back from a major injury; by the end of 2013, many considered them the NFL's best front line. The excellent *ChipWagon* blog posted video clips of what they call "Kelce porn" (don't worry, they're safe for work).[1] It's always fun to see your lineman pancake a linebacker, but it's *really* fun when he runs 20 yards downfield first.

Jeremy Maclin was considered a major risk before the 2014 season, coming back from an ACL tear at the position where speed and cutting ability is most crucial. He had a career year, matching the career year that (the uninjured and more talented) DeSean Jackson had had in the previous season.

Some injured prospects haven't worked out. Patrick Chung was a major liability at safety for the Birds in 2013, including the playoff loss, and Kenny Phillips never even made it out of training camp.

The jury is still out on some other players. Inside/outside linebacker Travis Long is coming off of two consecutive ACL tears, and his absence really hurt the team at ILB in 2014 when both starters (DeMeco Ryans and Mychal Kendricks) and top backup Najee Goode all went down with injuries. Goode and safety Earl Wolff have shown flashes of great skill but are both coming back

---

1   "#15 - Kelce Porn" by Ryan aka Chipwagoneer, *ChipWagon*, June 12, 2014.

from serious damage in 2014.

And no gamble is bigger than the trade of starting quarterback Nick Foles plus a second-round draft pick for Sam Bradford, also coming off of consecutive ACL tears—on the same knee. It's hard to see any other possibility the Eagles had to upgrade at quarterback, once Mariota proved unaffordable, but if Bradley gets reinjured or can't fully recover, the Eagles could be in very deep trouble.

The promotion for Shaun Huls and the new hires made it clear that the personnel changes and acquisition of injured players was not a coincidence; it's a deliberate strategy. The team is re-conceptualizing injury not as "bad luck" to be hoped against, but an inevitable part of the game that should be planned for and built into your training—and your player acquisition. Your reconditioning.

Everyone likes to quote Chip's mantra, "Bigger people beat up little people," but it's not as simple as that. Coach Kelly also wants fast, smart and versatile players.

But every team wants big, fast, smart, versatile players, so it's hard to find them. How does a coach come out ahead? He can compromise on one of his physical standards, hoping that a shorter or slower player might overachieve by will and intelligence, or he can draft smaller school players untested against top talent, and hope that they can make the leap against much better talent. The large number of college players—even from the SEC—who can't adapt to the NFL make the difficulty of that approach clear. Small school players essentially have to make two leaps, at the same time, even as they jump into adult life.

Seattle built a Super Bowl team on shrewd late-round draft picks (such as cornerback Richard Sherman in the fifth round), in part by applying the secretive SPARQ metric they developed with Nike to measure athletic potential.

Dallas seems to be getting every bad character player possible on the cheap, from Greg Hardy (domestic violence incident) to Randy Gregory (who tested positive for marijuana *at the Combine*, which he knew was an event that exists for the sole purpose of testing potential players).

The risks of that approach are obvious and increasing, as the NFL begins to crack down on domestic violence and other forms of abuse after highly publicized legal cases involving Aaron Hernandez, Ray Rice, and Adrian Peterson.

The Eagles are grabbing big, fast, talented players with injury histories and good attitudes. The hope is that Kelly's sports science program will give him an edge in reclaiming their potential. If it works out, it's a strategy to win a Super Bowl, to build a team of great players without compromise.

None of these strategies is guaranteed to be successful, but the Eagles' approach seems shrewder. Even if the Cowboys can successfully wrangle their wild bunch, they will at best be talented guys with sketchy character. Maybe Dallas will just embrace their new attitude, trade their white and blue uniforms for black and red, and call themselves the Bad Boys or the New Raiders. The Eagles' strategy has a higher upside, and seems like a smarter long-term bet.

If they are better at rehabilitating players than the rest of the league, it will be a very shrewd strategy. Not only will they get full-sized, athletic players with positive attitudes on the cheap, but those players will be motivated to stay with a franchise that will extend their career, and free agents will be inclined to come aboard.

ONWARD

Chip Kelly isn't talking about it, but what appears to be his master plan is slowly coming into focus. He signed a five-year contract in 2013. The goal is a Super Bowl; with this franchise, nothing less is acceptable, but that takes some building. 2015 will probably be a rough year, uneven at best just from all the changes. If Bradford or both new RBs or left tackle Jason Peters get injured, it could be ugly.

I believe Chip has a two-pronged strategy. The short-term plan makes the most of DeMarco Murray, Walter Thurmond, and some of the team's older veterans—Peters, Sproles and Ryans. They will help the team win, mentor the young'uns and establish Chip's offensive and defensive schemes over the next two to three years.

The long-term plan would appear to be a Super Bowl window from roughly 2016-2021, opening in the last two years of Chip's contract (and guaranteeing its renewal). That window is built around a great core of young players, including Alonso, Agholor, Shepherd and Rowe, Huff, Jordan Matthews, Jason Kelce, Lane Johnson and the entire DL. For a team built on culture, a group of high-character studs playing together for several years is the best possible situation.

Surprisingly, the 2015 off-season left the offense looking like the weakest unit of a team with a strong, rising defense and elite special teams. Until the quarterback position is settled, that's likely to remain the situation.

Chip Kelly's project in Philadelphia is so different from what anyone else is doing that it baffles people. But what he's doing is really very simple. Not easy, but simple.

What Chip Kelly is doing with the Philadelphia Eagles, just like what he did with Oregon, is so utterly basic and fundamental that it seems mysterious. Seth Wickersham of *ESPN The Magazine* put it brilliantly in a tweet:

> It seems like Chip Kelly is hellbent on proving that everyone else overthinks football, but he does it in a way that nobody can figure out.
> @SethWickersham. 4:14 P.M. November 27, 2014.

During the 2015 draft , Rich Eisen of the NFL Network spoke for a lot of reporters when he asked Kelly one final question at the end of an interview:

> Are you aware of how much we're thinking about what you're thinking? And does bring you any sort of glee, that we're wondering what you're thinking almost all the time, Coach Kelly?[1]

After a long pause, Kelly responded:

> I don't think about what I think as much as you think about what I think.

The four TV announcers laughed, especially when the coach followed up.

> CHIP KELLY: I had no idea where you were going with that question, Rich.
> {laughter}
> RICH EISEN: No! We're wondering! We're all wondering! We're wondering what are you thinking, I mean all the time. I wake up, I go to sleep. That's what I think.
> MIKE MAYOCK: {snorting with laughter}
> CHIP KELLY: Were you wondering what my answer was going to be to that question?
> RICH EISEN: Yes! Perfect example right there.
> CHIP KELLY: {finally cracking a smile} How'd I do? How'd I do?
> RICH EISEN: Fantastic. I'll give you an A grade on that one. Thank you, coach.

---

1 "Must See: Chip Kelly's Brilliant Remark (VIDEO)" by Chris McPherson, PhiladelphiaEagles.com, May 2, 2015.

Everyone took Kelly's answer as a smartass joke, but it was actually a very revealing answer.

> I don't think about what I think as much as you think about what I think.

Everyone else *does* overthink football. Thinking is what happens when you're not sure what you're doing. When you are sure, you don't think. You know, and you do.

Chip Kelly is pretty damn sure what he's doing. He has figured it out by relentlessly challenging every bit of conventional wisdom for twenty years, and his approach looks something like this:

- Learn everything you can about all the potential players.
- Focus on watching them play, not statistics.
- Get your best talent, and never compromise on measurables or character.
- Stay current on schemes and strategies, and build yours around your players.
- Train hard and fast.
- Study the hell out of your opponents and plan for their tendencies.
- Hide your own tendencies as well as possible.
- When in doubt, trust your gut, your experience and knowledge.
- Above all, no shortcuts. Do it right.

It's simple. But not easy. In fact it's the hardest way to do it. But if you do the work and put together a like-minded team, your odds of winning are much better. And the game is more fun.

All of which guarantees you nothing. Footballs take random bounces. Weather gets weird. Knees explode. Opponents find your vulnerabilities and pounce. This chaos is part of the game, and you have to accept it too.

All you can do is prepare as hard as you can, knowing that a big chunk of your plan will go wrong. You will get punched in the nose, and your plan will have to adjust. That's just how the game is played.

Chip Kelly got his nose bloodied in 2014. He made some tough calls, took his lumps and is still standing. Will he finally lead the Eagles to a Super Bowl victory? That will depend on how he negotiates the conflicting needs to hang tough and to adjust to reality. Will he be able to challenge his own hard-won insights the same way he challenges everyone else's? Can he make necessary adjustments—maybe accepting shorter defensive backs, or reconsidering the old-school macho stance on concussions—without losing his confidence and solidity?

Kelly's biggest enemy may be his own expertise. Fewer and fewer people can reasonably claim to tell the coach something he doesn't already know. Most people gradually lose the battle against rigidity as they age, even if they aren't experts.

So far, Kelly has done a remarkable job of escaping this tightening noose, in part by actively seeking out the perspective of his fellow coaches. But with each success and new power, he has fewer and fewer peers and most of them are his direct competitors in the NFL coaching ranks. The key will be his ability to stay open-minded and value his new experiences—such as losing three games in a row—and the knowledge they give him just as much as he values his old experiences.

If Chip Kelly manages to stay nimble and open-minded through all of this, it will be an incredible achievement. And he will be a very dangerous foe indeed.

ACKNOWLEDGMENTS

I owe a great debt to the many people who helped me with this book, including all of my sources (named and otherwise); Martin Clear; John, Ted and Carl Saltveit; Steve, Maryanne, Marcus and Lauren Troy; Linda Cooper, Andre Salz, Marc Grossman at Helium, Pat Ferro, Derek Boyko and the rest of the Eagles media office, and the crew at World Cup Coffee, especially Mike Smith. Special thanks to /u/Radatatin on Reddit and to Jim Keane for sharp-eyed error checking.

Tommy Lawlor and Jimmy Kempski gave me a forum and continue to be generous with advice and support. They are my on-going role models in every way. My colleagues at *Bleeding Green Nation* and FishDuck are tremendous, especially Brandon Lee Gowton, Brian Flinn, and Charles Fisher. And a special shoutout to the communities at BGN, /r/Eagles and *Iggles Blitz*—you all are three of the smartest and funniest groups on the internet, and I say that as someone who's been arguing online since 1991.

Nothing I do would be possible without the love and support of Anna, Rose and Olga. I love you. Thank you for listening to my endless anecdotes about Chip Kelly and the Eagles. You have to admit, they're at least *kinda* interesting. Finally, to my agent Rita Rosenkranz, who made this project possible, and to my editor Randall Klein, who collaborated and pushed and encouraged until this became a totally different and much better book.

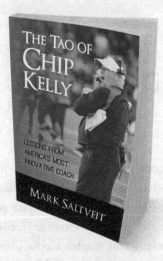